Flying From the Black Hole

Flying From the Black Hole

THE B-52 NAVIGATOR-BOMBARDIERS OF VIETNAM

Robert O. Harder

NAVAL INSTITUTE PRESS
Annapolis, Maryland

Naval Institute Press
291 Wood Road
Annapolis, MD 21402

First Naval Institute Press paperback edition published in 2013.
ISBN: 978-1-59114-386-4

The Library of Congress has cataloged the hardcover edition as follows:

Harder, Robert O.
  Flying from the Black Hole : the B-52 bombardiers of Vietnam / Robert O. Harder.
    p. cm.
  Includes bibliographical references and index.
  ISBN 978-1-59114-359-8 (alk. paper)
    1. Vietnam War, 1961-1975—Aerial operations, American. 2. Vietnam War, 1961-1975—Personal narratives, American. 3. Harder, Robert O. 4. Bombardiers—United States—Biography. 5. United States. Air Force—Biography. 6. B-52 bomber—History—20th century. 7. Bombardiers—Vietnam—History—20th century. 8. Bombardiers—United States—History—20th century. 9. Navigation (Aeronautics)—Vietnam—History—20th century. 10. United States. Air Force—History—Vietnam War, 1961-1975. I. Title.
  DS558.8.H384 2009
  959.704'348092—dc22
                              2009006329

21 20 19 18 17 16 15 14 13   9 8 7 6 5 4 3 2 1
First printing

To every individual who wore a uniform in support of Eighth Air Force's Arc Light and Linebacker operations, especially the truly forgotten guys—the B-52 bomb dump gangs, aircraft maintainers, and ground crews. Without those dedicated, highly skilled, and consistently overworked enlisted men, nothing would have ever gotten off the ground.

Contents

ILLUSTRATIONS

Flying From the Black Hole

INTRODUCTION

The story of rated, nonpilot U.S. Air Force flying officers has long begged a fuller telling. The origins of this "historiographic omission," if indeed that is what it is, can be traced all the way back to those first newspaper reports coming out of Kitty Hawk over a century ago. Since the very dawning of the air age that December of 1903, there has been a strong and still-persistent tendency among writers and historians to present aircraft operations almost exclusively from the viewpoint of the pilot.

In fairness to the scribes, it is a natural thing to do. After all, during aviation's formative years, there were only pilots operating aircraft (with perhaps the occasional mechanic or primitively trained "observer"). In those pioneering days, it was perfectly understandable for aeronautical journalists to focus the spotlight solely on the mechanical operator of the machine. As time went by, however, flight circumstances changed significantly, particularly after the introduction in the 1930s of modern, large complex aircraft requiring several additional, specialized aircrewmen. But by then the original public perceptions and writing conventions had already permanently hardened, and the older, established narrative styles and modes of expression remained largely in place. Even today, the term "pilot" is still regularly used by many writers to describe any flying officer serving aboard a plane.

Such deeply entrenched predilections are sometimes further reinforced by the absence of a clear understanding of what rated nonpilot aircrew members actually do, leading to a kind of default "the pilot did this," "the pilot did that" writing style. Still one more factor involves sizzle; the story arguably reads more dramatically if attention stays centered on the glamorous chap wearing the silk scarf.

The upshot of all this, whether intended or not, is that relatively few people today outside the American military community understand or are even aware of the crucial roles nonpilot officer aircrew—past and

1

present—have played and will continue to play in the armed forces of the United States. Such concerns aren't just about bruised navigator egos (though truthfully that is a part of it); erroneous perceptions can fuel serious misunderstandings that might spill over into national policy and human resource commitments. One current example: twenty-first century print and electronic media continue to insist that B-52 pilots are dropping bombs and launching cruise missiles on terrorist targets. And that last gets at the core of why I wrote the *Flying from the Black Hole*—to help set the record straight.

The long and unlikely path leading to my assuming this "spokesman" role began in the woods and lakes region of northern Minnesota. Following high school graduation, I entered the University of Minnesota at Duluth, where not coincidentally there was a U.S. Air Force Reserve Officers Training Corps (ROTC) detachment. I had a firm set of long-range goals in mind: Win USAF pilot wings and make the service my career. I was determined to follow in the deep footprints left by my mother's brother, Kelly Field Army Air Corps pilot and air transportation pioneer Orvis M. Nelson (founder of Transocean Air Lines, at one time the world's largest nonscheduled commercial air carrier).

Alas, a military pilot I was not to be, though later I did become a commercial pilot and an FAA-certificated flight instructor (CFI). After commissioning as a USAF second lieutenant, a pair of slightly myopic eyes instead set me on a course for navigator training, followed by bombardier school, and eventual assignment to the 306th Bomb Wing (B-52C & D) at McCoy AFB, Orlando, Florida. In addition to the Stateside practice nuclear war training sorties and Strategic Air Command Pad Alert duties every B-52 navigator-bombardier stood during the Cold War era, I flew 145 Operation Arc Light combat missions during the Vietnam War (1968–70).

Unfortunately for my youthful aspirations, the prospect of unlimited numbers of future rotations back to the Asian war, plus a scarcity of meaningful opportunities for someone holding my narrow specialty codes (in a pilot's Air Force), proved too much, and I resigned my commission. By January 1971, I was once again a civilian. After capping a long retail career as a vice president of Montgomery Ward & Co., Chicago, I became involved in real estate investment/management and, thinking there was still time to indulge a life-long ambition, decided to pursue a writing career. Which brings us directly to the effort in front of you.

One last comment before the narrative begins. An early reviewer of the manuscript called its author "passionate about the subject." I plead guilty. To all my fellow heavy bomber navigators and bombardiers, and yes, electronic warfare officers too—from World War II up to the War on Terror—I can only hope neither this book nor my version of events has let you down.

PROLOGUE: THE POOR PLAYERS

The Vietnam War–era B-52 Stratofortress carried a six-man crew. On some models, the tail gunner was alone and 150 feet to the rear of the cockpit; on others, he was forward, next to the electronic warfare officer in the front cabin's upper deck. The pilot and copilot on all models also sat on the upper deck, placed as close to the nose of the aircraft as was possible. These four crewmen were installed as one might expect in a military bomber, with windows and portholes available to scan the skies above and keep track of the good planet Earth below.

Toward the rear of the upper deck, back in its shadowy interior—behind the pilots, behind the jump seat, behind the bunk position, and just before reaching the electronic warfare officer's station—there was a square-shaped breach in the deck floor. This opening was about three feet on a side and it led down to an even darker, nether region below. In the dim light common to that part of the cabin—even on sunny days—it resembled nothing so much as a refuse trap, an uncovered sewer drain perhaps, where should a water hose be unleashed, all the flotsam and jetsam accumulated on the upper deck could be instantly flushed away.

It was down in this forbidding void, this "Black Hole of Calcutta," as it came to be known, that the B-52 navigator-bombardiers nested. From there, from within that claustrophobic and windowless den of black boxes, vacuum tube racks, radar scopes, instrument panels, and navigation and weapon delivery systems, the two Iron Bomb Artillerymen strutted and fretted their hour upon the Southeast Asian stage—until the agony at last came to an end and their kind was heard no more.

CHAPTER ONE

Operation Linebacker Two—The First Day

Andersen Air Force Base, Guam:
Monday, December 18, 1972

It was hot on The Rock. Hot in Agana city, hot in the surrounding villages, hot on the beaches, hot in the jungle, and hot on the handful of narrow roads that connected the tiny island's human presences. It was especially torrid on the northeastern tip, where several score of the world's largest bombers, the spear point of the most powerful aerial armada ever assembled, prepared for battle. Here the great strike fleet hunkered, like a school of black sharks at the ready, their tall, knife-sharp vertical fins menacingly erect.

A very long train of blue, school-type buses—just visible through the mirage-like shimmerings rising off the ramps, taxiways, and runways—emerged from behind a cluster of tropical-white buildings. The vehicles slowly weaved their way through the hundreds of vans, trucks, and motorized equipment units flitting hither and yon, the bus drivers using extraordinary care to avoid interfering with the several thousand frantic, overtaxed men charged with servicing the complex warplanes.

The three bomber crews shoehorned inside each bus, on tiny seats unaccountably designed for children, were miserable. Every window had been thrown open in a futile attempt to combat the stifling tropical heat. The men's flight suits had already turned a two-toned color—the standard issue light-green coloration now stained a dark wet under armpits and down backs. Instead of their usual cocky bantering, the airmen were morosely quiet, as if mourners in a funeral cortege. Even the blatant passing of bodily gases, close-quarter acts that had always before triggered vigorous and raunchy exchanges, were greeted with silent indifference.

The native Guamanian bus drivers moved from aircraft to aircraft, quickly off-loading their passengers. When empty, each vehicle immediately about-faced and scurried away, disappearing behind the white buildings in a manner suggesting their operators could not wait to distance themselves from the sinister black brutes. The six glum men left behind at each bomber heaped their equipment into one large pile at its nose, with more than one man squinting up at the machine through the sun's bright glare and wondering what ugly surprises his particular specimen might have up its sleeve.

Precisely eighty-seven D and G model B-52s were scheduled for takeoff, by far the largest number of heavy bombers launched from Guam at one time since the 1945 B-29 campaigns against the Japanese Empire. They would be joined over Indochina by forty-two additional B-52Ds out of U-Tapao, Thailand, where together the bombers would form up into three giant waves spaced four hours apart and initiate Operation Linebacker Two. The military objectives of these 129 Stratofortresses, with their combined bombloads in excess of a World War II thousand-plane raid, were unambiguous:

> By direction of the President, you are to commence at approximately 1200 Zulu, 18 December 1972, a three-day maximum effort, repeat maximum effort, of B-52/Tacair strikes in the Hanoi/Haiphong areas. Object is maximum destruction of selected military targets . . . Be prepared to extend operations past three days, if directed.

During these last hours before the opening round of U.S. president Richard Nixon's hoped-for master stroke to end the Vietnam War, the 12,000 uniformed individuals and untold thousands more civilians engaged in direct support of Eighth Air Force at Andersen Air Force Base had stepped up the pace to where their efforts and the outside air temperature had both reached boiling point. The stressed-out bomber crews had to force themselves to concentrate on their individual preflight preparations in the midst of an incredible array of distractions—the stifling heat, the eeee-whining of scores of spooling-up jet engines, a couple of hundred clamoring utility carts still servicing those bombers not yet operating under their own power, gasping air compressors with snake-like hoses that criss-crossed their way out to the horizon, screeching fan belts and burned rubber tires from a thousand motorized vehicles, and perhaps the most fearsome aspect of it all—the orders, shouts, curses, and tumult of a swarming human multitude.

The first order of flight crew business was for each pilot, also known as the aircraft commander (AC), and his ground crew chief to huddle in front of their bomber and discuss the machine's current condition. After whatever flagged maintenance issues had been addressed and resolved, the walkaround preflight could begin. The pilot and copilot slowly circled the plane with a careful eye, while the gunner hustled to the tail for an inspection of his Quad-Pack of .50-caliber machine guns. The electronic warfare officer headed for the rear of the aircraft as well, to a point under the 47 Section just forward of the gunner's compartment, where he checked his electronic countermeasures—the ECM antennas, flare ejectors, chaff dispensers, and all the other "spook stuff" that nobody but him understood.

The junior navigator-bombardier (called "nav") and the radar navigator/bombardier (called "radar nav") were responsible for inspecting the weapons. While the radar nav preflighted and armed the eighty-four 500-pound bombs in the sweltering, nearly oxygen-free bomb bay, the younger navigator checked the twenty-four external weapons—twelve seven-fifties under each wing—out in the relative open, where there was at least the suggestion of breathable air. The nav stayed braced in an upright position on the raised platform of a four-wheeled yellow B-4 stand while the gunner maneuvered him from bomb to bomb to ensure their general condition was good, the arming vanes weren't jammed or broken, and the bomb release shackles had closed properly. If everything was OK, the navigator pulled the individual red-flagged safety pins, prearming each weapon. From a distance, the exercise resembled nothing so much as one boy gaily pushing another around on a jolly rolling cart, except this was no fun and games; the work was dangerous and deadly serious. The stand's castored wheels often had a will of their own—in the manner of a balky grocery cart in a narrow supermarket aisle—and the gunner had all he could do to keep from either running his nav up against the long, sharp bomb-arming wires or having the entire business go flying down the tarmac. The activity normally produced lively exchanges between the two men, especially in regard to the gunner's directional competence, but on this day they grunted and sweated in gloomy silence.

B-52 aircrewmen usually finished their external preflights simultaneously—as if an orchestra conductor were standing at the aircraft's nose waving a baton—then one by one they entered the ship through the small hatch at the bottom of the airplane, located about ten feet aft of the nose. The pilots and electronic warfare officer (plus the gunner in G models) passed quickly through the nav-bomb compartment via a ladder to the upper flight deck and settled into their upward-firing ejection seats. The navigator-bombardiers brought up the rear, closing the hatch behind them before squeezing into their lower-compartment downward ejection seats. And squeeze it was, for the B-52 radar navigator/navigator station was a very tight fit, lacking even the tiniest hint of crew consideration and surrounded in all dimensions by radar sets, circuit breakers, switch panels, flight instruments, electromechanical computers, vacuum tube racks, bombing and navigation black boxes, and enough other miscellaneous equipment to mistake it for Fibber McGee's closet. The lower compartment was so diabolically devoid of space, light, and comfort that it was almost inevitable the place would become known as the "Black Hole of Calcutta," or, as time went on, simply "the Hole."

The bomber men might have been on the broiling subcontinent of India—Guam's midday heat had driven the temperature inside the airplanes to over 130 degrees Fahrenheit. The crews, breathing in superhot air through open mouths and already sopping wet from perspiration, were determined to make short work of their engine-start routines. Within minutes, they'd have all eight running, and the copilots could switch on their ship's internal air and finally cool things down.

The exquisitely choreographed, incredibly immense ground ballet occurring on December 18, 1972, had so far given every indication it was proceeding with nary a hitch and that the vaunted Strategic Air Command (SAC) was conducting the operation in its routinely efficient and professional manner. Casual observers almost surely would have sat back and relaxed—confident that the Big Push was in the most capable military hands America possessed and that all was well. Alas, such was not the case, not even remotely so, for unbeknownst to the tens of thousands of military personnel, permanent-party family dependents, and civilian Department of Defense workers watching and cheering on the sidelines in anticipation of what promised to be the most magnificent bomber launch ever witnessed, the battle itself was on the verge of becoming a colossal military disaster.

Only a few sharp-eyes noticed the terrible "oh-oh" moment. Just as the leading elements of the first wave began to taxi, scores of official staff cars raced frantically out onto the runways and halted the Elephant Walk. With bomber engines screaming into their naked ears, khaki-uniformed men carrying large briefcases scrambled out of the cars and ran over to the freshly opened entry hatches. Without word or ceremony, and in a manner faintly suggesting they were moving contraband, the officers pitched the cases up to the waiting navigator-bombardiers, then scurried back to their waiting vehicles.

Moments before 3 PM local Guam time, the throttles in the wave lead B-52D bomber were advanced. The noise and tension in the cockpit immediately escalated as the aircraft pawed at the departure hammerhead, shuddering and shaking from the strain of being held back. The navigator counted down to zero, the aircraft commander released the brakes, and the ship lurched forward. It rolled onto the active runway and turned ninety degrees to takeoff heading. The pilots made one last down-and-dirty instrument scan, then poured the cob to the eight J-57s. The balance of the first wave followed directly on the leader's heels at one-minute intervals. After each aircraft's gear was up and with Guam rapidly dropping away, the navigator-bombardiers frantically opened their just-received Top Secret cases and ripped out the contents.

The sorry chain of events that led up to what was increasingly looking like a slow-motion train wreck had started days earlier at SAC Headquarters in Omaha, Nebraska, when the command's leadership decided that only *they* were capable of planning the Linebacker Two mission, never mind that Eighth Air Force on Guam had been successfully selecting and bombing tactical objectives virtually unhindered for seven and one-half years. Omaha did take total control of the operation all right, but, in an extraordinary series of lapses, managed to bungle the job so thoroughly it leaves one breathless to this day. Numbed by two decades of antiseptic Cold War games, caught up short when permission to wage the unlimited air combat they had been whining about for years was finally granted, insulated from the realities of the hot conventional war their primary weapons platform was fighting a half world away, SAC HDQS not only dropped the ball, they kicked it out of bounds. The very thing SAC leaders had nagged their crews about for years—COMPLACENCY—had reared its ugly head in the He-Bear's Den itself.

Not only that, in a frightening preamble to even more malignant things yet to come, an astounding logistical snafu had occurred at the very moment the attack began. Every significant detail related to the strike brief—initial point, bomb run headings, target coordinates, simulated radar images of aiming points, and offset aiming values—*had only just arrived from Omaha*, way, way too late for even a glimpse of the data before takeoff. The Guam-based bombardiers' first look at everything they held holy did not come until after they were already on their way to North Vietnam.

The unprecedented Hanoi attacks would have been surrealistic under the best of conditions. A steady buzz had been building on The Rock since December 15, when a major operation warning signal was secretly transmitted to Andersen. By nightfall on the 17th, even the Guamanian bus drivers knew something big was cooking. Crews scheduled to go home were unaccountably held up, leaves were mysteriously canceled; crew transfers to U-Tapao, Thailand, the other B-52 base in the theater, were suspended without explanation; base security was beefed up; the maintenance tempo quickened; and 43rd and 72nd Wing senior staff members turned into deaf-mutes whenever anybody asked them what the hell was going on. Came the next dawn, the 18th, and the installation's general mood of deep uneasiness was as heavy as the early morning air. Late in the am the other shoe dropped; eighty-seven Andersen crews, 522 men, were literally jammed into the Arc Light Briefing Center in three separate groups spaced four hours apart. For-ty-two additional crews at U-Tapao assembled later in the day—they were much closer to Hanoi—for an identical dog and pony show.

Many of the heavy bomber aircrewmen, thoroughly confused between what was happening at the moment and National Security Adviser Henry Kissinger's "peace is at hand" rhetoric of late October, half believed they were going to be told the war was over and they'd be home for Christmas. Instead, the flyers were rocked by the news they would be bombing "Ha Noi," as the very first overhead slide made ominously clear by at last spell-ing the enemy capital correctly. Adam's Apples bobbed even faster when it was announced Press-On rules were in effect. ("All bombers are to press-on no matter what and despite SAMs [surface-to-air missiles] or MiGs if there is any chance of striking the target and recovering at an Allied base.") For the American Eighth Air Force, it was to be Schweinfurt, Regensburg, or perhaps even ghastly Ploesti all over again.

As the details of Omaha's lock-step, miserably-thought-out battle plan and air combat tactics rapidly unfolded, the crew's emotions progressed through sudden shock and went past a certain stoic acquiescence before finally arriving at open astonishment.

- Midair collisions between bombers are deemed a greater threat than North Vietnamese defenses, and the attack plan in all its rami-fications will reflect this factor.

- Accordingly, all bombers will attack in single file from the same initial point (IP), flying northwest to southeast.

- Accordingly, all bombers will fly at exactly the same airspeeds and altitudes between the IP and target.

- Accordingly, all three waves will attack precisely four hours apart, due to logistical and tanker considerations.

- Bombers will make a SAC combat break to the right after release, in accordance with standard doctrine, and exit the target areas to the south and west.

- Bombers will conduct no evasive action on the bomb run, with weapon delivery accuracy and associated collateral damage issues the overriding considerations.

The Andersen airmen watched glassy-eyed as the overhead slides flashed by, not quite believing either what was being visually displayed on the projection screen or what the Eighth Air Force staff was telling them. Although no one had verbalized very much since the brief began, the body language was coming through loud and clear—chairs scraped back and forth, people coughed nervously, furtive murmurs were delivered to neighbors, heads shook repeatedly, chins were stroked until red speckled, and eyes blinked like Navy semaphores. Of a sudden, and before anybody was even close to ready for it, the specific raid-profile segment of the presentation ended and the talkers moved on to other issues.

Fortunately for the thoroughly dazed flyers the balance of the briefing was routine and familiar stuff, giving them a chance to at least partially digest all that had come before. The time hack was given, the weatherman came and went, and Intelligence performed their usual song and dance. Just as things were wrapping up, however, a new shocker hit from out of the blue. The bomb/nav target study sessions scheduled to immediately follow the general briefing were canceled because *Omaha's detailed mission data, including the identification of the actual targets themselves, had not yet arrived.*

The crewmen simply stared at one another. Not only was SAC HDQS staff in over their heads on matters of attack tactics, *they had completely miscalculated the amount of time it took to transmit their precious plan through the chain of command and halfway around the world.* Suddenly, the screen went blank, the lights came up, and the obligatory, session-ending "Any questions, gentlemen?" was uttered.

"Why no evasive action?" one pilot reportedly blurted out, no doubt after a real struggle summoning the necessary boldness to ask the biggest and most obvious question. "We know we can get it steadied up prior to release." Clearing his throat, and in that very careful, self-deprecating manner a junior officer always uses when attempting to tell a senior leader he is full of bovine excretions, he went on to remind the bird colonel that, "We've been doing it in high-threat areas for some time now, sir."

"There will be absolutely no evasive action from IP to target," the wing commander said firmly. "We are determined that nothing be allowed to jeopardize mutual ECM support and cell integrity, nor to chance inflicting unnecessary civilian casualties."

Twenty-four hours later, when it was discovered that some crews had used evasive tactics anyway, that same colonel repeated that same no-evasion decree, adding, apparently on his own authority, that any man who violated it would be court-martialed (less than a day after that, a meek announcement filtered down from higher headquarters stating that evasive tactics were permissible after all). Perhaps in hindsight such an injunction could be understood, issued as it was in the heat of battle and coming as it did from a seasoned, competent senior officer who clearly understood the implications of what he was saying and honestly believed the mission required that kind of formal discipline. But for those highly trained and professional aviators sitting in that Andersen briefing room, men who had been entrusted with the safekeeping and delivery of nuclear weapons, men who in most cases had more B-52 combat flying experience than their commanders, men who knew exactly what the aircraft was capable of, to have had their lives held hostage to so arbitrary an order, and in a manner vaguely suggesting a lack of courage, was for them an unpardonable act.

The still mostly silent, though increasingly angry, crews now understood the die had been cast and that any further questions or implied criticism of the mission or tactics would only lead to an extended stay in the Chateau Bow-Wow. Just the same, while the SAC flyers were loyal soldiers and would do as they were told, the men remained flesh and blood human beings, genetically encoded with as strong a sense of personal survival as anyone else. Nothing could possibly have prevented what they were thinking:

"Easy for the Wing King to say no evasion maneuvers; he's not going."

"Has anybody besides me noticed that postrelease fifty degree break to the right slams us directly into a 100-knot headwind? Like throwing out an anchor when instead we should be getting the hell out of Dodge."

"Why not after the drop don't we just haul butt straight ahead for the Gulf of Tonkin instead of this bullcrap turn of a combat break to the right we keep using just because it's on the nuclear release checklist?"

"Do these people know a steep, slow turn over a million SAM launchers will cause all my electronic countermeasures to get pointed out into space?"

"Why can't we pump chaff at a surface-to-air missile? Why only at MiGs? Did somebody forget to buy enough of the stuff?"

"Are these not the same bomb run airspeed and heading tactics we've been showing them for years? They ain't exactly stupid down there."

"How come everybody has to come in at the same height? Is 37,000 feet the only altitude the airplane can fly at?"

"Talk about a scheduled parade. The bastards will be setting their watches to the timing between cells and waves."

"Old son, remember your pap telling you about the Marianas Turkey Shoot? Well, this here is gonna be the Hanoi B-52 Shoot."

And so it began, with the general agitation of the airmen so intense, the bitterness over the tactics so searing, the grumbling so widespread, that untrue rumors regarding crew mutinies during Operation Linebacker Two began circulating that day and have continued to persist nearly four decades later.

After the chaplain wrapped things up with a prayer, the aircrews filed out of the briefing theater. The buses were loaded, survival equipment and lunches picked up, the men delivered to their airplanes, and the preflights conducted, just as if it was a regular combat mission and everybody knew what they were doing. The clock ticked down to engine start time and the crews cranked up the turbines. It was only at the last moment that the radios had crackled with instructions to hold the bombers where they were, open the hatches, and prepare for hand-delivery of the just-received strike data.

Although staggered by everything that had transpired so far, especially the mind-blowingly clumsy—even reckless—attack tactics Omaha was insisting upon, the now-airborne B-52 aircrews settled down and, each on their own, determined to pick up the pieces. The gunners and electronic warfare officers compared notes and arranged for their ship's defense as best they could with what they had onboard, not knowing even at that late hour it would be woefully inadequate. The navigator-bombardiers feverishly crammed for what was to be the most important "exam" of their lives, with not much more than the equivalent of another student's cribbed notes. The dismayed pilots reviewed once again the obviously flawed approach to and exit from the target area and grimly manhandled their very heavily ladened bombers westward, jaws grinding away until their teeth hurt.

Most men kept what they were thinking to themselves, though a few cross words did spill into the open. One aircraft commander groused to his copilot that he thought SAC would have still launched the attack even if the targeting information hadn't shown up in time, just to save face, and that it would be a miracle if anyone found their target today. Operation Linebacker Two, he said, was about to become the "Cluster Fluke of all Cluster Flukes."

He was wrong about that last. It was worse.

CHAPTER TWO

A Booming Sound

The world's first "aerial attack" occurred nearly six centuries before the term "strategic bombing" was even coined. In northern France on August 26, 1346, 10,000 invading English knights and archers hurled themselves against 12,000 Frenchmen in a fight that would become famous as the Battle of Crécy. In addition to their regular arms complement of bows, arrows, crossbows, daggers, swords, and lances, the English had cooked up a little surprise, a fiendish new weapon so far removed from the accepted rules of engagement that its employment outraged the French.

The device was called a bombard, a word derived from the Latin *bombus*, meaning "a booming sound." One of the first cannons used in combat, it was a big, cumbersome piece, both mechanically unreliable and dangerous to operate. To modern eyes it was constructed bass-ackwards, which is to say the small end was at the breech touch-hole and the big end up front at the muzzle. As it happened, that bit of asymmetry was the least of the bombard's problems; because of the poor quality of gunpowder and crude cannon technology of the age, the tube's fearsome bark proved much worse than its bite. (The three pieces at Crécy did not contribute to the English victory.) Nevertheless, the genie was out of the bottle. From that day forward, the concept of "explosive bombardment"—whether from ground or air—became an essential component of warfare.

The principles of cannonade changed little through the following centuries, though the technology improved by leaps and bounds. Soon there were large siege bombards, sometimes called mortars, which once and for all replaced the ancient stone-throwing trebuchets and catapults. When it was discovered how to properly maintain the seal and pressure around the explosive material inside the cannon, the technique of ramming everything one item at a time down the muzzle gave way to the more efficient breech loading. The "bomb," what the delivered payload was called, also continued to be refined—progressing from whatever stones and bits of jagged metal could be stuffed down the barrel, to a fused, hollow metal ball filled with gunpowder ("bombs bursting in air"), to modern-day self-contained shells containing primer, explosive charge, and warhead.

The first recorded use of air-dropped explosives was in 1849, when the Austrian army hung "bombs" on hot air balloons in an assault against Venice, Italy. The results were negligible, however; most of the devices, equipped with slow-burning fuses, blew up harmlessly while still airborne. It wasn't until World War I that ground- and sea-based artillery, the primary bomb delivery systems up to that point, began giving serious way to flying machines. As primitive as those early twentieth-century heavier-than-air craft were, they still could outperform any contemporary siege gun. The most powerful rifled cannon of that time, Imperial Germany's famous Paris Gun, had a maximum range of but seventy miles, while even the most rickety wood and doped-fabric airplane could deliver heavy ordnance two or three times that far. Rigid airships (or dirigibles—as opposed to nonrigid and less-maneuverable blimps and unpowered balloons), especially those designed by Germany's Count Zeppelin, could strike even farther. His huge lighter-than-air ships were descendants of the Montgolfier Brothers' hot air balloon, which on November 21, 1783, became the first man-carrying vehicle to fly into the heavens.[1]

As it happened, one of the world's earliest strategic bombing campaigns was conducted in airships designed by the good count. In 1915, during World War I, Kaiser Wilhelm ordered a series of raids against Great Britain by the "L"-designated Zeppelins, an unprecedented feat of arms that electrified the world. Launched from bases in Germany, the Zepps traveled hundreds of miles across western Europe and the North Sea/English Channel to bomb targets in London and southern Britain. While the attacks did little actual damage, they nevertheless generated so much hysteria the English were forced to withdraw large numbers of their fighter aircraft from the French and Belgian fronts to meet the perceived threat at home.

Such fast-moving technological advances are a common wartime condition, and military nomenclature naturally evolves right along with it. After the Zeppelin raids made clear that long-range aerial bombardment was distinctly different from ground-based cannon in the manner it lobbed explosive devices, the words "bomb" or "bombing" began to refer only to ordnance dropped from the air, while "shelling," "mortaring," "cannonading," and "artillery fire" came into use to describe issue from surface cannon. Similarly, hand-thrown, smaller "bombs" gradually became "grenades."

The first weapons dropped from a heavier-than-air machine came in 1911 during the Italo-Turkish War, when Italian (German-made) Rumpler Taube's bombed Turkish forces at Ain Zara. The first truly "dedicated bomber airplane," however, is generally considered to be the 1914 single-engine British AVRO Type 504. A two-seater, it carried a pilot and observer (perhaps the original "bombardier"?) with a maximum takeoff weight of 1,574 pounds, meaning that after subtracting the weight of the machine, the two crew, and fuel, its payload was barely measurable. Not surprisingly, aircraft like the lightly weaponed AVRO, capable of just a few grenade/bombs hand-delivered over the cockpit side or through a trapdoor—after which a revolver or army rifle might be brought to bear, did not interfere very much with the enemy's capacity to make war.

Despite this early slow going, every Great War belligerent recognized the enormous potential of aerial bombardment, and it wasn't long before an airplane-building arms race broke out. The British hustled forward the de Havilland D.H.4 bomber, a vastly superior machine to the AVRO that boasted a 450-mile range with a 500-pound bomb load. Later came their Handley Page 0/400 "Bloody Paralyser," a two-engined behemoth that could haul 2,000 pounds of ordnance. Italy built a series of multiengine Capronis; Russia made a surprising contribution with an ahead-of-its-time four-engined Sikorsky; and Germany brought out their Gotha "long-range" bombers. The three-seat Gotha IV was especially impressive, able to carry 1,100 pounds of bombs with four hours endurance. The Gothas picked up where the Zepps left off, bombing London in the summer of 1917.

Which brings us to the aerial bombs themselves. The very first were crude in the extreme; more often than not they were either homemade explosive devices or had been adapted from regular army artillery shells. They came in all shapes and sizes, and some were quite odd looking. A few weren't even explosives; in 1914 the French successfully employed the wholesale dropping of pencil-sized steel darts, or *flechettes*. Don't laugh. Loosed from 1,500 feet, one of those little nasties could penetrate completely through a horse. There was also a shrapnel-spewing, hand-held contrivance shaped like a boxer's punching bag that was released as if one were flinging a water balloon over the side. Another was of the incendiary type, often dropped from Zeppelins, bearing a vague resemblance to an oversized street lantern (and with about the same destructive potential). At the low speeds of the early flying machines, bomb-design streamlining wasn't an issue, so any kind of device or configuration would work so long as it wasn't too heavy and blew up when it was supposed to. Most early-war bomb aiming wasn't of much account either; there were no aids per se—a man judged his speed over the ground, eyeballed the target, and released his grip about . . . mmm . . . now! As the Great War deepened, however, bomb aiming technology and techniques did improve significantly (subjects we will explore much more fully in later chapters).

By 1918 aerial bombs had assumed their familiar torpedo shape, though they still remained essentially cannon shells with fins. Indeed, converted 155-mm artillery ordnance was, for a time, the Allies' standard heavy bomb. Nearly all were HE (high explosive) devices, filled with TNT or its equivalent. (Blast concussion plus thousands of missile-like bomb casing fragments—shrapnel—caused the damage.) The largest used by either side in the war was the German 1,000 kilo bomb (2,200 pounds). Britain's biggest blockbuster was the 1,650-pound "SN," which housed a full 800 pounds of Amatol explosive.

Despite all the technical improvements the worldwide conflict had generated, it wasn't until the interwar period (1919–39) that bomber aircraft design itself really accelerated. Some of those changes revolved around improving existing Great War technology, but most of the advances would have been undreamed of just a few years earlier. They included much more powerful and lighter-weight engines, all-metal construction, enclosed cockpits, flaps, retractable landing gear, and the design evolution from high-drag, biwinged aircraft to streamlined monoplanes. With Germany denied an air force under the Versailles Treaty and France war exhausted (Italy, Russia, and Japan kept relatively low aviation profiles), the principal innovations in bomber aircraft manufacturing were now originating in either the United Kingdom or America.

One of the earliest and most successful of these newer machines was Britain's 1919 two-engine Vickers Vimy. While this breakthrough long-range bomber was too late for the war, it was immediately seized on by John Alcock and Arthur Whitten Brown to make the first nonstop flight across the Atlantic (St. Johns, Newfoundland, to Ireland), an almost forgotten epic voyage eclipsed eight years later by Charles Lindbergh's legendary New York-to-Paris solo crossing. Also, in the early 1920s, the clever U.S. airplane designer, Glenn Martin, came up with his two-engine Model GMB bomber, an improved version of which the court-martial–bound Billy Mitchell used to sink the "unsinkable" battleship *Ostfriesland*, thereby changing the nature and perception of air warfare for good. A fairly reliable way to measure one's success is by the number of imitators, and Martin had plenty, though most of the machines his designs inspired were of the kind that turn up in contemporary "aerial oddity" books.

The most successful of the Martin knockoffs was the two-engine Huff-Daland/Keystone bomber, boasting an ability to carry 1,500 pounds of bombs nearly a thousand miles. Unfortunately, and despite this substantial range and payload advance, the Keystone's speed and ceiling performance wasn't much improved from the heavy bombers of the Great War—their high-drag fixed gear and two giant wings made them inherently inefficient airplanes. All the same, the Keystone was as good as anything else then available (also the cheapest) and the U.S. Army Air Corps ordered two hundred of them. The Keystones remained the foundation of the American bomber force until well into the 1930s, though by that time their day was over and the worn-out, lumbering machines had been essentially reduced to training work. The author's uncle, Orvis Nelson, a 1934 aviation cadet who flew Keystones during his bombardment phase at the Kelly Field, Texas, pilot school (the "West Point of the Air"), said, "it was real work to fly them, and you always needed to remember they had but one speed—ninety miles per hour for take off, cruise, and landing."

The 1930s saw huge leaps in bomber development,[2] despite the U.S. economic depression and a puny American military budget. For once it was civilian market forces, the new "airlines," rather than a war that drove the changes in big airplane design. This new impetus came primarily from the Boeing Company and Douglas Aircraft. The Boeing 247, an all-metal, twin-engine, retractable gear, ten-passenger monoplane made its debut in 1933. The 247 was immediately successful, leading directly to the Douglas DC-3 (rolled out in 1935), perhaps the most famous airliner ever constructed, with 13,000 civilian and military versions built through 1968. Both the Boeing 247 and the "Three" could literally fly rings around the Army's Keystone (acutely embarrassing the military), and that was finally too much even for Congress. The long-obsolete, biplane bomber was finally replaced by the U.S. Army Air Corps' first all-metal, long-range, big-payload monoplane.

The rakish Martin B-10B was the sire of all World War II American medium and heavy bombers, its two Wright 775-HP radial engines giving it a maximum speed of 215 mph and a range of 1,240 miles. There were four crew positions—a pilot, radio operator/ventral gunner (lower forward), dorsal gunner (top rear), and, for the first time, a bombardier station in an omni-windowed nose—during World War II that location would become known as the "greenhouse." The pilots were required to take turns at the bombardier station, a duty they approached, at least initially, as an interesting change-of-pace novelty. The airplane's three .30-caliber Brownings were turreted (another first) and the internal bomb bay could hold 2,260 pounds of bombs. Yet, as advanced as the B-10B was,[3] it too very quickly became obsolete; the entire planet was ginning up for another world war. Its immediate replacement? None other than the legendary four-engine Boeing B-17 Flying Fortress.

A great deal has been written about the "Fort," and there are many documentary and fictional motion pictures showing the bomber in action, making it one of the best known of all combat aircraft. The B-17G, the widest produced version (Boeing, Douglas, and Vega/Lockheed built 8,860 copies of this series alone), was powered by four 1,200-HP Wright radial engines, could carry eight to twelve 500-pound bombs, and had a maximum range of 3,400 miles.[4]

Concurrently, over at San Diego's Consolidated Aircraft, another big new bomber was coming off the line—the four-engine B-24 Liberator. The B-17 and B-24 were fairly equal in performance and capability, with perhaps a small nod to the Liberators on payload and range. The B-17 was a stable, relatively "pilot-friendly" aircraft; the B-24 was considered a bit of a firetrap and harder to fly. As to which was the "better" weapon system, the answer depends on who the question is directed at. The government voted for the B-24, building about 18,000 of them in all versions (compared to fewer than 13,000 total for the B-17), the most of any World War II medium/heavy bomber. One thing everybody did agree on—the Lib (squat, boxy, clunky twin tails) wasn't as pretty as the Fort, and that took care of its popular reputation. The press always goes for the looker.

By the time the Flying Fortress and Liberator became fully operational (1937 and 1940, respectively), it was already clear the future in heavy bombardment aircraft rested with ever-larger and more sophisticated multiengine machines. Accordingly, and by late 1942, the B-29 Superfortress was ready. Easily the finest bomber built by anybody during World War II, the B-29 was the first American airborne weapon platform to have a pressurized cabin. Supported by an eleven-man crew, the B-29 was powered by four 2,200-HP reciprocating engines, cruised at over 350 mph, had a ceiling of 35,000 feet, and could either carry 20,000 pounds of bombs over medium distances or 10,000 pounds for nearly 5,000 miles.

The B-29 was one of a kind in its day; in late 1945 it was the only intercontinental atomic bomber in the world. The Superfortress was so far ahead of anything the Soviets possessed—they had become our new adversaries before the ink was dry on the war-ending paperwork—that Stalin stole one of them and had his engineers build hundreds of exact duplicates. The Tupolev TU-4 became the mainstay of the Soviet bomber force for several years.

Meanwhile, the Americans weren't standing still. As early as 1943, they had been secretly developing an even more impressive aircraft, a long-range strategic bomber so big it was nicknamed the "Aluminum Overcast." The Convair B-36 Peacemaker first flew operationally in 1948, and what a sight and sound show that nearly 400,000-pound behemoth gave to first-time onlookers! Operated by a crew of fifteen, it was powered by four General Electric jet engines and six Pratt & Whitney reciprocating propeller engines, with the latter mounted on the trailing edges of the wings in "pusher" fashion, as opposed to conventionally mounted "tractor" engines hung on the wing's leading edge.

The B-36 quickly became a Cold War political football and, as a result, much of the performance data published during its operational lifetime was an artful blend of the factual and the wishful. So much stuff was added and taken off the many different versions of the airplane (there were those variations that stayed on paper, and those that advanced to congressional subcommittee hearings, and those that were actually manufactured) that it's tough to get a definitive handle on the airplane's capabilities. Even a half century later, conflicting data about the B-36 continue to surface in modern reference works, a still-resonant echo of the contentious political and military climate at the beginning of the half-century-long confrontation between the United States and the Soviet Union.

The author's best stab at its most heavily produced version, the B-36D series, suggests a gross takeoff weight of 375,000 to 400,000 pounds, a top speed around 410 mph at 35,000 feet altitude, and about a 44,000-foot service ceiling. The airplane's range and bomb-load numbers are trickier to extrapolate. For example, several reference books claim it had an 86,000-pound bomb-load capacity, which theoretically was possible, though that left almost no available weight for gas—the bomber's resultant combat radius would be roughly from New York to Boston and back again. For the earlier B-36s, a 30,000-pound bomb load with a 3,500- to 4,500-mile range would be more reasonable; the later, more efficient Peacemakers were capable of hauling a twenty-one-ton Mark 17 hydrogen bomb for about 6,000 miles.

B-36 crews were quite fond of their aircraft, fiercely proud that during the Peacemaker's ten-year tour of duty there was "Never a Shot in Anger." (The bomber did not see action in the Korean War.) Unfortunately for the airmen, the U.S. government did not share their affection; the B-36 had plenty of operational problems, including the high cost of maintenance and downtime associated with its enormous complexity. The airplane's most serious issue, however, was its relatively slow speed and corresponding vulnerability to enemy interception, and in the end there was simply no way around that one. The last Peacemaker was flown to the Arizona "boneyard" smelter in early 1959.

The B-36 program put a period to the propeller-driven strategic bomber era. By the Korean War, the jet age had arrived, and the U.S. Air Force was eagerly awaiting the arrival of its sleek, almost fighter-like, B-47 Stratojet bomber. But events were happening so fast, even the B-47 would face a replacement before it had barely lost its new airplane smell. The newest new guy on the block was one of those rare kinds of airplanes that come along only once in the proverbial blue moon. Before it was even fully deployed it had revolutionized the very idea of long-range strategic bombing, indeed had created the parameters for an entirely new military concept that would soon be known throughout the world as "nuclear deterrence." Though no one had an inkling at the time, it was to become the most successful airborne weapons delivery system ever built.

CHAPTER THREE

The Big Ugly Feller

He was conceived over the long weekend of October 21–25, 1948, at the Van Cleve Hotel in, appropriately enough, Dayton, Ohio—the hometown of Wilbur and Orville Wright and the birthplace of all of aviation. His ancestors were a long line of distinguished Boeing aircraft; his multiple parents flesh and blood engineers and aviators; his midwives the United States Air Force and its newly created atomic bomber force, the Strategic Air Command.

The marriage leading to his conception was more of the "shotgun" variety than the result of a thoughtful, lengthy engagement. With the intensifying Cold War casting even darker shadows over the Western democracies and the need for a stronger bomber deterrent against the Soviets heightened, an anxiety-ridden U.S. Air Force, made a separate service only the year before, was completely bogged down in an aeronautical design/production swamp, with one foot stuck in the propeller-driven muck of yesterday and the other in the jet-rocket quicksand of tomorrow. Time had finally run out on all the dithering and hard decisions were required immediately.

The choices? Option A: stick indefinitely with the advanced models of the B-36 Peacemaker, a program already budgeted for and currently in heavy production. Option B: fully commit the nation to the about-to-be-rolled-out new six-engine B-47 Stratojet, a so-far, so-good performer, but essentially a medium bomber with some serious design limitations. Or Option C: scrap everything and start fresh with something brand new.

In mid-October 1948, a few good men—very few it seems in hindsight—were urgently summoned to Wright Field at Dayton to hash out the problem once and for all. It didn't begin well—by Thursday, the 21st, everyone was tired and thoroughly frustrated over the lack of progress. That evening, a half-dozen Boeing engineers were instructed by their Air Force counterparts to DAMMITCOMEUPWITHSOMETHING by Monday morning. Obediently, the engineers retreated to the Van Cleve and for three days and nights kept the lights burning brightly. From the first moment, the men agreed they were through retreading technologies; the job had to be done right and that meant a totally new kind of bomber.

On Monday, October 25, 1948, six exhausted individuals emerged from that Dayton hotel and proudly presented the United States of America with a new son, soon to be baptized the B-52 Stratofortress.[1] A robust prodigy that would weigh in at a staggering 450,000 pounds, the airplane instantly rewrote the book on strategic bomber design. Its unprecedented and most defining characteristics were to include four pods of twin, low-drag, turbojet engines (eight total); aerodynamically efficient swept-back wings; and several airframe structural advances that greatly increased the airplane's gross weight capability over all previous big-bomber designs. These engineering triumphs would result in astonishing performance payoffs: near-supersonic speed (630 mph), a 50,000-foot service ceiling, bomb loads that would eventually exceed 60,000 pounds (B-52D/H), and roughly a 6,000-statute-mile range. Even better—coupled with the new air refueling techniques coming on line—that already impressive range could be extended to infinity, or at least as long as the airborne crews could take it.

From the moment the new bomber's drawings were revealed to the Air Force, it was love at first sight, which made the long-drawn-out process of actually building the airplane that much more agonizing. The prototype YB-52's maiden flight did not occur until nearly four years later, when Tex Johnson and Guy Townsend quietly took the highly classified ship up at Boeing Field near Seattle. The test program accelerated rapidly after that, accompanied by all the problems that might be associated with so radical a new design. Difficulties included aileron control snags, elevator trim issues, cockpit layout changes, delays from subcontractors (eventually there would be 5,000 companies involved), and a host of other engineering obstacles, both major and minor. The process sounds fairly routine when recounted so casually in a brief space such as this; the people who had wrenches in their hands would say it was anything but.

The first production model, the B-52A, flew on August 5th, 1954, but it wasn't quite right, and only a handful of As were built. Most of the flagrant bugs were eliminated in the B and C models, and eighty-five of them came off the line.[2] It was with the B-52D, however, that everything came together—

reliable daily operations, full defensive capability, the latest in bombing and navigation systems, maximum payload configuration, and maximum range. Everybody was so happy with the D that Boeing's Seattle and Wichita, Kansas, factories feverishly cranked out 170 examples in 1955 and 1956. The E and F models that followed were essentially enhanced D models—chiefly, greater automation in the bombing and navigation system beginning with the E and more powerful turbojet engines starting with the F. A total of 189 of the latter two types were manufactured.

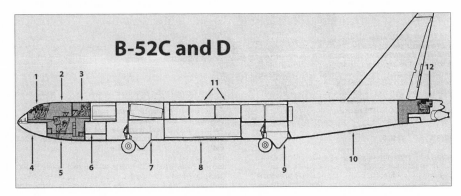

Fig. 1. B-52 C/D drawing/compartments. 1. pilot's station 2. bunk & celestial navigation station 3. EW officer's station 4. nose radome compartment 5. RN/nav station 6. alternator deck 7. front wheel well 8. bomb bay 9. rear wheel well 10. aft equipment compartment—"47 section" 11. fuel tanks 12. tail gunner compartment. (*Drawing modified from the illustration on Pages 1–6, USAF T.O. 1B-52C-1, 1970*)

The bomber was changed dramatically, however, with the B-52G. The most fundamental alteration involved the basic airframe itself, whereby the magicians at Boeing managed to lower the empty weight of the airplane while still increasing its overall gross operating weight. Simply translated, that meant it was able to carry more fuel, substantially increasing its unrefueled range. The primary external difference between the B-52G and the preceding models was its vertical tail fin, which had been reduced by eight feet (down to forty-feet high to save weight). Another thing a casual observer might miss was the gunner's relocation into the forward cabin, from where he would now operate his tail guns by remote control. Additionally, in what might be thought of as an uncanny stroke of prescience, there was also designed into the G a standoff launch capability for the soon-to-come Hound Dog and Skybolt nuclear-tipped air-to-ground missiles (AGMs), early forms of what we today call "cruise missiles."[3] This under-the-wing missile capacity not only increased the B-52's nuclear deterrent strength. but it also helped ensure the bomber's very long operational longevity. From late 1958 to early 1961, 193 G models were delivered.

The H series B-52, the "Cadillac" model, would be the designer's ultimate expression of the Stratofortress—bearing all the improvements and minus the baggage inherited from everything that had come before. The H's greatest advance—and mighty it was—was the replacement of the long-used turbojet engines with the outstanding new TF-33 Turbofan jet engines. Those superefficient babies not only reduced fuel consumption, they also boosted power by a good 30 percent, which was pretty much engineering Valhalla. A total of 102 Cadillacs came off the line; by the end of production in 1962, a grand total of 744 Stratofortresses had been manufactured.

The Vietnam-era B-52 had a basic crew of six—the pilot, copilot, radar navigator (primary bombardier), navigator (primary navigator), electronic warfare officer, and tail gunner. Those positions could be, and often were, augmented by up to three additional crewmen: the instructor pilot (IP), located in a jump seat between and a little to the rear of the two pilots; the bunk position (rarely used), behind the IP jump seat and on the left side of the fuselage; and the instructor navigator station down in the Black Hole. In case of a personal crisis, the instructor navigator (IN) seat also doubled as the forward cabin honey bucket, a circumstance that occasionally provoked off-color jokes at the occupant's expense. These last three stations were not particularly desirable in that they didn't have ejection seats; a condition made even more ominous by printed emergency procedures that plainly pointed out men seated in those positions had only modest chances of surviving a bailout.[4]

The tail gunner was the only enlisted man on the aircraft (and almost always was a staff sergeant or higher until the latter stages of the Vietnam War). He sat alone and in the rear of the airplane on the A through F models, and in the forward compartment next to the electronic warfare officer in the Gs and Hs. In charge of last-resort aircraft defense, his armament in the A through Gs was the MD-9 Fire Control System, a radar-directed package of four .50-caliber Browning M-3 machine guns housed in a tail barbette and bearing an effective range of about 1,500 yards. When they built the Hs in 1961–62, the .50-caliber guns were replaced by the more authoritative GE M61 20-millimeter six-barrel rotary cannon.

The gunner's tail compartment was an uncomfortable station. The quarters were cramped, and its independent life support system was notoriously cranky. Even more annoying was the backward-viewing ride; during flight, the tail was subjected to continuous seesawing, twisting, and whipping motions—

movements sometimes so severe they could and often did batter the gunner against the sides of his compartment. Conditions in the tail were even worse in low-level flight—to the point where other crew members could only shake their heads in wonder that any man could endure so much sustained physical abuse. The A through F model station did not have an ejection seat; in the event of an emergency bailout, "Guns" had to pull a handle to jettison his entire turret pod, then roll out into space through the gaping hole.

The B-52 tail gunner was the last in a long and honorable line of airborne manned gunnery positions, a tradition going all the way back to the early days of World War I. Every bomber built had always carried at least one machine gun. The Flying Fortress hosted a bunch of them—there was a gunner in the tail, two in the waist, one in an under-the-fuselage ball turret, one on a top turret above and just behind the cockpit, and, on most models, a nose machine gun operated by that jack-of-all-trades, the bombardier. The postwar B-36D Peacemaker, however, was the all-time "gunner champion," with a total of eight turreted positions.

A brief digression: Except for pilots and copilots, bomber crew positions and titles have always been fluid, their precise nature reflecting whatever modifications, additions, and subtractions were to occur in that period's generation of bombers. By the time of the B-52, many changes had already been made from the standard bomber crews of but a decade or two earlier. Gone were the flight engineers and radiomen; observers, bombardiers, and radar operators had been transformed into navigators and navigator-bombardiers; and nearly all the manned gunnery positions had vanished. Only the gun in the tail, a warplane's most vulnerable point of attack, survived in the B-47, a position that was also carried over into the B-52. Inevitably, the "bomber gunner" era had to come to an end. In 1991, concurrent with the breakup of the Soviet Union and the finish of the Cold War, the B-52 tail gunner position was eliminated in the remaining Gs and Hs (by then all the Bs through Fs had been attrited, gone to the smelter, or were a memorial), and the basic B-52 flight crew was reduced to five.

The second half of the defensive team was the electronic warfare officer. Like the radar bombardier, the EWO, or EW, or more commonly "E-Dub," traced his heritage back to the latter stages of World War II and the first "electronic countermeasures operators" employed by Allied forces to jam German radio signals. During that war, the code word for an EWO was "Raven," and from that point on and up to present day, their professional descendants have continued to refer to themselves as "Ravens" or "Crows."

Instead of hurling bullets or bombs, the B-52 "E-Double-U" (yet another nickname) machine-gunned the enemy with a dazzling array of electrons. He was the first line of bomber defense and, with all due respect to the gunner, the most important. Armed with a variety of seriously complicated black boxes, powerful transmitters, jammers, and other fake-out gadgets (i.e., radar screens, oscilloscopes, threat sensors, and tracking jammers to use against MiGs, missiles, and flak batteries farther out; chaff dispensers, flares, and other spooky stuff for close-in knife fighting), the EW had but a single focus: *Let No Harm Come to Thy Stratofortress.* Underappreciated during the Cold War, the electronic warfare officer would earn the respect he'd always deserved in the hot Vietnam conflict, especially during the Linebacker campaigns.

The pilot and copilot managed the crew, controlled the aircraft's operating systems, and flew the ship. Nearly all books currently in print about the B-52 present the bomber and its operation from the pilot's perspective, and it serves little purpose for us to stumble over the same, heavily trod ground here. (After all, this book is about navigators and bombardiers.) Having said that, however, rest assured the more important aspects of the pilot's role, especially as those functions pertained to crew relationships and bombing and navigation, will indeed be explored at considerable length later on. For the moment, suffice it to say the B-52 forward deck left-seater was not called the aircraft commander for nothing. He was captain of the ship in all respects—should he not be an exceptional leader and aviator then nobody was going to go anywhere to bomb anything. The copilot was his trusted assistant and implicitly an aircraft commander-in-training himself.

Finally, then, we come to the navigator-bombardiers, a combination of position names that hadn't been used to any degree until the B-47 was rolled out. The Stratojet not only reversed the trend of ever-larger crews in each succeeding bomber, but it also changed the way the Air Force described many of its nonpilot officer aircrew. What had been three navigation-type positions in the B-36 became only one in the B-47, the radar observer/navigator/bombardier, or "RO."[5] This crew integration experiment at the Stratojet's bombing and navigation station was successful, and it led directly to the idea of using two RO-types (to be called "navigator-bombardiers") in the more labor-intensive B-52 lower compartment. These individuals would have a relationship similar to that between the pilot and copilot—two men trained the same way, with the senior navigator-bombardier bearing ultimate responsibility for the collective effort of both.

In the B-52C and D models, the Black Holers were equipped with the AN/ASQ-48 Bombing and Navigation System (to be discussed at much greater length in the pages to follow). The B-52E through H models had available the later and more sophisticated AN/ASQ-38 BNS, which had been enhanced by greater automation and all the latest in digitized electronics and avionics. While there were many similarities between the two Q systems, the differences were still substantial enough to require completely different bombardier school curriculums.

Two quick asides: 1) The author has never seen or heard an explanation as to why the more advanced Q-38 had a lower nomenclature number than the preceding Q-48 system, and 2) Many old-time Q-48 bombardiers still insist their less-automated, more hands-on system had the edge on reliability and bombing results. So there you are—just a couple of more tidbits that can be added to the rich and storied history of the big fella.

Which brings us to the origins of the B-52's somewhat infamous nickname. The Air Force had officially dubbed it the Stratofortress, but that never really caught on, maybe because there had already been too many other "forts" along the way. Uncharacteristically for a warplane, the B-52 rolled along for quite some time without a popular handle, which in retrospect wasn't all that surprising given its very serious Cold War persona—the great Nuclear Shield of Democracy. By the time the dirty little Southeast Asian war had gotten up to speed, however, the bloom had gone out of the big boy's rosy cheeks and he was ripe for the picking.

Ironically—and according to the conventional wisdom of four decades ago—it was the fighter pilots, the bomber crew's so-called "little friends," who came up with a name that stuck. The jocks had intended it as a pimp job, a derogatory term they could hurl at those they deemed their "inferiors," the heavy bomber pilots. The occasion served as yet one more reminder of the vast (though usually latent) intellectual powers that had long resided within the Dilettante Air Corps, a priceless moment of inspiration the single-seat, ready-room kiddies were able to sandwich in between snapping towels at each other's butts and pulling on jumpy suits—all those crucial preliminaries to still another of their excruciatingly fatiguing nine-minute hops.

"Hey, Mr. Truck Driver," the fighter pilots would crow, "better roll that BUF, that big ugly "fellow," into the closest hog barn before it gets confused with a real airplane!"

The joke was on them. The "big ugly fellow" moniker (fellow rhymed with "sucker") fitted the personality of the giant, middle-aged airplane to a tee. The bomber crews, displaying their usual maturity and equanimity, recognized a fine opportunity by promptly turning the entire business on its head—they deflected the intended slur by simply embracing the gag name as their own.

Naturally, the stiff-necks at SAC headquarters in Omaha opposed any kind of informal nickname for their precious bomber, especially one not acceptable in mixed company when spoken in its original form. But that was like trying to stop an avalanche, so Air Force public information officers went into damage control mode instead, using what today is known as positive spin. Whenever newspapermen requested an explanation of this BUF/BUFF expression they had begun to hear, the bright-eyed public information officer would affect a knowing chuckle. "It's an affectionate term," he would stage-whisper to his fellow propagandists, "meaning the Big Ugly Fellow." Or Flying Fellow, or Friendly Fellow, or Fat Feller, or any combination thereof except what the last word actually was.

The crews recoiled at this prevarication of their bomber's new handle, along with its implied sissification. They were proud of the vulgar alias, holding very dear their own perceptions and world view of what it meant. Oddly enough, some bomber types discovered they were reluctant to say aloud this new nickname, even among their own, perhaps subconsciously anxious the machine might overhear the remark and attempt to exact revenge, an anthropomorphic tick not uncommon when airmen and their planes become intimate.

When the men who flew the B-52 *did* choose to publicly refer to the aircraft, the matter was usually handled with circumspect indirectness. And if the new acronym/name did come up in the exchange, it would be spoken without emotion or flamboyance and most often expressed in a "lower case" sense. Which is to say: If the last bomber flown had not been in an ornery mood and determined to kill him, and if the crewman was feeling on the generous side, he might neutrally regard it as the "Buf," the big ugly fellow. On those other occasions, however, when the machine was suspected of unpredictability or showed signs of outright treachery and the discussion made it necessary to mention the airplane at all, then an oblique term such as "that thing" was more likely to be used instead—as in "we were on a low-level Oil Burner Route last week when the terrain avoidance radar crapped out, and that thing tried to drive us through a mountain."

In any event, and no matter what anyone might have intended at the start, the "Buf/BUF/BUFF" nickname became firmly established during the Vietnam War and has now endured for four decades, with no sign of it giving way.[6] Short in form but limitless in meaning, it has come to represent the sum of all the love, hate, superstition, anger, fear, respect, and pride both past and present B-52 bomber aircrews feel toward their big ugly feller.

CHAPTER FOUR

LeMay

For the majority of Americans in 1955, the year the Stratofortress became fully operational, the terms "B-52 bomber" and "Strategic Air Command" were already interchangeable household expressions, synonyms for the Cold War's premier nuclear deterrent force. Few other phrases of that time generated the same graphic images of national life or death—indeed, of life and death for the entire planet. Looking back today at those high stakes of a half-century ago, it is difficult to comprehend the doomsday monolith most people simply referred to as SAC came to pass largely through the efforts of a single man.

He was an American air force officer named Curtis E. LeMay, one of those exceedingly rare military leaders who could be characterized both as a general's general and an individual the lowest ranking enlisted man would follow down the barrel of a cannon. He earned his third star after fewer than twenty years of active service, the tenure it normally takes for even fast trackers to achieve lieutenant colonel. His World War II combat record was nothing short of magnificent—he was the man who firebombed Japan into submission, coming out of the war with the kind of "tough as nails" reputation even Gen. George Patton would have envied. The glowing effectiveness reports in his personnel jacket were well deserved, for LeMay was just as capable and rugged as he looked and acted, all the way down to his bulldog countenance and ever-present cigar.

One day in the mid-1950s, so a revealing (likely apocryphal) LeMay story went, the general was conducting one of his dreaded flight-line reviews. While strolling past a B-52, he decided to make an up close and personal bomb bay inspection, a lit cigar clenched firmly between his teeth. The conscientious but temporarily insane crew chief raised an objection.

"General," he blurted, "you can't smoke this close to the aircraft."

LeMay shot back, "Why the hell not?"

The crew chief was beside himself. "Because, sir, the plane might explode!"

LeMay slowly withdrew the cigar from his mouth, sternly eyed the young man, and said, "Son, it wouldn't dare."

In 1946 an increasingly belligerent Soviet Union was daring the United States of America into yet another war—this time an atomic war. The American Army Air Force responded by completely refashioning itself into three brand-new combat organizations: The Air Defense Command (ADC would provide "homeland security" in the form of aircraft detection, identification, interception, and destruction, using fighter/interceptors), Tactical Air Command (TAC was to supply fighter/bombers, transports, and recon at battlefield level to interdict enemy forces and provide close air support to ground troops), and the Strategic Air Command (SAC was responsible for the intercontinental delivery of atomic bombs).[1]

From the very beginning, this newly formed Strategic Air Command was deemed so critical to national security that it received its own unique chain of command, one under the direct operational control of the president of the United States. Gen. George C. Kenney was appointed SAC's initial commander, and he remained in charge for the first two years, content with using the World War II B-29 Superfortress as his "foundation" atomic bomber.[2] However, after the creation of an independent United States Air Force in 1948 and arrival of the first of the very-long-range B-36 Peacemakers, U.S. leaders realized SAC had to be brought to another level. The Cold War was ratcheting up—the Soviet Union had become even more bellicose, China was on the verge of falling to the Communists, and the Berlin Airlift was in full swing. A newly fearful America needed the kind of general in charge who would literally put the fear of God into its enemies. The nation gave LeMay the keys to its atomic bomber fleet.

He took command on October 19, 1948, and wasted not a moment in signaling his independence by moving Strategic Air Command's headquarters out of the Washington, D.C., political hotbox and into the North American hinterlands near Omaha, Nebraska. (The move, he said publicly, was necessary because the Soviets could too easily hit the East Coast.) The relocation wasn't a bad idea on a couple of levels: an Offutt Air Force Base location made it more difficult for either Russian bombers or the Pentagon to interfere with LeMay's ambitious plans. No one had the temerity to seriously question the move, then or later, and the headquarters remained at Omaha throughout SAC's lifetime.

LeMay made his presence felt from the get-go, never easing the pressure on himself or his people during the decade he served as SAC's commander. From the first, he made clear the primary mind-set he required of his men: "We are at war NOW!" That quote was no Air Force public information officer sloganeer talking; that was pure LeMay himself. He sincerely believed the nation was in a neck-deep fight to the death. The general backed up such bold talk with quick action, making sweeping changes throughout the SAC organization.

He saw to it that new bomber bases were established around the continental United States while simultaneously accelerating the delivery of the sleek new B-47 jet bombers. Centralized command and control procedures were put into effect. Comprehensive training programs were implemented, augmented by clear-cut organizational goals and objectives enforced by rigid testing and high performance standards. During World War II, only selected men had led waves; in LeMay's SAC, each crew was required to be "pathfinder" qualified. Every in-flight procedure and emergency contingency was anticipated, the required activity and responses spelled out in explicit detail. Conformity and standardization were the watchwords—individual crew initiative was not only discouraged, it also became punishable. The idea of anyone taking a B-52 for a joyride would have conjured up images of a firing squad.

On top of all this, LeMay was a triple-rated officer (one of the first), having held pilot, navigator/observer, and bombardier aeronautical ratings since before World War II. He could talk nuts and bolts with anybody on the crew, and they, in turn, quickly learned there would be no snowing the commanding general.

The changes weren't all strictly business. Important morale and career-enhancing motivational programs were introduced, most notably better pay, improved base housing for both officers and enlisted men, and the aircrew "spot promotion" system, whereby, for example, a permanent first lieutenant who received outstanding effectiveness reports could become a temporary captain, with full pay and benefits for so long as he maintained his superior performance.[3]

Contrary to what one might instinctively want to believe, LeMay's inflexible, doctrinaire approach actually worked quite well in fighting the Cold War—the question of whether or not to employ nuclear weapons and perhaps destroy all of mankind in the process left zero margin for error. Unfortunately, those same policies were to have near-devastating consequences when SAC became enmeshed in the conventional Vietnam conflict, as we shall see in coming chapters. Of course, in the beginning, no one could have forseen any such thing. All the SAC men knew at the time was that their commanding general was hell on wheels and they had better stay razor sharp if they wanted to be a part of what promised to become a unique and elite military unit. Which

Fig. 2. The SAC emblem and the command's founding general, Curtis LeMay, as he looked in the 1930s when a junior officer helping to develop the Air Corps' formal navigator and bombardier training programs. (*Courtesy National Museum of the U.S. Air Force*)

is precisely what came to pass. Within a few short years, LeMay's leadership, his iron discipline, and the nation's commitment to provide SAC with the finest air weapon systems available resulted in pure Damascus steel—the most powerful, combat-ready bomber force in the world.

In 1948 SAC rostered just 52,000 personnel and 837 assorted aircraft. LeMay had only thirty-five first-line B-36s and about the same number of B-50s (essentially beefed-up B-29s); the rest of SAC's planes were nearly all of World War II vintage. When he turned over the helm on June 30, 1957, to become Air Force vice chief of staff, the Strategic Air Command had 224,000 troops and 2,700 aircraft in its inventory, including 127 still-operational B-36s, 1,500 B-47s, and 243 B-52s. By 1957 midair refueling techniques had become firmly established, and SAC also maintained a stable of airborne tankers organized in dedicated squadrons attached to each bomber wing. At that time, there were 742 of the KC-97 Stratofreighter propeller-driven tankers (a spin-off of the B-50) and 24 of the newly operational KC-135 jet-powered Stratotankers.[4]

By 1960, long after LeMay had gone to the Pentagon (his huge leadership shadow colored SAC's heart and mind for years after his departure), one-quarter of all Strategic Air Command bombers and tankers were on fifteen-minute alert, standing by to launch at the sound of a klaxon. In addition, a certain number of nuclear-armed bombers were constantly rotated on round-the-clock airborne alert, ready to instantly attack the Soviet Union should the Go Code be received. During this same period, SAC's intercontinental ballistic missile (ICBM) arm also became operational, with two-man launch teams embedded in "silos" beneath the North American prairies—standing the same kind of alert as the bomber crews—ready to fire nuclear-tipped ICBMs at a moment's notice.

The bleak prospect of Armageddon served LeMay's cause well. The American people gratefully wrapped their arms around the security blanket known as SAC. Carefully noting this phenomenon, the U.S. Air Force leadership began standing shoulder to shoulder with LeMay on his budget requests, eager for their branch to gather in as many defense dollars as possible. LeMay/SAC was not at all bashful about expending this political capital, soon running roughshod not just over other Air Force generals, but the Army, Navy, and Marines as well. There were unintended consequences to this—for example, a strong case can be made that LeMay's disdain for any kind of fighter aircraft, both as SAC commander and as Air Force chief of staff, set Tactical Air Command and Air Defense Command so far back it affected national security. Air Force Vietnam-era fighter pilots to this day still blame SAC's early dominance of the USAF for their relatively poor showing against the North Vietnamese MiGs (i.e., compared to the Korean War and Naval Aviation's results in Vietnam).

LeMay did not believe in fighting Korean or Vietnam-type "brushfire" wars and strongly resisted allowing SAC to become involved in them, though he eventually had to cough up a couple of B-29 air groups for Korean interdiction. He never wavered in his devotion to the "massive retaliation" doctrine as the only necessary counter to Communist aggression. This attitude put him increasingly at odds with the John F. Kennedy and Lyndon B. Johnson administrations, which believed the world struggle was evolving more into a series of tactical skirmishes; they subscribed to the "domino theory"—one nation falling to Communism would lead to the adjacent country going down, and so on. LeMay considered that kind of thinking rubbish—the only thing that mattered was to keep waving the big stick at Russia and Red China. Until Vietnam went out of control, he had his way. The man's military reputation was so fearsome and his popularity with the American people so high, even presidents were afraid of him.

The general's dedication to "his" Strategic Air Command was total; the stories about him, told both in and out of the military, became the stuff of legends. Any one of them revealed more about the fellow than a basket of air power books. An early favorite came during those electric months following the B-52 design unveiling at the Van Cleve Hotel. It seems an engineering team from Wright Field was determined to make an Omaha pilgrimage to pitch LeMay on taking one last look at an improved version of the B-47. The Stratojet was already in full production by then, and, so the thinking went, if additional performance improvements could be garnered from this already ongoing program, then no new bomber would be necessary and huge sums of money could be saved. The SAC commander would have none of it; he was fully aware of both the abilities and limitations of the B-47 and had concluded that airplane in any form simply wasn't capable of doing the job the B-52 could. Furthermore, he didn't want any distractions to interfere with the future development of the Stratofortress. Midway through the briefing, LeMay lost what little patience he might have started out with and stopped the proceedings cold: "Just how deep does a program have to be buried before you dumb sons-a-bitches at Wright Field will stop digging it up?"

Later, after the first prototypes X and YB-52s had been constructed, the general learned Boeing had placed the two pilot seats in the same tandem manner as the B-47, that is, one pilot in front of the other, fighter style. LeMay objected strenuously to this, believing bomber pilots should be seated side-by-side for communication and crew coordination purposes. One can just hear him privately saying that the change was absolutely necessary because, dammit, that's the way it was *supposed* to be! All 742 production B-52s were built with side-by-side pilot seating.

On yet another occasion, back in the days when there were still more propellers than jet engines on the flight line, LeMay decided to test the resoluteness of his airplane guards. After approaching a weaponed bomber without first seeking permission or showing his credentials, the general was challenged by an armed sentry. LeMay, who was dressed in mufti, acted pugnaciously.

"Don't you know who I am?" he bellowed.

The guard stood his ground. LeMay became even more verbally aggressive, and made a move toward the airplane. The guard unslung his weapon and leveled it at LeMay.

"Sir," the guard said, shaking in his boots because he did not understand what was happening or precisely who this maniac thought he was, "if you do not stay where you are, I will shoot!"

LeMay immediately dropped his "saboteur" pose, identified himself, and promoted the astounded guard on the spot. The story, like all the others, traveled through SAC at light speed.

There were many such LeMay anecdotes; all of the ones that gained long-lasting currency had the implicit approval of (or even originated with) the commander himself. He used them to make a point, no matter how outrageous the incident might seem to others. Usually everybody understood his underlying message, though sometimes the buccaneer approach got him into trouble, especially during the Kennedy and Johnson administrations when he was Air Force chief of staff.

LeMay came off sounding like a raving lunatic during the 1962 Cuban Missile crisis; after the Russians had backed down, he was purported to have suggested that we "go in on Monday and make a strike anyway."[5] When the Vietnam War began heating up, he grumbled publicly that Johnson and Secretary of Defense Robert McNamara were pussyfooting around militarily. "We are swatting flies when we should be going after the manure pile." Later a much more damaging statement was attributed to LeMay (a comment apparently intended for his biographer's ears only) that said he favored "bombing [North Vietnam] back into the stone age." Johnson finally had enough, and LeMay was retired in 1965 after thirty-five years of military service.

The general's admirers have always wished that in retirement he would have, as Gen. Douglas MacArthur put it, quietly faded away. It was not to be. For reasons never clear, LeMay agreed to become independent and segregationist George Wallace's vice presidential candidate in the deeply fractious 1968 election. (LeMay once commented late in life his motive had been to take votes away from Humphrey and throw the election to Nixon, despite the logic of his conservative candidacy having the opposite effect.) Although nothing in LeMay's service record has ever suggested he was a bigot, that unfortunate political act nevertheless put a permanent stain on the great man's legacy.

The "father of SAC" died on October 1, 1990. Less than two years later, following the breakup of the Soviet Union, his beloved, but no longer necessary "child," passed into history with him. On June 1, 1992, the Strategic Air Command was disbanded, its men, equipment, and remaining B-52Gs and Hs absorbed into the newly created Air Combat Command. The Gs were themselves retired soon after the first Gulf War, leaving only the B-52Hs to carry the torch into the new millennium.

As this is written, and granting one's perspective comes from a short historical distance, a powerful argument can be made that in the end, Curt LeMay's lifework was vindicated, that the Cold War he fought so valiantly for so long did not just end but was instead *won*. And that the Soviet Union lost the contest primarily because it went bankrupt trying to compete—economically and militarily—with America and its vaunted "triad" nuclear defense: the undetectable submarine force armed with Polaris-type missiles, the nearly invulnerable, underground North American ICBMs, and the nation's most versatile deterrent—LeMay's B-52 bomber. One would be hard-pressed to find a single individual who crewed a Strategic Air Command Stratofortress between 1955 and 1992 who isn't proud to have been a part of that victory.

CHAPTER FIVE

Early Navigators and Bomb Aimers

Having a singularly outstanding war machine like the B-52 to build a Strategic Air Command around was one thing; possessing properly trained flesh and blood personnel to deliver its payload to precisely the right place at precisely the right time—with 100 percent reliability—was quite another. Along with the establishment of strong ground support programs and dependable nuclear "fail-safe" procedures, probably the most difficult hills for Gen. Curtis LeMay's embryonic SAC to climb were anywhere-in-the-world navigation and accurate bomb dropping.

For us to properly understand how those challenges were met, we must start at the very beginning. The science of navigation—or perhaps art, arguments still continue about which it is—has been around for at least three thousand years. Phoenician and Greek sailors were the first to codify the "getting from Point A to Point B" problem, finding their way across the Mediterranean by using crude charts, the North Star, and a rough form of "deduced" navigation, a term later corrupted either by accident or design into the modern expression "dead reckoning" (DR). (Early wags claimed it came about because "if you didn't reckon right, you're dead.") The Romans gave a name to the discipline, combining the Latin words *navis* and *agere*, meaning "ship" and "direct" respectively.

The first navigation aid was most probably Polaris, or the "pole star," which could be relied on to stay fixed in an almost due north position—the most meaningful constant in the heavens. Likely a few clever mariners also learned to make educated guesses at their relative earthly locations, using the sun, moon, and certain other celestial bodies. The careful observation of ocean currents, cloud formations, and wind patterns arrived next (think Polynesians). The earliest man-made device used was the compass. That little item surfaced about a thousand years ago when it was discovered (and no doubt attempted

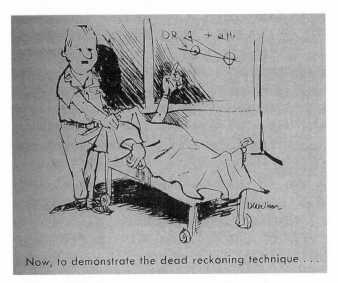

Fig. 3. The Navigator Magazine, USAF, Mather AFB, CA, Spring 1968. (*Author's collection*)

to keep secret) a magnetized iron needle floating on a cork in a bowl of water always pointed toward north. This was especially useful in seas like the murky North Atlantic, where ships could sail for weeks without seeing the stars.

The basic question of which way to point the bow had thus been determined, but what about how long it would take to get from A to B? Said another way—how fast was the vessel going? Most maritime historians credit the sixteenth-century Dutch for coming up with the answer. The Netherlanders called it "heaving the log." The idea was to tie knots in a rope at equal intervals, attach a heavy piece of wood at rope's end, toss the wood over the side, and then count the number of "knots" that slipped through a sailor's hand during a fixed period of time (measured by an hourglass). The more "knots" that went by, the faster the ship traveled.[1]

Later—after compasses and the first speedometers had been invented—astrolabes, cross-staffs, and ring dials came along, which were observational devices that enabled sailors to calculate the approximate local time and/or measure the altitude (angle) between the horizon and the sun, a value conveniently equivalent to the latitude of a high noon observer.[2] In 1735 the Englishman John Harrison perfected an accurate chronometer. (He called it a watch; we would think of it as a clock.) Harrison's invention at last made it possible to use celestial bodies to determine a ship's longitude,[3] something marine navigation had long needed if for no other reason than to cut down on the many costly shipwrecks caused by location uncertainty during close approaches to land. A few decades later, just after the American Revolution, a mathematical genius, Nathaniel Bowditch, published *The American Practical Navigator*. Coupled with the development of more precise sextants and octants,[4] this book paved the way to modern maritime navigation by providing important computation techniques, tide tables, and, most valuably, accurate astronomical tables—all of which greatly improved the quality of latitude and longitude positions obtained through celestial observations.

While early twentieth-century aviators had essentially the same navigational requirements as sea voyagers, their operating circumstances were quite different. Ocean ships progressed slowly and in two dimensions; airplanes were comparatively fast and moved in three. Celestial computations and observations onboard ship could be done relatively leisurely, often with a daily set of noon sun lines (one azimuth change shot just before noon, one at noon, and one just after noon) and perhaps a nighttime three-star fix or two.[5] Airplanes, conversely, demanded frequent and continuous position updates, a nearly impossible physical feat, especially for the first pilots, who almost always were the sole operators of their frail, highly unstable machines. They could afford neither the time nor the distraction, nor could they physically carry out mariner-style navigation and still fly the airplane. The plain fact was the early birdmen had to devise some kind of a new flying navigation system.

What they came up with, at least for flying over land, not only met their needs but it also was easy to use: lay hands on a good map, strap it to a leg, and while airborne compare its markings with any prominent landmarks seen below. It worked so well that nearly all of the original airmen promptly adopted the technique; the more alert grasped the additional wisdom of map-highlighting a few of the more conspicuous surface features before departure, instinctively understanding even then that preplanning was essential to sound flying—something aviators still call "staying ahead of the airplane."

Favored map-reading checkpoints during and just after World War I included small towns (names appeared on water towers and train depots), dams, odd-shaped lakes, large rivers, and all the many train tracks that gridded the nation. (There were few trunk highways in those days.) Comprehensive railroad maps were used most often early on, the rails themselves often called "iron compasses." Operating at night became more difficult, though still possible, especially if there was a moon; electric light beacons and bonfires positioned along well-traveled routes were found to be helpful.

Taken altogether, then, this read-the-map/look-at-the-ground/compare-against-the-map-again process came to be known as flying by "pilotage." Coupled with basic DR techniques,[6] pilotage formed the basis of nearly all aerial land navigation until paneled flight instruments and radio aids became available.

By the 1920s, it was becoming more and more apparent that for aviation to get beyond puddle-jumping Jennys, itinerant barnstormers, and flying circuses, much more sophisticated pathfinding capabilities were going to be required. Fortunately, a few well-educated, progressive-thinking, navigation-minded birdmen had been hard at work on just that.

One of the first was nonpilot Arthur Whitten-Brown, he of the aforementioned 1919 transoceanic flyers, Alcock and Brown. Brown, a World War I British observer who had been shot down (and permanently lamed) used his spare time while a German prisoner of war to study overwater navigation. After his release, he sought out decorated Royal Air Force pilot John Alcock, who shared the same dream of flying nonstop between North America and the British Isles (and winning the London *Daily Mail*'s £10,000 prize). Brown offered his services as ship's navigator, which Alcock eagerly accepted. Largely self-taught, Brown used his own methods of dead reckoning and celestial navigation to guide the Vickers Vimy across the stormy, forbidding North Atlantic. His navigation kit consisted of little more than pencils, plotter, dividers, maritime charts, and sextant. Extensive precomputations were required at that time for airborne celestial observations, and as a consequence, Brown restricted himself to just four bodies: the sun, the moon, and the stars Vega and Polaris. Soon-to-be Sir Arthur's unprecedented air navigation feat would speak for itself; he hit Ireland almost dead on course.[7]

In the United States, also not long after the World War I armistice, U.S. Army 2nd Lt. Albert F. Hegenberger was directed to establish the Instrument and Navigation Branch of the Air Service at McCook Field (part of the hallowed ground that subsequently became Wright Field, then Wright-Patterson AFB, then the National Museum of the USAF at Wright-Patterson AFB). Hegenberger and his small group identified the cockpit instruments needed for safe and reliable military flying, encouraged manufacturers to build prototypes, and then tested those new devices under actual conditions. Significant advances were made along many fronts, including more accurate airspeed meters, better compasses, sextants customized for airborne celestial observation use, and dedicated air navigation maps.[8]

In addition, good magnetic compasses finally became panel installed, replacing the previous jury-rigged or hand-held devices. Pitot tubes (small, hollow pipes that scooped in air directly from the forward slipstream) and static ports (air pressure sensors neutrally located on the side of the fuselage, set at 90-degree angles from the pitots) combined to provide a more reliable means of determining airspeed and altitude than either a pair of wind-watery eyeballs peering down from an open cockpit or a strip of metal attached to a wing strut that measured wind resistance by how much it bent. Also, the Sperry Company (founded in 1910) was by this period churning out high-quality gyroscopes, which were found to be excellent mechanisms for maintaining a steady aircraft heading and flight attitude and would eventually prove critical to modern bomb sighting.

By the end of the 1920s, the standard cockpit instrument panel had essentially evolved—an integrated package of meters located directly in front of the pilot that old-timers still refer to as the "steam gauges." They included the magnetic compass, altimeter, air speed indicator, vertical speed indicator, turn and bank coordinator, heading indicator (gyrostabilized), and attitude indicator (gyrostabilized artificial horizon).

In 1927 Hegenberger and another Air Corps lieutenant, Lester Maitland, put their new instruments, equipment, and knowledge to good use when they hopped into a Fokker trimotor and made the first flight from California to Hawaii. Only a month earlier, the cunning Charles Lindbergh had conquered the Atlantic on nothing but pure dead reckoning, though even he understood he was lucky not to have gotten lost—Hegenberger and Maitland never would have found those isolated Pacific dots on straight DR. Following his successful 1927 Hawaii flight, Hegenberger and two other Army instructors were ordered to start up the first pilot navigation school at Wright Field, next door to where he'd done his earlier instrument work.[9]

It was Hegenberger who later brought the Army's attention to famed marine navigator Harold Gatty. From "down under" (Tasmania), Gatty was trained at the Royal Australian Naval College and served in the Australian merchant navy, where he first began contemplating aerial navigation by the stars. Gatty's initial fame had come from surveying Pan American's flying boat Pacific routes in the very early 1930s. But it was his subsequent work in the development of the "Type B-2 Groundspeed & Driftmeter," along with his institutionalization of dead reckoning/celestial navigation procedures, precision use of in-flight instruments, and improved charting/logging techniques, that had aroused Hegenberger's interest and led to Gatty's deep involvement and permanent influence on American military aviation. Not without ample reason did the great Lindbergh himself call Harold Gatty the "Prince of Navigators."

With Gatty now in the lead, the Army Air Corps authorized the opening of two additional pilot navigation schools (increasing the emphasis on instrument flying and celestial observations) at Langley Field, Virginia, and Rockwell Field, California. By late 1935 the training of pilot-navigators had advanced to the point where civilian Gatty was able to pass the baton on to Army Lt. Thomas Thurlow, whose assistant was another promising Army Air Corps lieutenant named Curtis LeMay. Thurlow and LeMay continued to build on Gatty's exceptional accomplishments, widening the scope and sophistication of the training and thereby setting the stage for the successful introduction of America's first official "multicrewed" bomber, the Martin B-10B.

In 1933 air navigation received another boost when the U.S. Naval Observatory first published an aviator's version of their *Nautical Almanac*, dubbed the *Air Almanac*. To use the *Air Almanac*, one applied the local "Zulu," or Greenwich Mean Time, to that day's calendar page and extracted the Greenwich Hourly Angle of the celestial body to be observed. This information was then used to interrogate the Navy Hydrographic Office's Sight Reduction Tables, which were astronomical compilations (descended from Bowditch) that provided certain data derived from the latitude, declination, and hour angle of selected navigational stars. By combining the technical information extracted from these two volumes and incorporating it into Gatty's simplified celestial fix computation scheme, many of the complex mathematical pre-computations faced by early observers like Arthur Whitten Brown were eliminated. Assuming the availability of an accurate watch and reliable sextant, the American military aviator now had all the resources necessary to determining his position anywhere on earth.

All these multifaceted improvements had paved the way for one last great leap forward into the modern era—the advent of electronic navigational aids, which permitted all-weather "blind flying." The first major rollout of this long-sought capability came in 1929, when the four-course radio-range was introduced. A direction-finding apparatus, the new system co-opted the same low AM frequency technology used by the popular commercial radio stations that were just beginning to sweep the country.

Boiling radio range down to its essence, there were two pairs of Morse code antennas (four total transmitters) broadcasting simultaneously from a single station (often located on an airport). Each pair of transmitters created an electronic "figure eight" signal pattern that was sent out about a hundred miles, with the two "eights" perpendicular to each other. While one pair of transmitters dotty-ditted the letter *A* (. -) and the other broadcasted an *N* (- .), the pilot tried to steer his airplane into one of the four zones (or lobes) where the two eights overlapped. If he heard dot-dash (*A*), he was to turn one way, if it was dash-dot (*N*), turn the other. If it was a steady hum (meaning the airplane was inside a lobe), the pilot knew he was "on the beam" (and the desired airway). When the airplane crossed directly over the transmitters, there was a "cone of silence," which confirmed station passage (another of those cherished navigation "fixes"). And that was "radio ranging."

Pilots of the day swore by *"A-N,"* a common shorthand term for the aid. There were problems, of course—just as one's garage radio crackles, spits, and fades whenever a thunderstorm passes over, likewise did the radio range. The sound of rain beating against the fuselage often made it difficult to hear the *A*s and *N*s, and crystallized snow created such a loud, steady hissing that it often was enough to close down the range. Mountains were a problem, weakening and sometimes even splitting the beams, which resulted in an entirely new set of hazards. Naturally, such interruptions were all the more likely to occur when everything else was going wrong with the airplane, the seriousness of the transmission degradation directly proportional to the seriousness of the emergency. Still, radio ranging was far better than anything else that had so far come down the pike, and it was universally embraced by all of aviation.

Radio direction finding (RDF) followed on *A-N*'s heels, and then later ADF, or automatic direction finding, both based on similar low-frequency radio-ranging technology but with many additional refinements that provided even safer all-weather, day or night flying. Later, after World War II, the same concept would be used to develop very high-frequency and omnirange-bearing (VOR) and distance-measuring equipment (DME), along with every pilot's true love, the instrument-landing system (ILS), which did as much to bring reliably scheduled airline service as speedy, above-the-weather jet aircraft.

Now, all of these wonderful instrumentation and navigation advances were just terrific insofar as meeting the domestic requirements of American military aviation and civilian air transport. As early as the mid-1930s, both airline and Army Air Corps pilots had been able to consistently guide their aircraft to any point in the continental U.S. by way of a reliable network of land-based radio-ranging stations. But there still remained one very large and grave concern. In spite of the progressive (overwater) navigation training at least some of the Army's pilots were now receiving, could the Air Corps actually function effectively outside of the North American continent?[10]

It wasn't a theoretical question. Most of the world beyond the Americas was already sliding into chaos—both Imperial Japan and Nazi Germany were on the move, their territorial ambitions seemingly growing by the day. Army leadership had little doubt that if an air war had to be fought, it wasn't going to happen over Des Moines. Clearly, and without much more delay, military aviation had to rethink and reorganize its aircrew navigation training programs and requirements to meet the coming global threat. What's more, long-range navigation was only the half of what was increasingly on the U.S. Army Air Corps' mind during the 1930s. There was also the matter of thoroughly coming to grips with its equally difficult-to-handle first cousin: precision bombing.

The extraordinarily complex nature of *that* problem came to light at the start of World War I. Three fundamental issues quickly became apparent: 1) the airplane must maintain a direct course line to the target so the weapon does not fall to the left or right; 2) because of the forward momentum of the aircraft the bomb has to be released at a precise instant somewhere in advance of the target so when it arcs out and downward it will not fall long or short; and 3) wind, aircraft speed, altitude, and platform stability (plus much more) dramatically affect 1 and 2.

The first attempts at solving these problems came in 1915 when a British professor-cum-artillery lieutenant, Henry Tizard, developed a simple bombsight with two rigid aiming bars mounted on the side of the fuselage. The pilot sighted along them until they lined up with the target, consulted his stop watch, and then tripped the release lever at the appropriate moment. Another rudimentary bombsight was manufactured by none other than the Edison Phonograph Works of Orange, New Jersey. A simply made, folding mechanical device containing no internal motors, it was mounted on the side of the fuselage, with the pilot leaning out into the slipstream and somehow managing to peer through it. Neither of these devices even pretended to address above item 3, and it followed that the results were not much improved from the squinty-eyed windage and guesswork methods of 1914, though several thousand of Tizard's "CFS 4" bombsights were nevertheless manufactured. Probably the most important contribution of these early mechanical devices was in legitimatizing the very idea of more sophisticated bomb aiming.

The first at least reasonably effective bombsight is generally acknowledged to have been developed by the Royal Navy in 1917 and subsequently adopted by the U.S. Army in 1919. Designated the "Mark 1," it incorporated methodologies that for the first time seriously attempted to compensate for ground speed and drift. It had a significant drawback, however; it was necessary for the pilot to crisscross the target at 90-degree angles to get the proper drift readings to do the drop calculation. (Navigators would later term this a "double-drift" procedure.) Flying a relatively slow-moving warplane back and forth across a target in a hot war zone is not a very practical method of bombing people doing their best to prevent same.

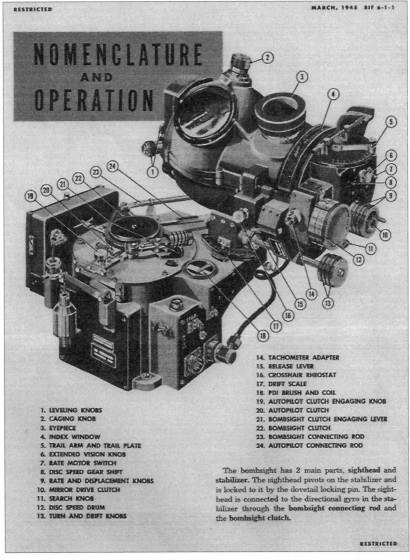

RESTRICTED   MARCH, 1945 BIF 6-1-1

NOMENCLATURE
AND
OPERATION

14. TACHOMETER ADAPTER
15. RELEASE LEVER
16. CROSSHAIR RHEOSTAT
17. DRIFT SCALE
18. PDI BRUSH AND COIL
19. AUTOPILOT CLUTCH ENGAGING KNOB
20. AUTOPILOT CLUTCH
21. BOMBSIGHT CLUTCH ENGAGING LEVER
22. BOMBSIGHT CLUTCH
23. BOMBSIGHT CONNECTING ROD
24. AUTOPILOT CONNECTING ROD

1. LEVELING KNOBS
2. CAGING KNOB
3. EYEPIECE
4. INDEX WINDOW
5. TRAIL ARM AND TRAIL PLATE
6. EXTENDED VISION KNOB
7. RATE MOTOR SWITCH
8. DISC SPEED GEAR SHIFT
9. RATE AND DISPLACEMENT KNOBS
10. MIRROR DRIVE CLUTCH
11. SEARCH KNOB
12. DISC SPEED DRUM
13. TURN AND DRIFT KNOBS

The bombsight has 2 main parts, sighthead and stabilizer. The sighthead pivots on the stabilizer and is locked to it by the dovetail locking pin. The sighthead is connected to the directional gyro in the stabilizer through the bombsight connecting rod and the bombsight clutch.

RESTRICTED

Fig. 4. Norden Bombsight (*U.S. Army Air Forces, Bombardier's Information File 6-1-1, March 1945*)

In the middle twenties, both the Army Air Service Engineering Division's "Bombsight Type D-4" (designed by Georges Estoppey) and the "Sperry C-1" bombsight appeared. The D-4 was built on the same mechanical/stopwatch-timed principles as the Mark 1, while the Sperry Company made use of a promising, though difficult-to-perfect new gyroscopic technology. Although both were deemed "better" than the Mark 1, the blunt truth was that in any conditions other than ideal, the D-4 could not hit the broad side of a barn and the C-1 simply never worked properly.

The big breakthrough finally came in 1931–33 with the invention of the transforming, gyrostabilized "Norden Mark XV Bombsight." The XV's preliminary results so impressed Army brass that a dedicated bombardier cockpit station was installed in the new B-10Bs then coming on line. (Navigators did not receive a dedicated station until the B-17.) To everyone's delight, the Norden thoroughly proved out operationally in the Martins, and it and its successor models were subsequently installed in the greenhouses of the B-17 Flying Fortress heavy bomber, B-25 Mitchell medium bomber, B-26 Marauder medium bomber, B-24 Liberator heavy bomber, and nearly every other U.S. bomber of World War II.

The XV's maker was Carl Norden, a Dutchman who came to the United States in 1904 and went to work for Elmer Sperry making ocean liner gyrostabilizers. A brilliant engineer and ambitious, Norden left the Sperry Company in 1915 to set up his own company and had already been awarded several patents for aerial torpedoes before turning his attention to bombsight invention. From 1931 on, when the XV was first revealed, all the way into the 1940s, Norden continued to make improvements on his amazing device. The American military remained fearful throughout the 1930s and for most of World War II that the enemy would somehow get hold of one, discover the sight's secrets, and turn it against the Allies.

That worry was justified, for Norden's achievement was of enormous and lasting significance (so much so that the Sperry Company immediately began working on a similar bomb-aiming device, coming up with its own "Sperry S-1" in the later 1930s).[11] Until the Model XV finally appeared, the vexing, inherent trigonometric difficulties in obtaining consistent bombing accuracy had simply defied a really good solution. After all, just exactly how *does* one place various types of gravity-propelled weapons on specific earthly targets when releasing them from fast-traveling airborne vehicles operating in three dimensions? As anyone who has ever had anything to do with the proposition can testify, it's a lot tougher than it looks on paper. A partial list of the many variables would include the size/weight of the bomb, shape of bomb, manner of releasing bomb, malfunctioning bomb, wind/drift, turbulence, aircraft altitude, aircraft speed, defective aircraft, defective bomb-aiming equipment, ballistics computation error, human aiming error, flak-induced aiming error, and Murphy's Law.

Norden's answer had been to design a complete bomb-aiming system rather than another single-dimensional-approach device, which would have assuredly led to yet one more dead end. This new system was built around what today would be characterized as an optical/mechanical analog computer. It had two primary components: the sight head (what you looked through) and the stabilizer (like the tiny otolith "balance" organs in the human inner ear, spinning gyros kept the Norden in three-dimensional equilibrium). These major hardware elements were supported by a complex array of knobs, dials, levers, cranks, cams, mirrors, tiny motors, and a multipower telescope (the optics).

Greatly simplified, here's how it worked. About thirty minutes from the target, the bombardier took up his position in the greenhouse. Preparatory to arrival over the initial point, he entered his ballistics and other precomputation data (accounting for many of the variables discussed above) into the Norden system. Once on the bomb run, he positioned himself over the bombsight and grasped an appropriate knob with each hand, pressing an eye against the optical eyepiece. If his estimated inbound heading, wind values, estimated time of arrival (ETA), and other precomputations were at least close to matching actual conditions aloft, his crosshairs would already be in the general vicinity of the aiming point. Using the course and range knobs, he would then manually crank the hairs across his field of view until they lay atop the aiming point. If the precomputations (especially for wind) had been off a little—they, of course, always were—he could "kill" the actual drift and speed differences by continually dragging the crosshairs back to the target, allowing the Norden computer to neutralize the disparities. This coordinating on the target of a vertical (course line) crosshair with a horizontal (release line) crosshair came to be called the "synchronous method," a phrase that was carried over into the B-52 era. Considerable manual dexterity and not a little finesse were essential. As Bruce D. Callander, a World War II B-24 bombardier and former editor of the *Air Force Times*, put the matter: "It was roughly equivalent to trying to tune a radio and adjust the temperature in a shower at the same time."

Once the bombardier was satisfied he had acquired the target, he notified the pilot he was ready to take over the airplane. The pilot then threw a switch on his instrument panel, slaving the airplane's autopilot to the bombsight crosshairs. After that, if the bombardier moved the hair placement, the plane would obediently turn to follow. When the To Go (TG) meter ran down to zero (aircraft straight and level for the final thirty seconds), the Norden permitted the bombardier to either manually "toggle" the weapons loose at the flip of a switch or allow the system to automatically release the bombs when the horizontal and vertical hairs crossed one another over the aiming point. (The latter technique eliminated the human element in deciding that exact instant when the weapons should be dropped.) Once the release lights started blinking, the bombardier called "bombs away!" After the weapons were clear of the ship, the pilot took the airplane back from the Norden/autopilot and exited the target area.

The Norden sight wasn't perfect. By late 1943 it had picked up something of a reputation for occasionally pitching out "bad bombs" (i.e., yielding an unfavorable CE, or circular error; hits within two hundred feet when dropped from 12,000 feet were considered an acceptable to good mark in a B-17). Machines are machines and certainly the nearly 44,000 Norden bombsights built were not all created equal. Nevertheless, in most cases, inconsistent bombing results were usually more a function of a man's skill than the equipment itself. Which is *not* to say the Norden wasn't a fragile piece of goods. If it was dropped or otherwise mishandled, as sometimes happened, its working parts could get screwed up, and if they did then, yep, you bet, whether tail-end Charlie or pathfinder bombardier, the ordnance was going to get scattered all over hell's plantation.

When push came to shove, however, the Norden could be relied on. There was no better testimonial to this than a combat mission flown on August 6, 1945, when a B-29 Superfortress bombardier, using M9B Norden Bombsight Number Victor 4120, successfully dropped the world's first atomic bomb against a belligerent. A little over two decades after that event, the author, then a raw first lieutenant navigator-bombardier, found himself assigned to the same squadron as the bomb aimer of that B-29, a gray-haired, soon-to-retire full colonel named Thomas Ferebee. Along with a number of other freshly manufactured Black Holers, he was privileged to sit at the elbow of Ferebee and hear the full story of the *Enola Gay's* drop on Hiroshima from The Man's own mouth. The encounter would be seared into his and the other young men's brains forever, they understanding even at so tender an age that such a relatively "primitive" optical aiming device was still capable of accurately delivering a nuclear weapon.

Yet the Norden wasn't the final word in World War II bomb-aiming technology; not by a long shot. Big things were happening in the European theater, with even more scientific breakthroughs following an already long string of British technological achievements.[12] Among the new innovations were two radically designed navigation and bombing systems, both scheduled for roll-out in 1942–43. Their code names were Gee/Oboe and H2S.

Even today, few people are aware of how important ground-based electronic radio aids and airborne radar mapping were to the success of Allied bombing raids against Occupied Europe and Nazi Germany (and indeed, how much they would mean to the British and American nuclear bomber forces in the still far-off future). The British "Gee" navigation system was a brand-new radio beacon scheme (though with many similarities to the American *A-N* radio-range) that allowed an airplane to locate its position by timing the delays (measured in milliseconds) between three sets of ground-based transmitters sited fifty to one hundred miles away from one another. Initially, these sites were in southern England; after D-day they were moved to the continent, dramatically extending Gee's useful range. At the risk of oversimplifying what was a fairly complicated system, the Gee stations (a master and two slave transmitters—no need to go any further into that part of it) each broadcasted an electronic "hyperbola" on a designated frequency. This hyperbola was the radio energy pulse radiating outward, something like the ripples caused when a stone is dropped in calm water. Each of the three ripples had a value that, when intercepted by an aircraft receiver, could be translated into how far in miles the airplane was from each transmitting station. It was fairly accurate—at a distance of 250 miles, Gee (the name apparently was derived from the word "grid," roughly the form these hyperbolic lines took on a Gee chart) could provide navigators with a three-sided electronic ellipse of between one to six miles in size, with the airplane located somewhere inside it.

Despite this relatively good positioning, Gee wasn't accurate enough for precision bombing. That would have to come from still another radio-based system, designated "Oboe." Using essentially the same kind of electronic interrogation/answer technology used today in identification friend or foe (IFF) transponders, Oboe transmitted from a pair of English stations (actually there was a chain of these coupled-up transmitters) that were always called "Cat" and "Mouse." The Oboe radio frequency bandwidths were quite narrow; each of their individualized electronic pulse packages brimmed with chirping Morse Code dots and dashes. The Cat station kept the bomber moving on the correct track to the target (as with *A-N*, if you heard dots, turn one way; if you heard dashes, turn the other; if you heard a solid tone, you're "spot on"), while the Mouse station signaled when to release the pay-

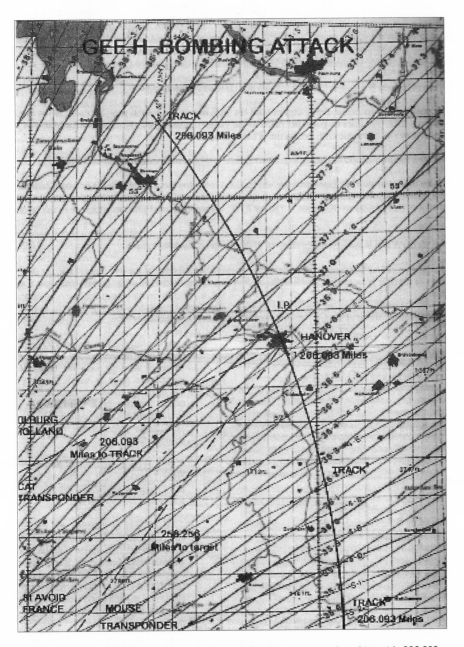

Fig. 5. Assume target in Hanover: CAT transponder distance to track and target is 206.093 miles. MOUSE transponder distance to bomb release point is 258.256 miles. (*Courtesy John Howland and the AFNOA, as reprinted in their newsletter "DR Ahead," October 2003*)

load. Late in the war, scientists found a way to combine Gee and Oboe into a single system called Gee H.

This "through-the-cloud-bombing," as it was called, was a godsend, for the Norden bombsight could only be operated in clear weather and was almost always restricted to daylight operations. Gee/Oboe, however, could be used at night and in any weather. It was also just as accurate as the Norden, with a published standard circular error of 120 yards at a broadcast distance from the station of 250 miles. Overall, there was just a single serious drawback, albeit a very big one: The Oboe operators in England could only handle one aircraft at a time.

Which was a primary reason why both the Royal Air Force's Bomber Command and the American Eighth were pleased to also have the "H2S" bombing and navigation system in their arsenal. That was a strange designator even for a wartime code word—odd enough, in fact, for us to ponder over it for a moment. Perhaps it was nothing more than a random acronym selected by security people to help obscure the technology's true nature. Or possibly "H2S" was derived from some technical aspect of the project that only the engineers could identify with; or maybe somebody simply uttered a throwaway remark that happened to stick to the wall. (One story had a British Lord commenting he thought the entire program "stunk"—H2S being the chemical symbol for hydrogen sulfide, or rotten egg gas.)

The only thing that mattered, of course, was what H2S was: the first ground-mapping radar used in combat, made possible by the 1940 invention of the cavity magnetron by British scientists John Randall and Harry Boot. The cavity magnetron was the first practical apparatus that could make microwaves, which doesn't sound all that impressive (though it did eventually lead to that convenient instant oven we enjoy in our modern kitchens) until it's understood how much more powerful radio detection and ranging (radar) became with the mechanism. Early researchers were amazed to discover that the magnetron allowed their test radar to pick up a submarine periscope from six miles away.

Even richer pay dirt was struck when the magnetron was conjoined with a sophisticated cathode ray tube, and both of those components were connected to a scanning antenna on the bottom of a flying machine. The result was a detailed, black and white rotating-map display of every natural and man-made feature that passed beneath the aircraft. Tuning controls were added to aid resolution and scope interpretation and—voila![13] When Field Marshal Hermann Goring learned about H2S late in the war, he exclaimed, "My God! The British really can see in the dark!"

Fig. 6. Surface features converted to "paints" on mapping radar, in full-scan mode. (*USAF Manual 51-40, vol.1, August 1968*)

Returning to our earlier discussion regarding the insular nature of the 1930s-era U.S. Army Air Corps, it's important to further stress how tiny American's air forces were before the opening of European hostilities, with just a few hundred mostly obsolete bombers in its entire inventory. Furthermore, as late as the summer of 1939, dedicated (i.e., separate) non-pilot navigators and bombardiers were not required crew members on U.S. bombers; the airplanes were still relatively simple to operate, and the Army's overall defense responsibility remained exceedingly modest. Up to that point, pilots performed these other aircrew duties; whatever additional instruction they required was conducted fairly easily and inexpensively via supplemental on-post training at the squadron level.

But with the advent of the "modern" B-10B, all that began to change. Although many Gatty-Thurlow trained pilots had displayed a good aptitude for bomb aiming, plotter, and divider work, including how to use a sextant and compute three-star fixes, the Army now realized there was no way a man could fly a modern bomber and handle heavy navigational/bombing work-loads at the same time, and that would be even more the case with the soon-to-arrive and more complex B-17. What's more, the intricacies of Norden-type bomb aiming had also underscored the need for more formally trained men to function as separate bombardiers. The final straw: it made very little sense to require expensively trained pilots to perform jobs other rated aircrew-men could do as well or better and at far less cost.

Everything came to a head when World War II erupted in Europe. The U.S. Army Air Corps was immediately faced with an enormous buildup in size and complexity, requiring huge numbers of freshly recruited aircrew-men to be trained in many flight specialties to operate the thousands of new bombers slated for construction. It was at that moment the positions of "navigator" and "bombardier" were officially created. Once and for all pilots were removed from all other flying duties. (Simultaneously, the positions of flight engineer, radio operator, and the gunnery stations were evolving inde-pendently within the enlisted ranks.) Additionally, in an attempt to enhance the public prestige of and aid recruitment to the new aircrew positions, the Army had by 1941 established formal and separate aeronautical ratings for navigators, bombardiers, aerial observers, combat observers, and technical observers. These officer airmen were further authorized to wear distinctive wing badges on their uniforms, putting them on at least some level of par with the pilots.[14]

In 1940 and with Pan American World Airways' assistance, the Army Air Corps opened its first formal nonpilot navigation school at Coral Gables, Florida. That same year, the first formal optical bombardier school was also installed at Lowry Field, Colorado. In early 1941 an even more comprehen-sive bomb school opened at Barksdale, Louisiana. And then, in the immediate aftermath of Pearl Harbor, it was decided to transfer Air Corps bombardier training from Barksdale to a big new prototype post near Albuquerque, soon to be designated Kirtland Field. Many more navigator and bombardier schools were to follow. By 1945 over 50,000 men would win their navigator wings; another 48,000 would pin on bombardier badges.[15]

The selection and training of these navigators and bombardiers began with a series of rigorous mental and physical tests, after which those candi-dates chosen to begin a program were enlisted into the Army and assigned to a training post. Before June 20, 1941, they were servants of the U.S. Army Air Corps; subsequently the official paperwork informed them their employer was now the U.S. Army Air Forces. There were few already-com-missioned officers in the early programs; nearly all candidates were cadets, and their training was designed to not only turn them into aircrewmen but "officers and gentlemen" as well. All the trainees, no matter what their rank, were required to first complete a ten-week "preflight" course. This ground activity included physical conditioning, hand combat and personal weapons training, military traditions and protocol, officer responsibilities, aviation theory, and an introduction to navigation.

After preflight, the in-depth work began. The course for those assigned to the navigator schools ranged from fifteen to twenty weeks, depending at that moment on the needs at the war fronts. The nav trainees had the fundamentals of pilotage, dead reckoning, radio-range navigation, and celestial navigation drummed into their heads literally day and night. Each man could expect a total of about one hundred airborne training hours in an AT-7 "Navigator" aircraft.

The bombardier course was initially set at twelve weeks. Later, after the training programs got fully up to speed, every bombardier candidate could expect eighteen weeks of concentrated effort after preflight. As one would expect, bomb school students spent the bulk of their time learning the mechanics of bombing in general and the operation of the Sperry and Norden optical bombsights in particular. Later in the war, the emphasis in many schools shifted away from Norden-type optical bombing to the more advanced H2S bombardier/radar observer training. In those days, bombardier candidates were not expected to also be navigators, except perhaps in an emergency, and as a result they received only rudimentary instruction in pilotage and dead-reckoning techniques.

Besides the heavy desk work, optical bombardier trainees spent a lot of time working with a customized ground simulator. Bruce Callander, the Liberator bombardier mentioned earlier, described how that "sophisticated" training device worked: "The simulator resembled a house painter's scaffold with a bombsight on top. The self-propelled trainer moved slowly across the floor of a hangar as the bombardier steered it with the knobs of his sight. He aimed at a cardboard target mounted on a small moving box and, as the trainer passed over this 'bug,' a solenoid-driven pen dotted the hits on the target."

Most World War II bombardier students flew their training missions in AT-11 "Kansan" airplanes. Both the navigator's AT-7 and the bombardier's AT-11 were modified versions of the C-45, which in civilian life was a Beechcraft Model 18. This airplane was about the size of a modern twin-engine, propeller-driven business airplane, with an old-fashioned-looking double tail similar to the B-25 (i.e., Doolittle bomber), though it had a tiny tail-dragger landing wheel instead of the tricycle gear on the Mitchell. These nav/bomb school planes weren't very big—gross weight was a little under 10,000 pounds, max speed about 215 mph, and they had to struggle to reach 20,000 feet. The cockpits were small, with just enough room for two or three students, an instructor, and a pilot.

Washout rates ran at about 20 percent for navigator trainees and 12 percent for the bombardiers. Those men deemed unfit for the work were sent directly into other assignments as enlisted men; others who still showed promise were "washed back" into the next class, and a surprising number of them went on to finish the program, which actually improved the washout rate, though one would not learn that from the officially reported statistics. After each man successfully completed the full course, he received his aeronautical rating as either a bombardier or a navigator and was commissioned an Army second lieutenant.[16]

A few days later, with the easy part now behind him, the newly rated officer would be on the way to his assigned unit, where he would receive additional type-training in a specific aircraft. Only after that would he become a fully qualified Army Air Force bomber aircrewman and declared ready for combat.

CHAPTER SIX

Training the Cold War Magellan

By the later 1950s, with World War II rapidly receding in the rearview mirror and the B-52 Strategic Air Command bomber age growing ever larger in the front windshield, the U.S. Air Force had consolidated nearly all of its many nonpilot flying officer training schools into just three locations. These were Harlingen Air Force Base at Harlingen, Texas; James Connally Air Force Base at Waco, Texas; and Mather Air Force Base at Sacramento, California. The previous training programs of Army Air Force/ U.S. Air Force aircraft observers, technical observers, combat observers, ECM "Ravens," navigators, bombardiers, and radar (H2S) operators had likewise been reconfigured into three primary specialties: navigator, radar observer/ bombardier, and electronic warfare officer.

In the B-52 those first two jobs saw even further refinement. Entry-level Black Holers were required to be formally cross-trained—first as a navigator, then a radar bombardier. The Buf's electronic warfare officer was also obliged to first hold a navigator aeronautical rating before he could become eligible to attend the six-month EWO school. By the time the Vietnam War had gotten up to full speed, the majority of active-duty nonpilot SAC officer aircrewmen had received their training under this framework and at one of the above three bases.

In the mid-1960s, the Harlingen and James Connally navigation schools were closed, and Mather (affectionately known as "Mother") Air Force Base became solely responsible for all Air Force navigation, bombing, and electronic warfare officer training.[1] Mather held that role until the station was permanently closed in 1992 and Randolph Air Force Base, Texas, was selected as its replacement (and where similar schooling continues to this day).

The men selected for navigator training during the 1950s and 1960s arrived from one of four routes: Aviation Cadets, Officer Candidate School (OCS), Reserve Officer Training Corps, and the Air Force Academy. Aviation Cadets, the elder statesman of the four, traced its organizational roots all the way back to World War I. From the first and throughout the following decades, it was an on-again, off-again program—both for pilots and observers—its production robustness dependent on however strong the war winds were blowing at that particular moment. Aviation Cadets had the least-demanding education prerequisites of any of the four paths (a college degree was not always necessary), and the syllabus for Aviation Cadets called for the making of officers and navigators simultaneously. The men began as and remained enlisted personnel until receiving their commissions and aeronautical ratings.

A brief aside: As late as 1960, the majority of B-52 aircrew were still "brown shoe" types; that is, men trained during the World War II era and before the creation of an independent Air Force in 1947 (the Air Force regulation shoe was black). Many of these former Army men did not hold a college degree, having come up the hard way through Aviation Cadets, and were quite "old" when compared to the captains, majors, and lieutenant colonels of a decade later. The average age of a Buf crewman fell dramatically as the brown shoes began retiring in the later 1960s.

The second alternative was OCS, or Officer Training School (OTS), as it was also called. A young man so inclined toward Air Force OCS—and many were in those days of universal selective service—would first need to earn a four-year college degree, enter into and successfully complete a three-month officer training program at Lackland AFB in San Antonio, Texas, and then, if qualified, be sent to navigator school. Upon graduation from nav training, the already-commissioned student officer would receive his aeronautical rating.

The third option was ROTC. Here the civilian college freshman voluntarily enrolled himself in his school's cadet detachment, and if he stayed the course for the full four years, earning a minor in Air Science along the way, received his commission as a second lieutenant in the U.S. Air Force. Like the OCS graduate, he was then eligible for assignment to navigator school as a student officer. By the early 1960s, approximately four out of the five new Air Force officers entering the service were coming via ROTC.

The final route to wearing Air Force navigator's wings, and by far the most desirable from a career standpoint, was to secure admission to the Air Force Academy at Colorado Springs, Colorado. (The first class graduated in 1959.) The appointment itself was very difficult to obtain, to say nothing of surviving four years of an extremely rigorous academic and physical curriculum.[2] About 85 percent of academy appointments came from the recipient's congressman or U.S. senator (the vast majority were competitive, merit-based selections); the balance through other routes such as direct presidential appointment, honor graduates of military schools, and sons of Medal of Honor winners. Naturally, any candidate, no matter how much clout he might have initially had, still needed to pass the entrance examinations on his own.

A United States Air Force Academy (AFA) commission was preferred over all others for two very practical reasons: 1) it was understood by everyone the AFA was, in the words of its first superintendent, "training generals, not second lieutenants," meaning whether the man stayed in the service or not he had one heck of an item on his resume, and 2) Academy graduates were awarded *regular* commissions as opposed to the reserve commissions received by Aviation Cadets, OCS grads, and ROTC cadets,[3] which meant that not only was a twenty-year minimum service pension virtually assured (reserve officers could be released anytime), but Academy alumni might also expect a faster promotion track.

Undergraduate Navigator Training (UNT), the school's formal name, was for the great majority of freshly commissioned student officers their first duty assignment. The exceptions were mostly limited to pilot eliminees and foreign officers (many from the Republic of South Vietnam during the 1960s). Contrary to conventional wisdom, only a small percentage of the men were pilot school washouts, though it *was* true that, deep down, nearly every navigator trainee counted himself a disappointed pilot candidate. In nearly all cases, the cause of that disappointment was traceable to eyesight—specifically the lack of 20/20 uncorrected vision. No matter that all the other mental and physical qualifications were the same for both navigators and pilots, the eye test was an absolute deal killer; if one did not have "perfect" vision, one was simply not admitted to UPT (Undergraduate Pilot School).

Despite the deep disappointment most of the fellows felt in having to "settle" for nav school, every trainee took solace in the knowledge that at least he would serve in the air, and his military rank/financial compensation were equivalent to a pilot's. Pay and allowances for an Air Force bachelor buck lieutenant after the first flight school sortie (qualifying him for hazardous duty, or flight pay) ran about $5,300 a year, an OK entry level salary for the time. During the Vietnam War, the average B-52 Black Holer—call him a married captain on combat duty with over eight years service—made a much more respectable $11,000 per year.

In the mid-1960s, that kind of "captain money" was but a fantasy to the new brown bar navigator trainees arriving at Mather AFB,[4] though the size of their paycheck was not the uppermost thing on the fellows' minds. Excitement and apprehension were the leading emotions of the moment. Fortunately, there was little time to dwell on either. The young men were streamed into their new work on a dead run, and that intensity did not let up in the slightest over the next thirty-eight weeks.

Preflight was the first phase, as it always had been and always will be during flight training. Here the student was introduced to his new environment—basic aerodynamic theory, the atmosphere, and the general nature of the vehicles operating in that unnatural, gaseous realm above the earth's surface. There was also a good deal of physical activity, which continued throughout the entire course and was not restricted to the then-popular Canadian 5BX calisthenics regimen. Combat judo (hand-to-hand fighting) was a lively course that most of the boys enjoyed and, along with team sports, provided excellent conditioning. The rifle range spiced things up; the men were introduced to several hand weapons, with special emphasis on the Smith & Wesson .38 revolver (an item common to survival kits). Everyone shot for record, and a few earned their Small Arms Marksmanship Ribbon. Water survival and life raft courses in the base pool brought confidence in one's ability to live through an over-ocean bailout, despite occasional sessions that degenerated into something resembling preschoolers playing with their rubber duckies.

Mass assemblies in the high-altitude pressure chamber, where groups of student navigators were collectively introduced to the dangers of hypoxia (lack of oxygen) and the effects of expanding gases within the human body, provided olfactory experiences never to be forgotten. Vertigo was demonstrated by means of a special chair (pompously called a "vestibular apparatus") in which the student was strapped and then, like a top, spun rapidly round and round until an instructor abruptly brought both to a halt. Watching the occupant thrash about after the little gyros in his inner ear had tumbled (see Norden bombsight discussion in chapter 5), his senses transmitting urgent but erroneous information to his brain that he was still spinning, demonstrated with memorable clarity the hazards of spatial disorientation.

The most adventurous activities were the practice ejection seat ride, jump training, and parasailing. It's one thing to watch a movie actor (supposedly) eject from an airplane on the silver screen; it's quite another to actually be lashed into a forbidding-looking seat positioned atop a powerful explosive and have that charge ignite under one's keister. It helped a little to know the entire practice ejection exercise would last less than a minute; the ring was pulled and the seat rocketed up a long vertical rail, then coasted back down to earth once its energy had been spent. A single ride sufficed—both to understand how the mechanism worked and to strive diligently from that day forward never to have to use it for real.

Parasailing/jump training got the adrenaline thoroughly flowing. Detailed instruction with regards to rigging and harnessing, followed by leaps into a sawdust pit from off an elevated platform, all were preparatory to the subsequent parasailing phase, which did a good job of simulating an actual parachute jump. Students were often apprehensive the first time they were launched hundreds of feet into the air from behind a speeding jeep, though after completing their prescribed three "jumps," they usually came back begging for more. The parasail, a training aid adapted from the recent development of a new thrill-seeking sport by the same name (or was it vice versa?), was essentially a standard parachute with the forward panels removed. Once it had billowed full and assumed the characteristics of a lifting airfoil, the jeep took off, and the chute yanked the tethered student into the air after only a few running steps. When the towline went slack, the trainee floated earthward while instructors bellowed orders from the ground:

To explore controllability of the descent:
"Tug on the left shroud lines for a left turn! The other way to go right!"
To prepare for the PLF, or parachute landing fall:
"Legs together! Knees bent! Eyes on the horizon!"
To survive the procedure:
"DO NOT UNDER ANY CIRCUMSTANCE," came the warning over the bullhorn, "PULL YOUR CANOPY QUICK RELEASE LANYARD UNTIL AFTER, I REPEAT AFTER, YOUR FEET TOUCH THE GROUND!"[5]

After the preflight phase, the student navigators began in earnest to learn their new trade—chart work, solving wind problems, time and heading dead reckoning, Morse Code, cockpit instrumentation, and how to use plotter, dividers, and circular slide rule. Various types of simulators were used to assist the fellows in absorbing as much of this new knowledge as was possible before they were transitioned into actual airborne conditions.

After many weeks of ground preparation, the trainees were at last ready for their first flight in a T-29C "Flying Classroom." The curriculum called

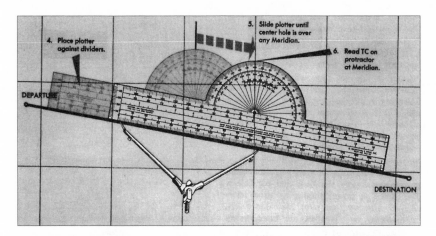

Fig. 7. Circular slide rule, plotter, and dividers—The navigator's basic "dead reckoning kit." (*USAF Manual 51-40, vol. 1, August 1968*)

for a total of forty training sorties, the first half dozen consisting of visual "pilotage," or map-reading flights. The next dozen would incorporate the same basic navigation procedures (called BNP) learned in the pilotage phase, but instead of looking out the window to determine where the airplane was, the student used a mapping radar set (another descendant of H2S) to establish his position. This radar scope interpretation (RSI) work turned out to be much more difficult than any of the men had anticipated; being able to properly compare/connect the "snowstorm" of indistinct, white-on-black radar screen returns with the cultural and topographic features depicted on an aeronautical chart took a great deal of practice. There was more than "a little" getting lost on these radar missions in particular, something that was allowed to happen by the instructors and pilots to drive various lessons home.

The T-29C pilots, all active-duty Air Force officers, were an essential part of the training process; from the first sortie forward, they expected the student navigator to conduct himself as a fully trained professional aviator. That included competently briefing the full mission before takeoff, then subsequently directing all elements of the actual flight to a successful conclusion. The trainee was given his head; pilots almost never interfered with compass directions, airspeeds, and altitudes radioed to the cockpit by the student lead navigator—each man took his turn—unless there was a safety of flight issue or an egregious error involved. Incidents involving the latter, "ah shucks" moments every trainee experienced at least once, became deeply memorable. To wit:

> Student lead navigator with worried look and sweaty forehead pressed against his mapping radar hood is directing the T-29C southbound down the Central Valley of California. Instead of turning the ship east toward Needles as he is supposed to, he radios the pilot a reciprocal heading he has mistakenly picked off his circular slide rule (Type MB-4A Computer, Air Navigation, Dead Reckoning). Airplane is now steaming hard for the Pacific. Pilot lets it go until the T-29C crosses the coast and is about to bust through the Air Defense Identification Zone (ADIZ).
>
> "Ahhh, lead nav, pilot here. Maybe before we go too much farther it'd be good to check our gas and make sure there's enough to make it to Honolulu."

The Tango Two-Niner Charlies were as good for this kind of work as the mercifully indulgent pilots who flew them. The military version of the Convair short-haul civilian airliner, the Flying Classroom looked a lot like a DC-3 that had been equipped with tricycle landing gear (as opposed to the Three's small, nonretractable tail-dragging wheel). The T-29s were workhorse propeller airplanes driven by two Pratt & Whitney Wasp Radials that furnished a 270 mph cruise speed, 1,800-mile range, and service ceiling of 30,000 feet. There was room in the cabin for three or four instructor navigators and fourteen student stations, each with its own dedicated work table, five-inch radar screen, and instrument panel. Five driftmeters, essentially upside-down periscopes bolted to the floor that allowed students to align a reticle on a ground object and "kill" (measure) the airplane's drift, provided a means to obtain the actual winds aloft. Overhead, two glass-bubble blisters were positioned along the fuselage centerline. These transparent canopies came into play about midway through UNT, when sextant observations replaced radar mapping as the student's primary method of "fixing" the aircraft's position.

The sun and star celestial training phases (i.e., "Day Cel" and "Night Cel") were eagerly looked forward to, usually kicking off one bright morning in the observation area (it looked something like a tennis court) adjacent to Bleckley Hall,[6] Mather's main classroom building. While the boys dutifully milled about in either Air Training Command's (ATC's) approved clockwise direction for even or counterclockwise for odd calendar days, the instructors solemnly handed each man his personal issue of the apprentice navigator's Holy Grail—the MA-2 Hand Held Sextant.

"Jeez, it's heavier than I thought!"

"How in hell are you supposed to hold it steady in turbulence?"

"I can't see a damn thing through this eyepiece."

"How do they get the bubble in there?"

"Look at all the wheels, dials, and watchamacallits!"

"A guy said if we break or lose one we got to pay for it."

"How much?"

"Over a grand."

"SHEET, man!"

Later that same day the fellows were introduced to the sixty celestial bodies the United States Air Force had drafted into service.

"Gentlemen," the instructor began, "you may set aside your college astronomy textbooks regarding star identification. The old constellation names first used by the Greeks are not practical in terms of our modern observational needs. Those of you who have tried to locate individual stars using the mythological figures know what I'm talking about. It's like an ink blot test; the spots, dots, and squiggles can mean anything. Furthermore, when the ancients gave certain star patterns such names as Orion, the Hunter; Leo, the Lion; Taurus, the Bull; and the always popular Virgo, the Virgin [pausing for the expected tittering], they clearly had other things on their minds."

If the instructor was a major or higher, the chuckles would last longer than the joke deserved. After the class settled down, a lengthy slide show and lecture commenced.

"As it turns out we can salvage a little from out of the ancient star naming system. The Pleiades group and Ursa Major and Minor are important. The latter two, also known as Big and Little Dipper, are especially useful in orienting the celestial navigator."

The gray, industrial-sized GAF projector whirred and up came the next image. "As you can see, we have constructed a memory device, one that we trust everyone can identify with." The instructor would clear his throat theatrically to be certain he had the trainees full attention. "From now on, gentlemen, I want you to think of the heavens as Yankee Stadium!"

Everyone could see right away the night sky had been arranged to look like the players, coaches, umpires, and selected fans in a baseball park. The instructor would start the detailed discussion by thrusting his pointer at the "manager" sitting in the dugout, assign "him" a star name, and explain that body's place in the firmament. After allowing the class a few moments to digest the information, he then moved on to the "man" in the on-deck circle, followed by the umpire, catcher, and batter. The projector would whir and click, whir and click.

"This next slide depicts our first baseman, Charlie Pollux. Standing next to him is Eddie Castor, the runner for the opposing team. Now compare what you see on the screen with your own star charts."

All eyes fell to the desktops.

"Notice how close together the twin stars of Pollux and Castor are located. While finding them isn't difficult, great care must be taken to avoid confusing one for the other, so carefully note their relative brightness and positions." The class would murmur in comprehension.

After rounding out the infield, the instructor moved to the "star" outfield.

"Observe how deep this fellow plays. That's because a power hitter is always at the plate when we are searching for—" He paused and cupped an ear, anticipating these bright young men would be looking ahead in the text.

"Mickey Diphda in left field," the class recited in unison.

"Very good, people," the beaming instructor said. "Mickey is way, way out there, with few other stars around him. You won't use the Mick very often, but on those nights when you've got solid cirrus above and every other body is obscured, you'll be plenty glad to know where he is."

The recognition sessions continued until the entire class could show 100 percent reliability in identifying all the navigational bodies, especially the favorites—the planets Venus and Jupiter, and the stars Polaris, Capella, Arcturus, Rigel, Vega, Betelgeuse, Aldebaran, Antares, and good old Sirius, the brightest nonplanet body in the night sky. After another heavy review of ground procedures, the students were sent back into the air, where they would slog their way through yet more long days and sleepless nights until finally able to claim mastery over the secrets of celestial navigation.

The key to that success could be summarized as follows: Carefully observing the preflight ritual of exactly synchronizing one's watch to Greenwich time by placing a phone call to the government's official clock ("This is WWV in Fort Collins, Colorado. At the tone, the correct Zulu time will be—"); learning how to properly extract and compute preobservation data from the *Air Almanac* and Sight Reduction Tables; accurately plotting dead reckoning positions crucial to sextant prepositioning; acquiring the manual dexterity necessary to making good sextant observations; actually being able to *find* the body while peering through the sextant eyepiece; obtaining reliable mathematical resolutions to all the observations; and, finally, the accurate plotting of that arithmetic result—three charted star lines forming a tight "fix" triangle. (You were somewhere in the center of it at the computed time of observation.)[7] All of this, by the way, had to be accomplished while enduring the distractions and physical discomfort that invariably accompanied every training flight—including the constant and very fatiguing engine and slipstream noise, bumpy air, poor cabin lighting, student congestion in the aisles upsetting tight shooting schedules, balky observation dome safety harnesses making one even more late for the precomputed shot that couldn't wait, and the inevitable, pitiless instructor hovering over a shoulder—red pencil at the ready.

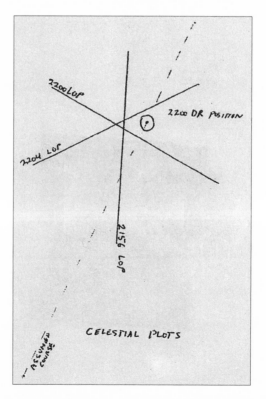

Fig. 8. Dashed line represents assumed course; the aircraft's assumed dead reckoning (DR) position at 2200 Zulu is as marked. Using that DR point as a baseline, three celestial observations are made four minutes apart and the lines of position (LOPs) plotted, with the aircraft's actual position at 2200Z somewhere inside the resulting triangle. The smaller the plotted triangle, the more confidence the navigator has in the quality of his observations. (*Courtesy Ken Ablett, from his booklet, "The Way It Was," 2004*)

Becoming proficient in day and night cel was at the heart of navigator school; once successfully accomplished, the student was on the home stretch. For most men, the celestial phases were the most satisfying part of their entire training—deliciously elemental disciplines that relied almost solely on an individual's wits for success. While electronic and radio navigational aids like ADF, VOR, DME, and over-water LORAN (LOng RAnge Navigation used radio pulsing transmitters similar to "Gee") were sometimes more accurate and easier to use, none offered as much nourishment to a pathfinder's soul as the lights of the Cosmos. In the years ahead, through many lonely and dangerous flights and after all the other fancy radio equipment had either broken down or was otherwise unavailable, the well-trained celestial navigator would come to view the sun, moon, planets, and stars as his most loyal and trustworthy friends.

CHAPTER SEVEN

Stratofortress Bombardier Training

Successfully completing UNT and winning navigator wings was the end of formal schooling for a majority of the men.[1] After a few days' celebration and home leave, they headed directly to operational assignments throughout the various U.S. Air Force commands. Most went to MATS (Military Air Transport Service), redesignated Military Airlift Command (MAC) in 1966, where they filled navigator chairs in large multiengine airplanes such as the C-124 Globemaster, C-133 Cargomaster, and C-141 Starlifter. Others went to Tactical Air Command's C-130 Hercules, SAC's KC-135 Stratotanker, and to certain reconnaissance aircraft (spy ships), as typified by the EC-121 Super Constellation. A few drew wild cards, especially as the 1960s deepened, like guiding the AC-47 "Puff the Magic Dragon" Gunship (yet another incarnation of the venerable Douglas DC-3) over hostile Southeast Asian jungles.

The balance of the freshly frocked also had new assignments, but their orders came without benefit of scenery change. These were the fellows headed for either Electronic Warfare Officer Training (EWOT) or Navigator-Bombardier Training (NBT), advanced schools located right there on the "Mother" campus. Some of the boys had asked for the duties, others were going in spite of their wishes; all knew what graduate work at Mather meant. With the exception of a handful of NBT types who would be selected for a RO position in the backseat of a recon/fighter/bomber like the RF-4C Phantom (the Navy called him a radar intercept officer, or RIO), everybody in bomb school was headed for SAC and the B-52 Stratofortress.

In years past, bombardiers had been trained under the assumption they would be assigned to one of several light, medium, or heavy bombers in the American inventory. Their instruction programs reflected that condition by building in enough course flexibility to accommodate differences in the aircraft types. No more. By the mid-1960s, the B-47 was gone and the limited production supersonic B-58 Hustler was on its last legs (a cool-looking bird and faster than blazes, but fatally burdened with insufficient payload and range capability—Curtis LeMay had to hold his nose when the politicians ordered it operational). The light/medium B-57s and B-66s were more recon aircraft than bombers, and anyway they were about finished as well. All of which meant there was only one place left for new bombardiers to end up. If anyone with an assignment to navigator-bombardier training still had doubts about that, the foreword in the NBT Student Study Guide quickly dispelled them: "This Guide was designed to guide you through the accomplishment of required procedures during your [simulator] trainer and flight missions. [The training is] based on current Strategic Air Command and B-52 procedures modified only where necessary to make them compatible with the T-29 airplane."

The long path leading to the specialized training the boys were about to receive had begun with the World War II–era B-29. The first "intercontinental" bomber, the Superfortress had been equipped with both the latest Norden-type optical bombsight and a more advanced version of H2S/H2X,[2] the American-built AN/APQ-7 "Eagle" bomb/nav system. The Eagle's radar equipment and avionics gave some of the best target resolution and bombing

Fig. 9. (USAF, from the introductory page to Radar Navigator's/Navigator's Manual, T.O. 1B-52C-1-1-2, 1970)

accuracy to date, but it came at a price. Its under-the-fuselage, wing-shaped antenna (presumably generating the Eagle moniker) was so big and unwieldy (spanning seventeen feet and weighing 1,000 pounds) that neither the crews nor maintenance could properly deal with it, and after the war the entire Q-7 system had to be revamped.

When the B-36 "Aluminum Overcast" was introduced in the late 1940s, its upgraded and enhanced AN/APQ-24 radar navigation and bombing system required support from three nav-bomb types—a navigator, a radar operator/bombardier, and someone called a "co-observer."[3] An unusual American aircrew position that reflected the overall complexity of the airplane, the co-observer's navigation and bombing duties were largely consistent with that of the airplane's copilot, who was also a distant third in his own pecking order behind a supernumerary aircraft commander and the left-seat pilot.

The B-36 Peacemaker's then "state-of-the-art" Q-24 radar lasted but a few short years before giving way to the more automated B-47's "K" system, which allowed a single crewman to both navigate and bomb. As advanced as the K was, however, it proved too unreliable to carry over into the new B-52s, so once again the engineers had to go back to the drawing board. The result was the MA-6A bomb/nav system, which was installed in the B-52A and B models. Although it was a big improvement over the K, the MA-6A still wasn't quite up to snuff. Really good Stratofortress lower compartment equipment didn't arrive until the mid-1950s, when at last the AN/ASQ-48 radar bombing and navigation system became available in the C and D models.

The Q-48 BNS (bombing and navigation system) was the cat's meow. We will speak a good deal more about this system in subsequent chapters, but here's a quick preview. According to Air Force Tech Order 1B-52C-1-1-1, it was capable of providing "automatic navigation, solution of the bombing problem, rendezvous with other aircraft, radar presentation of the surrounding area, and terrain avoidance (TA) capability to aid in flying at very low altitudes." In short, everything.

The B-52 "Dash One" Manual went on to explain how the Q-48 operated as a totally integrated network:

[After inputting the aircraft's latitude and longitude] the BNS continuously determines the aircraft position and can supply the autopilot with a heading error correction for automatic navigation to a desired destination. [It] can determine the time to go to the bomb release point and can supply the autopilot with a heading error correction to enable it to direct the aircraft to this point. [A related subsystem called] the MD-1 astrocompass refines the best available true heading from the BNS or N-1 compass to provide a more precise true heading reference by sighting on and tracking a celestial body. [Another related subsystem called] the APN-108 Doppler Radar provides ground speed and drift angle.

As mentioned in chapter 3, fresh arrivals to Mather's bomb school during the 1960s were immediately separated into two groups. One would study the older B-52 AN/ASQ-48 bombing and navigation system (C and D models), the other the more advanced AN/ASQ-38 BNS (Es through Hs). The men quickly grasped that in either system the essence of their work was going to revolve around that old UNT bugaboo, radar scope interpretation—RSI—coupled with an exhaustive study of bombardment systems, weapons and their ballistics, and really hard-core radar mapping and celestial navigation.

The men found the tone at NBT different from the UNT of Bleckley Hall.[4] Where before they had been regarded by the faculty and base staff as "students," at bomb school they were treated as fellow officers and professional aviators. A few had already advanced to first lieutenant (unless a fellow screwed up, a silver bar was automatic at eighteen months service), and both the candidates and their instructors wore wings. The crucial dynamic in play now was not fear of washing out, but of the timely acquisition of a new and intricate skill that not only was important to a man's career progress, but also if imperfectly learned and/or understood, it might very well cost him his life.

NBT candidates flew fourteen training missions in the T-29D, the bombardier version of the Flying Classroom. Gone were the astrodomes, driftmeters, small five-inch radar sets, and one dozen plus "dead-reckoning" plot desks—replaced by just six bombardier trainee and instructor stations, each with a tiny desk, a "K" system optical bombsight, and a bulky MA-6A bombing radar set. The practice flying sorties were designed to build on the many ground simulator hours each man had already undergone, hammering home all the many challenges and permutations of radar navigation, radar bombardment, and in-flight maintenance procedures.[5]

Exactly as in the B-52, the T-29Ds had an all-purpose "tracking handle" that served as the bombardier's primary control device. Embedded on the radar navigator's side of the bombing and navigation console/desk,[6] this flexible, six-inch-high vertical handle suggested a fighter pilot's joystick, both in looks and functionality. In a similar manner to the way the knobs and cranks on the Norden bombsight allowed the optical bombardier to freely move the mechanical crosshairs anywhere in his field of view, the manipulation of the tracking handle allowed the radar operator to direct his electronic crosshairs to any spot on his screen. Handle deflections to the left moved the crosshairs to the left; swinging it to the right caused the crosshairs to follow accordingly; pushing the handle forward "threw" them farther out in front of the aircraft (i.e., toward the top of the radar screen); and so on. Wired to the electromechanically operated tracking computer, the tracking handle provided a means for the radar navigator to, among other things, determine wind and ground speed, "fix" the aircraft's exact position, refine aircraft heading input, and furnish the pilot with an emergency airborne radar approach (ARA) to a blind landing. Most important, it served as the primary aiming instrument on the bomb run.

And that worked something like this on the T-29D: After the prefigured data was loaded into the various black boxes and computers and the airplane was inbound to the target, the radar nav/bombardier threw his electronic crosshairs out in front of the airplane and "acquired" (laid them on and kept them on) the aiming point. With that act, the onboard computers began determining the bomb release line (BRL) by continuously absorbing the effects of wind, altitude, weapon ballistics, and other associated variables. As the bomb run proceeded and heading corrections were needed (e.g., the bombardier moved his crosshairs a little), that new heading data was automatically relayed to the pilot's deflection indicator (PDI). When the pilot detected his PDI needle drifting left or right, he immediately recentered it. The bombardier continued to "synchronize" his crosshairs on the aiming point, and the pilot kept centering the PDI; when the To Go meter ran down to zero, the release sequence was initiated. Strategic Air Command B-52s used essentially this same process as their primary nuclear weapons delivery method, officially dubbed the Radar Synchronous Bomb Run.

While the Q-38 NBT trainees went their separate way using the newer E through H model equipment, the Q-48 guys focused attention on the APS-108 radar, the same one they would see in the B-52Cs and Ds. It had three primary controls: receiver gain, video gain, and antenna tilt. Receiver gain adjusted the signal to bring out land/water contrasts and cultural features, video gain controlled the overall brightness, and tilt allowed the operator to direct up/down power on a specific return. While learning to use these tuning controls was challenging in itself, it was (once again) the radar scope interpretation that proved the most difficult technique to master. The bewildering blur of lights, darks, and shadows the student navigator had wrestled with on his low-power UNT radar scope was child's play compared to the complex echoes presented on the NBT bombing radar sets. After many weeks of nearly despairing he was ever going to catch on, the light bulb in the candidate's head would finally come on, and the white electronic mush displayed on his radar screen magically transformed itself into buildings, towns, dams, bridges, mountain peaks, lakes, rivers, and coastlines.

Five months after the starting gun, with their technical skills honed about as well as Mather could be expected to get them, the bomb school trainees turned to the final phases of the course: the Human Reliability Program and a four-week Special Weapons School. On this matter of "human reliability"—SAC had a tendency to dress that idea up by putting it forward as some kind of a formal course, apparently in an attempt to give the American press and public a larger comfort zone as to the quality of man it was entrusting to handle nuclear weapons. The issue became even more a concern during the early 1960s, after the release of such popular, but almost dangerously misleading Hollywood films as Fail-Safe and Dr. Strangelove. Human reliability screening, at least as it was handled during the Vietnam War era, was more than anything else a commonsense evaluation of a man's fundamental character, with a particular emphasis on the following: overall conduct and performance to date, Officer Effectiveness Reports (OERs), instructor flight reviews, informal peer comments (yep, gossip), even minor legal trouble, history of or current chemical dependencies, and domestic unrest (wife trouble). The fact was any erratic, unreliable, dishonest, or dishonorable behavior during the enormous stresses associated with one and a half years of flight training would almost certainly have already surfaced and been red-flagged. (It happened.) Background checks had already been conducted by the FBI and Air Force OSI (Office of Special Investigations) when the trainee was assigned to UNT. Those inquiries were, of course, reopened; before a man could graduate from NBT, his security clearance had to have been upgraded to Top Secret. Certain official questionnaires and forms had also to be filled out and signed by the candidate, testifying to his loyalty to the United States and to the moral and legal obligations he was now undertaking.

Once this security vetting had been satisfactorily concluded, the almost-trained bombardier received his first look at the B-52's strategic payload, a one-month course conducted just a few blocks away at Mather's Special Weapons School. There it was the incredible horrors of thermonuclear devices were removed from the theoretical and brought chillingly and personally home. Day after day the fellows were exposed to highly classified, graphic images and accounts of not only what atomic bombs did to military targets, but their terrifying effects on nature, cities, buildings, homes, and . . . humans. The young officers (there was little horseplay during these weeks, the mood unusually somber) were told of the MARK-28, the most widely used thermonuclear device in the American inventory, with an adjustable yield that averaged one megaton. Each of the four MK-28s a B-52 could carry packed fifty-five times the punch of the weapon that destroyed Hiroshima. They learned of the MK-39, four times more powerful than the MK-28. And of the hideous, world-shattering 25 megaton MK-41, with six times the yield of the MK-39. The emotional effect of Special Weapons School was profound; there would never be a time when a B-52 navigator-bombardier's knees did not quiver and the back of his neck did not tingle when preflighting and/or prearming a nuclear weapon.

After NBT and the welcome passage of another graduation ceremony, the fellows were sent to the U.S. Air Force survival school, a requirement for all combat aircrewmen. Stead AFB near Reno, Nevada, had been selected for this work during the Korean War, and that is where prospective new B-52 Black Holers went until 1966, when the school was transferred to Fairchild AFB at Spokane, Washington.

The three-week-long survival course concentrated on postejection events, central to which was the reinforcement of an officer's sworn duty to observe the Code of Conduct and to receive instruction on various escape and evasion (E & E) schemes.[7] Recovering and hiding the parachute, determining the extent and treatment of personal injuries, avoiding capture, and ground-to-air radio communication with SAR (search and air rescue) were followed by tips on individual night and day ground navigation, food/water gathering, and more ground-to-air signaling when the Jolly Green Giant rescue helicopter made its joyous appearance above the life raft or jungle canopy. In the event one became a prisoner of war, the men received instruction on what to expect, information they were allowed to give to captors (yes, it was officially limited to name, rank, and serial number, though everybody knew that narrow injunction wouldn't stand up to bamboo shoots under the fingernails), and exposure to mock interrogations by "enemy" intelligence officers.

Although a valuable, potentially life-saving experience, everyone was glad to have done with "Snake School." Next stop—the Central Valley of California and Castle Air Force Base. It was to be at Merced, while assigned to the 4017 Combat Crew Training Squadron (CCTS), that the boys would finally get their first dance with the B-52 Stratofortress.

CHAPTER EIGHT

Welcome to the Big Leagues

I n 1955 the Strategic Air Command decided on a single location to serve as
the B-52 Stratofortress aircrew training center, a kind of transitional "halfway house" for all the new people transferring into SAC from either Air
Training Command or other Air Force flying jobs. Castle AFB near Merced,
California, with its 300-foot-wide by 12,000-foot-long runway and adjacent
93rd Bomb Wing facilities, was chosen. Castle's core unit was designated the
4017 CCTS and the course ran for three months, at the conclusion of which
the attending pilots, copilots, radar navigators, navigators, electronic warfare
officers, and gunners were awarded their B-52 "type ratings."[1]

To the particular dismay of the young men arriving fresh from Mather (via
survival school), the first six weeks at Castle turned out to be yet one more
round of ground school drudgery. The boys could only watch in envy as, just
beyond their classroom windows, the more-advanced classes were out on the
field getting actual batting practice while they were stuck with more preflight,
textbook, and simulator preparation.

After a seemingly never-ending review of the fundamental skills learned at
UNT and NBT, the course's academic attention finally got around to the B-52.
Understandably enough, the initial focus was on the bomber's emergency procedures and life support systems; SAC wanted at least a modicum of assurance
the greenhorns wouldn't promptly kill themselves if an emergency occurred on
their maiden voyage. This phase was followed by exhaustive sessions in mission
planning, lower compartment familiarization, radio protocols, aircraft electrical and hydraulic fundamentals, crew coordination procedures, and a host of
other topics. At long last, after hope had nearly vanished, the much-anticipated
moment arrived—first flight as a crew member in the big boy!

The author's personal experience on that memorable day might be as good a way as any to summarize what Castle was all about. It began with a hectic and confusing early-morning meeting of students and instructors during which everyone took turns briefing their particular roles in the coming mission. As there would be three first-time trainees aboard—a copilot, navigator, and gunner—safety of flight issues were topmost on the aircraft commander's agenda.

"Now listen up, people. If it becomes necessary to leave the aircraft, I will give the command, firmly and in the clear. There will be no anticipation of this action, which is to say any statements or questions over the interphone are never to include the word BAILOUT. Misuse of that word in the heat of an emergency can easily result in a misunderstanding leading to tragic consequences. It is to be used only by your aircraft commander in the context of an actual order to begin the activity. Is that clear?"

Yes, Sir!

"Should it become necessary for me to give the order to leave the airplane, this is the controlled departure sequence: Gunner blows his rear turret and steps out whenever he is ready. In the forward cabin the navigator ejects first, then EW, followed by the copilot. Extra crew members are to immediately proceed to the open hatch door at the navigator's station and manually bail out. The radar navigator will notify me after all extra crew have departed, and he will then eject. I will be the last to leave the aircraft." What went unsaid, but was keenly noted by all during this fine speech, was that the AC's tidy little scenario assumed there would be enough time to accommodate his orderly exit.

After three hours of intense preparation, the crew was bussed to the waiting B-52. After what was at best a tentative preflight inspection (no memory of it survives, because this was his first exposure to the thunderous noise and general confusion of a Stratofortress flight line), our hero managed to locate the entry hatch door. After first bumping his head on an underfuselage antenna next to the hatch opening (a rite of passage), he scrambled up the steps and entered the aircraft. The pupils in his eyes were still calibrated to the bright valley sun, and there were several anxious moments of groping around in the near-absolute darkness until he at last located his station. Before his butt had even made contact with the cushion/survival kit, the IN (instructor navigator)—he who had been waiting impatiently in the left-hand radar navigator's seat—embarked on a rapid-fire introduction to the lower compartment. The rookie heard none of it, having become totally fixated on the closed-in jungle of instrumentation that literally surrounded him on all sides. Although warned in advance of just how small the B-52 cockpit spaces were, he was still astounded to discover that such a huge aircraft could be so terribly devoid of elbow room on the inside.

Fig. 10. This cartoon was making the rounds during the mid-1960s at the 4017th Combat Crew Training Squadron, Castle AFB, CA. (*Courtesy of the artist, Jerry Thompson*)

Despite having had six weeks to make a thorough study of the egress system, our subject couldn't figure out how the straps, belts, buckles, and cords on his "brain bucket" and Weber downward ejection seat all fit together. After a series of clumsy gyrations and false starts, he finally wrestled on the harness of the seat-installed parachute and cinched its straps tight around his chest and groin. He remembered to test the ankle restraints to make sure they would snap shut when tapped just so, then fingered the all-important trigger ring between his legs. He had a vague notion there was more to do, but that thought disappeared amongst all the hand waving and gesturing coming from the man on his left.

The instructor navigator's lips were moving, but no sound was coming through. It dawned on the trainee that despite having had enough presence of mind to carefully fit his helmet on his head, he had neglected to hook it up to the ship's radios. He fumbled furiously with his cord jack and intercom panel, until purely by chance got it configured correctly. Although relieved to have now joined the general business in progress, he became newly discomfited upon realizing he couldn't separate out what his instructor was saying from all the other pilot/ground crew/control tower radio chatter. Moments later, yet another, even more intense burst of rapid-fire directives issued from the instructor navigator, who was becoming increasingly frustrated over his inability to penetrate the student's thick covering of gray matter. Before the IN's spirited monologue could fully conclude, the engines started and the main hatch door slammed shut. The startled navigator hurriedly buckled his seat lap belt, an act that also caused him to become suddenly and acutely aware of his very greasy sausage and egg breakfast.

The taxi began and the chaotic interphone and ground control radio chatter of a few minutes earlier shifted into a somewhat calmer exchange between the instructor pilot/aircraft commander and copilot, the latter also on his first ride. The young flyer was having as much difficulty understanding the goings-on up in the front office as the rookie nav was down in the lower compartment.

"You will find, lieutenant," the instructor pilot (IP)/aircraft commander was saying to his right-seater, "that this machine is not to be confused with a regular airplane. It does not act on the ground nor function in the air like other aerospace vehicles. It has, in fact, all the flying characteristics of a Mack truck."

"Yessir!" the copilot said, in the accepted student-responds-to-instructor manner.

"Now," the IP continued, having thoroughly warmed up to his task, "while we are taxiing along twiddling our thumbs and taking in the sights of Castle Air Force Base, why don't you refresh my memory regarding the B-52's special features?"

Like the clueless slug sitting in the downstairs navigator's chair, the copilot was at that moment having difficulty recalling his own name. "Sir," the lieutenant at last said, finally remembering what he'd read in the Dash One, "the aircraft is characterized by swept wings and empennage, four underslung nacelles housing eight turbojet engines, a quadricycle main landing gear, and a tip gear near each outboard engine."

The IP's left forefinger tightened around his mike trigger switch on the control column. "And what keeps everything in the ship functioning?"

"Sir, the aircraft's primary electrical power is 205-volt alternating current. There is also the engine air bleed pneumatic power that operates the hydraulic, air conditioning, and alternator packs."

The copilot had been studying the manual, which meant the IP had to work a little harder to trip him up.

"OK, let's talk about our first critical phase of flight. Explain to me the difference between rotation and unsticking on takeoff."

The right-seater was completely absorbed with keeping the beast headed down the middle of what appeared to him an incredibly narrow taxiway and hadn't a clue what had just been asked. After a long and painful silence, the IP declared victory and rendered his question rhetorical.

"When you took off in one of those light-footed T-38 jet trainers back in flight school, you rotated the nose up when flying speed was achieved, after which the bird lifted off and continued its climb out in a nose-up attitude. This machine, on the other hand, is reluctant to leave the ground in the first place, requiring a great deal of persuasion before it finally agrees to unstick itself from the runway. When that happens, and if it pleasures the gods, the B-52 will remain in a level attitude while, like an elevator, it gradually ascends into the heavens."

"Yessir," the copilot said absently, distracted by something out his right-hand window.

"Stop worrying about the outrigger gear," the IP said sternly, "or you'll drive us off the road. Those wing tip wheels will follow along good and proper if you keep the airplane rolling down the centerline."

"Yessir . . ." The resolve in the right-seater's voice was weakening.

The instructor pilot and copilot continued on with a wide range of cockpit and crew coordination issues, nearly all of which did not directly apply to the Black Holers. The navigator forced himself to stop listening; he had plenty of his own problems, not the least of which was the growing discontent in his stomach.

"OK, nav, time to figure your seventy-knot data," the IN was saying on their private intercom channel, referring to the decision-speed call the navigator always gave the pilot on takeoff roll.

"Sir," the nav said, running his forefinger over the entering arguments on a chart in his yellow checklist, "it computes to 14.8 seconds."

The navigator was to announce "Fourteen point eight seconds, NOW!" when that many stopwatch ticks had expired after the aircraft commander had made his own call of "Seventy knots, NOW!" Before this decision speed was reached, roughly ninety knots, the bomber could still be stopped within the limits of the runway. After the nav's NOW call, however, the airplane was committed to the launch. No matter what.

While the speed check was an easily performed duty, it was an altogether critical one, for there was no more vulnerable time for a B-52 than on takeoff. That realization, coupled with the nav's growing conviction he was about to give his life over to a giant firetrap, touched off an even more intense wave of gastrointestinal distress. To make matters worse, a steady blast of nauseat-ingly hot air from the lower compartment heating duct was blowing directly into his face. All the while the big ship continued to sashay left and right as it lumbered down the uneven and seemingly endless taxiway.

"Aircraft is stopped and brakes set," the copilot finally announced, to the navigator's enormous relief.

The before-launch catechism between IP and copilot now began.

"Water injection pump switches on."

"Trim set, checked for takeoff setting."

"Air brakes off."

"Flaps one hundred percent, lever down."

"Fuel switches set."

"Windows and hatches closed and locked."

"Flight instruments set."

"Generators set."

"Rudder pedals and control column adjusted and checked."

"Crew, remove ejection seat safety pins. Stand by for takeoff."

And with that, the big ship waddled onto the active runway and began its fifty-second takeoff roll.

The navigator gripped his stopwatch with both hands, waiting anxiously for the pilot's seventy-knot call. The airplane continued to gather momentum.

"Nav," the IN suddenly said over their private channel, "you forgot to thread the parachute zero delay lanyard through your lap belt." He was point-ing at the dope's tender midsection.

Thrown into complete confusion, with the airplane bucking up and down in the opening stages of its attempt to become airborne, the nav flipped his stopwatch on the worktable and, using both hands, began reassembling the buckles and straps on his ejection harness.

"Seventy knots, NOW!" the pilot announced.

The nav's mouth dropped open. He looked at his unstarted stopwatch, then stole a glance at the IN. The latter sadly shook his head and held out his right hand, brandishing the backup decision-speed timing mechanism.

"Pilot, fourteen point eight seconds, NOW!" the IN announced at the correct instant.

"Committed," the aircraft commander responded matter-of-factly, as if he had expected the nav to blow the call.

The ship staggered into the air at 137 knots, with the copilot at the controls. The wings rocked alarmingly for nearly half a minute—as if the thing was a spirited horse testing an unskilled rider—until the bomber finally submitted to the full-deflection control inputs. Everything settled down after that, and the climbout proceeded uneventfully, with the pilots doing most of the work. Downstairs, the nav's primary job during this phase was to monitor altitude and heading, and to at least pretend he was keeping a running position on his chart.

When the altimeter showed the airplane approaching 12,000 feet, the navigator, after stomping his right foot several times in an attempt to find the floor mike switch, squeaked out his "Passing through 12,000 feet" call, the signal for the crew to go on oxygen. At the same moment, with the ship bouncing and pitching through a stretch of clear-air turbulence, another gale of gut-churning, kerosene-perfumed hot air erupted from the nav's overhead heating duct. It was too much for the occupant of that seat; with a mighty heave he upchucked the undigested remains of his breakfast on the worktable in front of him.

The instructor navigator's eyes widened, but he said nothing. Less than a minute later, the young man cut loose again, this time on the forward instrument panel.

The IN unsnapped his oxygen mask and yelled across the lower compartment, "You OK, nav?"

The navigator gamely nodded his head but he felt awful and no doubt looked the same. After what seemed forever, the aircraft leveled off at cruise altitude and settled in for a short run to a practice aerial refueling, though sans any meaningful directional assistance from the lower compartment right seat. In an inspired move coinciding with the moment the copilot made contact with the tanker's boom, said same navigator noisily deposited yet another load into his box lunch, the only container he could get his hands on in time. It was at this point the IN sighed heavily, put his pencil down, and leaned back in his seat.

Despite having succumbed to motion sickness, the nav was not so far gone he couldn't translate the instructor navigator's body language. He had busted his first mission. The only question remaining now was whether or not the young man would live through the balance of the flight. He could expect no early return to Castle—the copilot and gunner-in-training still had their work to do. Green-faced and miserable, the nav had not in his wildest dreams imagined how disruptive and disorienting the B-52 could be.

After the air refueling exercise, he cinched it up and got through a two-hour Day Cel navigation leg. Although it was clear the IN was no longer keeping score, there remained the matter of self-respect. Actually, his final sun line and ETA didn't turn out too bad, giving him a slight lift. He had even begun to entertain an idea the worst might be over, when the ship abruptly dropped to the deck. The "Oil Burner" route, the low-level portion of the flight, was more excruciating than anything that'd come before. The turbulence and vibration while traveling four hundred miles an hour at five hundred feet was so bad, the rook couldn't keep the instrument panels in focus, and he had to fall back on straight time and heading for all turns.[2] As if it were a low-level bomb run checklist item, his nausea once more boiled to the surface at the 120-second To Go call. At that point, he could only think of what a Mather brown bar had once said about the morning after a hard night of partying: "At six am, I was afraid I was going to die. At nine am, I was afraid I wouldn't."

At long last, the bomber arrived back over Castle for "transition," as the syllabus characterized touch and goes. No matter everyone's already deep fatigue, the copilot was required to practice takeoffs and landings for two hours. While the rest of the crew endured, the front office right-seater did his utmost to prove Boeing built the world's best landing gear. It was midway through this final torture, with the spatial disorientation effects of the UNT vertigo chair now looking like a quiet evening in a rocking chair, that the hapless would-be Black Holer began seriously entertaining notions of suicide. On the final go-around, as an exclamation point to an already perfectly symmetrical day, he managed one last regurgitation, an especially juicy round lubricated by all the water he had been drinking to stave off dehydration. The glob arched skyward like a giant wad of chewing tobacco and landed squarely in the IN's lap.

"Lieutenant," his weary instructor said, as the crew bus trundled the sweat-soaked men off to debriefing, "they ought to give you an award for the six most spectacular barfs I have ever seen on one nine-hour flight." The officer looked down, making a face at his soiled and smelly flight suit. "The Vomit Cross with Five Oak Leaf Clusters."

The wretch could barely mumble the obligatory "Yessir."

The conversation turned serious; the IN wasn't so sure his charge would be able to hack the program. "Believe it or not, we do get a few washouts at this stage. The thing is a hard witch to ride."

The idea of washing out after nearly two years of fearsome toil was, to put it mildly, utterly repugnant. Shameless groveling ensued, after which flight surgeons and squadron commanders were urgently lobbied for a refly of mission one. Fortunately, there was a war on. Refly granted.

Amazingly, or maybe not so amazing—similar first flight experiences had happened to others—everything went swimmingly on the second try. As did the balance of the one dozen flight training missions required to graduate from Castle. In the very end, the subject recovered at least a portion of his personal dignity; he never got airsick in a B-52 again.

A couple of days before wrapping up CCTS the fellows began hanging around the Operations office, waiting for word on their permanent base assignment. The Q-38 troops would head for one of the many newer-equipped wings; Q-48ers did not have as many choices, with fewer squadrons still outfitted with the older Cs and Ds. For once, a man's personal preference regards a particular base was taken under consideration, an unexpected and pleasant new experience. Most important, the end of Castle meant the end of the training merry-go-round and a beginning of life in the *real* Air Force.

Or so the boys thought. Only after arriving at their operational stations would the men learn they still faced up to an additional three months of hard training, one final great melding before they were officially joined at the hip with a specific model bomber and a permanent crew.

CHAPTER NINE

Getting SAC'emcised

Strategic Air Command's principal organizational unit was the wing, typically composed of several ground support squadrons, at least one tanker squadron, and at least one bomber squadron. Each of the flying squadrons maintained about fifteen to seventeen planes. In 1964, on the eve of SAC's involvement in the Vietnam War, there were forty operational squadrons of B-52s, married to an equal number of tanker squadrons. Some thirty-five bases throughout the continental United States and Puerto Rico were host to SAC wings. Twenty-three of the bases accommodated the newer B-52E through H models, while the remaining dozen supported the older Cs and Ds, the number of latter locations declining with each passing year concurrent with a planned C model phaseout.

SAC's tanker aircraft, by this time all Boeing-built KC-135s, had four-man crews—pilot, copilot, navigator, and boom operator. As previously noted, the B-52s carried six men. Using an approximate ratio of three crews for every aircraft, along with assuming an average of sixteen planes in each tanker and bomber squadron, the number of individuals in each of these flying units can be extrapolated at approximately 192 tanker and 288 bomber crewmen. A little more math tells us that out of a quarter-million active-duty personnel in the Strategic Air Command during the mid-1960s, there were about 7,680 tanker and 11,520 bomber Combat Ready SAC aircrewmen, just 8 percent of the command's total force.

From out of this huge nationwide pool of bases, people, and airplanes, it was to be the B-52 D model squadrons that would shoulder nearly the full brunt of the conventional war in Vietnam.[1] This happened for several reasons. In the overall SAC nuclear deterrent context, the older Ds were considered more expendable than the newer-built, technically updated bombers. Also, there were a lot of D models still around, over 150 of them; by using large numbers of a single model within a combat theater, important maintenance and logistical efficiencies could be realized. Most important, the D model was capable of undergoing what was called a "Big Belly" modification, allowing it to carry a staggering total of 108 conventional bombs weighing 60,000 pounds (the equivalent payload of twelve B-17Gs).

This decision to use the B-52Ds almost exclusively in Vietnam would come at a high cost to its aircrews. Because there were significant differences between it and other Stratofortresses, men assigned to the newer models could not directly transfer from their airplane to a D model without first going through a formal transition school, a major barrier to Southeast Asian deployment. Also, SAC had a responsibility to maintain its commitment to airborne and pad alert against the Soviet threat; the newer ships and their crews were best suited to fill that deterrent role. Further, combat squadrons function more efficiently when there is little personnel turnover, especially at crew level; wholesale transfers of E through H model crews in and out of D units would have taken that advantage the other way. As a consequence of all these factors, though it might not have been initially planned that way, the largest burden of the Vietnam War fell on the roughly 3,500 to 4,000 aircrewmen in the older D model "Q-48" bombers.

Not surprisingly, this circumstance resulted in a good deal of unrest within the D model community. Both the crews and their families came to resent the "pass" most of the E through H crews received during the long years SAC conducted "iron bomb" operations in Southeast Asia. Their gripes were legitimate: before the nation's longest hot war was at last concluded, large numbers of D crewmen would rack up five, six, and even seven combat tours. For some of those men, the price was too high: not a few came back to broken homes.

Readers may be scratching their heads at this point, wondering how it was these same airmen could have been sent back to the war over and over. It was indeed a neat trick (dare one say stroke of genius?), pulled off by way of the military's six-month temporary duty (TDY) policy, which limited such assignments to a maximum of 189 days, without limiting their number. Thus, by avoiding the nuisance of a permanent change of station (PCS) move, SAC not only retained full ownership of its crews and airplanes (i.e., it did not have to turn them over to theater commanders), but also the national rule limiting involuntary Southeast Asia (SEA) war service to one year was bypassed—technically, a B-52 crewmen could be ordered back to Vietnam an infinite number of times.[2] As noted above, for a significant percentage of the men, it very nearly did become infinite. Many wound up with three hundred combat missions, some had over four hundred, and as incredible as it might seem, one or two B-52D crewmen were credited with five hundred-plus heavy bomber combat missions.

By 1969 the pissing and moaning over these repeated TDY rotations had gotten so loud that even the people down in the Omaha bunker could hear it. As a result, the RTU program was established (Castle's Replacement Training Unit), which called for a certain number of either volunteers or selectees from Q-38 wings to be run through D model transition training at Castle (or its equivalent) and then sent to the Pacific as "augmentees." Although this program spread the pain out a little, the cadre D wings still continued to carry the brunt of SEA operations all the way to the end of the war.

Fortunately, those eager, just-out-of-school Q-48 navigator-bombardiers of the mid-1960s were blissfully unaware of what lay before them. The only thing they knew for certain after leaving Merced was that their carcasses were headed for one of the following D model Air Force bases: 7th Bomb Wing at Carswell, Texas; 22nd BW at March, California; 28th BW at Ellsworth, South Dakota; 70th BW at Clinton-Sherman, Oklahoma; 91st BW at Glasgow, Montana; 92nd BW at Fairchild, Washington; 96th BW at Dyess, Texas; 99th BW at Westover, Massachusetts; 306th BW at McCoy, Florida; 454th BW at Columbus, Mississippi; 461st BW at Amarillo, Texas; or the 509th BW at Pease, New Hampshire.

By the time the fellows had arrived at one of these wings, they were all at least first lieutenants, their peach fuzz long gone. Twenty-three or -four years old now, the majority were married, some even with a baby or two. Many were as much adjusting to the rigors of domestic life as they were to their budding careers. On most bases, family men were provided with Capehart or Wherry housing,[3] which usually was a fairly decent one-bath, two- or three-bedroom ranch-style home. When such quarters were not available, the families had to live off base, making do as best they could with a not always adequate housing allowance. The bachelors had it a little easier, having only themselves to worry about. The BOQ (bachelor officers quarters) suited some, at least for a time, though most of the fellows paired or tripled up with other bachelor officers in off-base apartments. But married or not, with or without government housing, there still loomed the matter of meshing in with the operational Air Force without stripping a gear.

Much of that process was quite mundane. As a single example, what sort of uniform was our young navigator-bombardier expected to wear when reporting to his squadron commander for the first time? What with all the chaperoning during his training years, that kind of question had always before been answered for him. The nonrated first lieutenants at his new base, having been at the station since the day they were commissioned, already had such things thoroughly scoped out, including probably the combination to the Command Post (CP) safe. A new nav-bomb guy, caught up in yet one more unfamiliar whirl, had all he could do to even locate the CP. Always before, routine business had been prescribed; now the Mather/Fairchild/Castle itinerant was expected to figure out the correct uniform of the day for himself.

Seemingly trivial matters like proper uniforms were not to be taken lightly. If one failed to observe basic, everyday military protocols, one could be sure of receiving the Air Force's equivalent of a Scarlet Letter. There were four styles of clothing in our just-arrived flying officer's closet he could dither over: 1) Mess Dress—a tuxedo if you will—for those rare formal occasions, 2) Class "A" Blues, with single-breasted suit coat, tie, and brimmed service cap, 3) 1505s, a more informal, khaki-colored "desk" outfit with short sleeves, open collar, and soft blue overseas cap that could be tucked under the belt, and 4) fire-resistant Nomex flying suits—ye old "green bag"—worn with either the overseas cap or wing-approved baseball cap. If it was summer, he would report to the commanding officer in his 1505s; if stationed in the American South, he might very well go the same way even in winter. In the North, in the winter, it would be Class As. Footwear was also strictly regulated—the Mess Dress, Class As, and 1505s all required brightly shined, low-quarter black shoes and blue regulation socks. Combat boots were to accompany flight suits, either laced or quick-donning (zippered).

The first day or two at a new base was always hectic. In between attending to his official duties, a man somehow had to sandwich in scouting parties, either by auto or on foot, to "fix" such important locations as the administration and personnel buildings (to make damn sure they knew you were there and regular paychecks were forthcoming), squadron offices, base operations, control tower, base exchange (BX), cafeteria/mess hall, barber shop, dry cleaners, post office, and the Officers' Club. On every base, the "O" Club was the unquestioned center of off-duty socializing; here always one could find good food, drink, convivial friends, cultural programs, dances, and the always deeply refreshing postflight Happy Hour.

Once established at the base and routine matters had been attended to, each newly arrived officer was ready to turn his full attention back to the B-52. During that first interview with his squadron commander, nervously listening to "God's" pronouncements and praying his fly wasn't open, he learned the bomber crew force was divided into four categories:

1. Noncombat Ready—New people were assigned to one of these crews, usually formed with a mixture of experienced crewmen and rookies, though sometimes all six were fresh out of Castle.[4] They might receive a designation such as Crew NR-40.

2. Ready—The entire crew had undergone all the training required and was certified Combat Ready. An example would be Crew R-35.

3. Experienced/Excellent/Elite (every wing seemed to define it differently)— An intact crew that had been together for a lengthy period and done a good job. They could be Crew E-15.

4. Select—The very best crews, those who had been eligible for the coveted "spot promotions" during the LeMay era. Variously called Standboard, Stanboard, Staneval, or Standardization and Evaluation, by any name they were, frankly, the cops. The top six guys in the squadron became Crew S-01.

Assembling a new B-52 crew wasn't a casual matter. It was essential the men be highly compatible; in all likelihood, they would be kept together for years. Serious personality clashes among those who worked so closely together and spent so much time with each other, especially on nuclear alert, were simply intolerable. Furthermore, it was nearly impossible for a SAC airman to separate himself from his mates socially—because of the crew's very close-knit association, an individual and his loved ones became inextricably bound to the extended families of the other five men. SAC monitored these interpersonal relationships continually, a policy that had nothing to do with "touchy-feely"—it was critical to the national deterrent mission that a nuclear-armed strategic bomber crew function as a single, cohesive organism.

Strategic Air Command squadron commanders wasted no time in getting their NR crews certified B-52 Combat Ready, a process other Air Force pilots and navigators referred to as "getting SAC'emcised." Which meant that in addition to yet more flight training in the Stratofortress, every new officer had to receive extensive instruction in the wing's Positive Control procedures (i.e., the precise courses of action required by everyone on everything related to nuclear weapons) and demonstrate he thoroughly understood SAC's rigid two-man policy when in the vicinity of thermonuclear devices (aka "No Lone Zones" around a "cocked" aircraft). He was further expected to maintain a high level of personal conduct on and off duty, guard against COMPLACENCY whenever dealing with Positive Control procedures, and be satisfied with nothing less than ZERO DEFECTS in his own performance. There would be no letup on any of this, either before or after achieving Combat Ready status.

While a thorough understanding of these matters was critically important, the flight training itself remained at the core of combat crew readiness. Planning for a new crew's first sortie began several days before takeoff (as would every SAC practice mission they flew from then on), when the navigator made a pilgrimage to base operations (Ops) to learn the profile/objectives of the coming flight. The information he received from Ops was always bare bones, consisting of little more than the takeoff time, air refueling rendezvous location and time, high-level bombing times and location, specific low-level "Oil Burner" route and entry time, pilot's "touch and go" practice duration, and final landing time back at the starting point. All other aspects of the flight the navigator had to figure out for himself, including determining forecast winds, drawing up the charts, ensuring avoidance of restricted airspace, preparing the mission log, and planning all the en route altitudes, headings, turn points, and leg times. It invariably took at least one solid workday to do this, while meanwhile the other five guys were out drinking beer around the pool—a condition of employment no Buf navigator ever really stopped resenting. The load didn't ease up in flight either; the B-52's Black Hole right-seater was arguably the hardest working man on the airplane.

Twenty-four hours later, the entire crew would meet for a full day of joint mission planning. The burden now shifted to the copilot, especially as regards analyzing the weather, securing en route clearances, fuel planning, and calculating the ship's weight and balance. Everyone outlined in detail their scheduled activities; the aircraft commander explained what he expected and specific areas to work on. Additional crew or instructors on board would discuss their requirements and expectations. At some point in the session, especially on flights during the early stages of the overall combat crew certification process, the pilot would make a throat-clearing speech reminding his new crew that their paramount objective was to mold themselves into a smoothly running team that could successfully operate the aircraft while producing consistently reliable scores in navigation and bombing—the two being inextricably bound together. For in the final analysis, their sole purpose in life, the only reason these men were putting themselves through this incredible exercise and the nation to such great expense, was to possess the capability of delivering nuclear weapons on demand—precisely on target and at precisely the scheduled time anywhere in the world.[5]

Keeping that time was the job of the navigator. His most important aid in getting it done was, logically enough, a good watch. Usually he wore two, one on each wrist; his backup timepiece likely was a Japanese-made Seiko purchased during one of his TDY rotations to Okinawa ("24 carats for 24 dollars"). The second watch represented insurance; although the government chronometers were accurate, it would have been inconceivable for a SAC magellan to be caught out with an errant time or a stopped hand. Both the civilian and military watches used were surprisingly uncomplicated affairs, their most important feature an ability to stop the second hand and synchronize (or "hack") it exactly. There was no need for one of those heavily advertised European-styled wristwatches—an item often foisted on the unsuspecting as required kit for aircrewmen. Ostentatious and overwrought, they typically offered up such things as the current hour in twenty-four time zones, calendar settings, an alarm, puzzling star data, and sometimes even those always helpful signs of the Zodiac. Not only irrelevant to the mission, such clutter was potentially an obstacle to determining the precise time, which was the only thing that mattered.

With the mission planning completed, the rookie Q-48 navigator and his newly formed crew were now ready for their first flight. Perhaps the most efficient way to illustrate how it might have gone for them is by joining a typical B-52D certification practice sortie already in progress. The crew has completed their air refueling and celestial navigation leg and are now somewhere over the (simulated) polar icecap. The (simulated) "Go Code" has been received and authenticated and the HHCL ("H" Hour Control Line) was just crossed.

Down in the Black Hole, the two men turned the pages of their yellow-paged, spiral-bound checklists to: Weapons Preparation for Release (Nuclear). While the rest of the crew members installed thermal curtains on their windows, the nav-bomb team covered up their optical bombsight, cutting off as much as possible the terribly blinding light that would accompany a nuclear blast.[6] Over the next several minutes, certain system switches and circuit breakers are accounted for, and then the serious "call and respond" began.

NAV: "Release circuits disconnect?"

RN (radar navigator): "[Simulate] seal broken."

NAV: "Special weapons manual lock handle?"

RN: "[Simulate] pulled and stowed."

NAV: "Special weapons lock indicators?"

RN: "[Simulate] indicate unlocked."

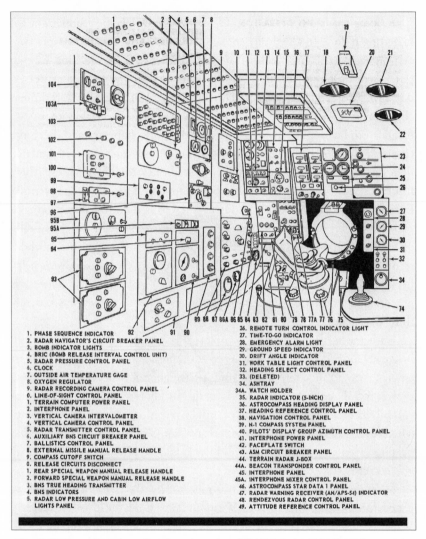

1. PHASE SEQUENCE INDICATOR
2. RADAR NAVIGATOR'S CIRCUIT BREAKER PANEL
3. BOMB INDICATOR LIGHTS
4. BRIC (BOMB RELEASE INTERVAL CONTROL UNIT)
5. RADAR PRESSURE CONTROL PANEL
6. CLOCK
7. OUTSIDE AIR TEMPERATURE GAGE
8. OXYGEN REGULATOR
9. RADAR RECORDING CAMERA CONTROL PANEL
0. LINE-OF-SIGHT CONTROL PANEL
1. TERRAIN COMPUTER POWER PANEL
2. INTERPHONE PANEL
3. VERTICAL CAMERA INTERVALOMETER
4. VERTICAL CAMERA CONTROL PANEL
5. RADAR TRANSMITTER CONTROL PANEL
6. AUXILIARY BNS CIRCUIT BREAKER PANEL
7. BALLISTICS CONTROL PANEL
8. EXTERNAL MISSILE MANUAL RELEASE HANDLE
9. COMPASS CUTOFF SWITCH
0. RELEASE CIRCUITS DISCONNECT
1. REAR SPECIAL WEAPON MANUAL RELEASE HANDLE
2. FORWARD SPECIAL WEAPON MANUAL RELEASE HANDLE
3. BNS TRUE HEADING TRANSMITTER
4. BNS INDICATORS
5. RADAR LOW PRESSURE AND CABIN LOW AIRFLOW
   LIGHTS PANEL

26. REMOTE TURN CONTROL INDICATOR LIGHT
27. TIME-TO-GO INDICATOR
28. EMERGENCY ALARM LIGHT
29. GROUND SPEED INDICATOR
30. DRIFT ANGLE INDICATOR
31. WORK TABLE LIGHT CONTROL PANEL
32. HEADING SELECT CONTROL PANEL
33. (DELETED)
34. ASHTRAY
34A. WATCH HOLDER
35. RADAR INDICATOR (5-INCH)
36. ASTROCOMPASS HEADING DISPLAY PANEL
37. HEADING REFERENCE CONTROL PANEL
38. NAVIGATION CONTROL PANEL
39. N-1 COMPASS SYSTEM PANEL
40. PILOTS' DISPLAY GROUP AZIMUTH CONTROL PANEL
41. INTERPHONE POWER PANEL
42. FACEPLATE SWITCH
43. ASM CIRCUIT BREAKER PANEL
44. TERRAIN RADAR J-BOX
44A. BEACON TRANSPONDER CONTROL PANEL
45. INTERPHONE PANEL
45A. INTERPHONE MIXER CONTROL PANEL
46. ASTROCOMPASS STAR DATA 1 PANEL
47. RADAR WARNING RECEIVER (AN/APS-54) INDICATOR
48. RENDEZVOUS RADAR CONTROL PANEL
49. ATTITUDE REFERENCE CONTROL PANEL

Fig. 11. Radar navigator's and navigator's station. (*USAF, 1-4, 1-5, T.O. 1B-52C-1, 1967*)

NAV: "Special weapons prearming check?"

RN: "Tested, complete."

NAV: "Bomb indicator lights?"

RN: "Off, tested."

NAV: "Bomb release mode selector switch?"

RN: "Normal, safetied."

The ship continued to bore on until it was one hour before the initial point, when the men turned to their Before Pre-IP checks. That action list included

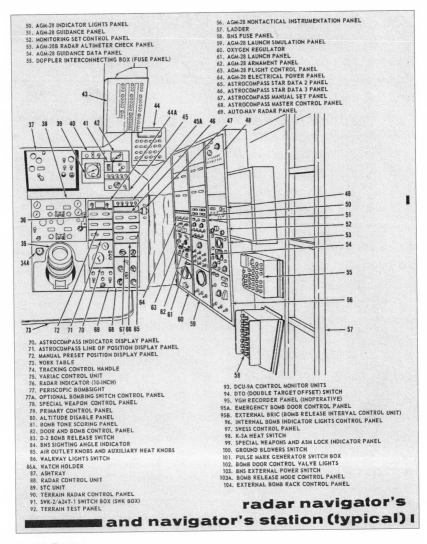

50. AGM-28 INDICATOR LIGHTS PANEL
51. AGM-28 GUIDANCE PANEL
52. MONITORING SET CONTROL PANEL
53. AGM-28B RADAR ALTIMETER CHECK PANEL
54. AGM-28 GUIDANCE DATA PANEL
55. DOPPLER INTERCONNECTING BOX (FUSE PANEL)

56. AGM-28 NONTACTICAL INSTRUMENTATION PANEL
57. LADDER
58. BNS FUSE PANEL
59. AGM-28 LAUNCH SIMULATION PANEL
60. OXYGEN REGULATOR
61. AGM-28 LAUNCH PANEL
62. AGM-28 ARMAMENT PANEL
63. AGM-28 FLIGHT CONTROL PANEL
64. AGM-28 ELECTRICAL POWER PANEL
65. ASTROCOMPASS STAR DATA 2 PANEL
66. ASTROCOMPASS STAR DATA 3 PANEL
67. ASTROCOMPASS MANUAL SET PANEL
68. ASTROCOMPASS MASTER CONTROL PANEL
69. AUTO-NAV RADAR PANEL

70. ASTROCOMPASS INDICATOR DISPLAY PANEL
71. ASTROCOMPASS LINE OF POSITION DISPLAY PANEL
72. MANUAL PRESET POSITION DISPLAY PANEL
73. WORK TABLE
74. TRACKING CONTROL HANDLE
75. VARIAC CONTROL UNIT
76. RADAR INDICATOR (10-INCH)
77. PERISCOPIC BOMBSIGHT
77A. OPTIONAL BOMBING SWITCH CONTROL PANEL
78. SPECIAL WEAPON CONTROL PANEL
79. PRIMARY CONTROL PANEL
80. ALTITUDE DISABLE PANEL
81. BOMB TONE SCORING PANEL
82. DOOR AND BOMB CONTROL PANEL
83. D-2 BOMB RELEASE SWITCH
84. BNS SIGHTING ANGLE INDICATOR
85. AIR OUTLET KNOBS AND AUXILIARY HEAT KNOBS
86. WALKWAY LIGHTS SWITCH
86A. WATCH HOLDER
87. ASHTRAY
88. RADAR CONTROL UNIT
89. STC UNIT
90. TERRAIN RADAR CONTROL PANEL
91. SWK-2/A24T-1 SWITCH BOX (SWK BOX)
92. TERRAIN TEST PANEL

93. DCU-9A CONTROL MONITOR UNITS
94. DTO (DOUBLE TARGET OFFSET) SWITCH
95. VGH RECORDER PANEL (INOPERATIVE)
95A. EMERGENCY BOMB DOOR CONTROL PANEL
95B. EXTERNAL BRIC (BOMB RELEASE INTERVAL CONTROL UNIT)
96. INTERNAL BOMB INDICATOR LIGHTS CONTROL PANEL
97. SWESS CONTROL PANEL
98. K-3A HEAT SWITCH
99. SPECIAL WEAPONS AND ASM LOCK INDICATOR PANEL
100. GROUND BLOWERS SWITCH
101. PULSE MARK GENERATOR SWITCH BOX
102. BOMB DOOR CONTROL VALVE LIGHTS
103. BNS EXTERNAL POWER SWITCH
103A. BOMB RELEASE MODE CONTROL PANEL
104. EXTERNAL BOMB RACK CONTROL PANEL

**radar navigator's
and navigator's station (typical)**

Fig. 11. Part two.

about twenty-five items—the bulk of which related to getting more switch positions in the right place, cross-checking headings and ground speeds, and making sure the navigator still knew where the aircraft was located.

That last was greatly aided by the information presented on the navigation control panel, positioned directly in front of the nav and just above his five-inch radar scope. This panel provided the downstairs team with a running dead-reckoning position, using heading information synthesized from the MD-1 Astrocompass (which was continuously locked on to a celestial body) and the N-1 magnetic compass, both of which were augmented by ground speed and drift angle supplied from the APN-108 Doppler Radar (which sensed the aircraft's movement relative to the earth's surface). The data was assimilated by the bombing and navigation system (BNS) and then translated into a self-updating latitude and longitude display on the navigation control panel. Black Holers referred to these lat/long readouts, which, again, continuously showed the aircraft's assumed current position, as "the counters."

Despite the heading corrections, gyroscopic stabilizing, and Doppler inputs flowing into the navigation control panel, the counters still required regular updating (i.e., timely corrections supplied by "fixes"). Three primary methods were used: 1) a manual counter update using the coordinates obtained from a very recent celestial fix, 2) a manual update based on a radar range and bearing the RN took from off a known ground point, or 3) an automatic update using the radar navigator's tracking handle to get what was known as a ground position indicator (GPI) fix.

A GPI fix (the most commonly used method) was accomplished in this manner: The RN identified a known land feature on his ten-inch radar screen, laid the electronic crosshairs on its radar echo, and then sent the coordinates of that return directly into the BNS computers. The computers took a "back bearing" from the GPI point and figured out precisely where the airplane was at that moment. The navigator then manually input that hard information (i.e., the aircraft's known current position) into the control panel, which promptly updated his counters.

Although considerably simplified, this was the way the B-52D nav/bomb team kept track of their ship's passage across the earth's surface.[7] Yet, while plenty good enough for getting the bomber from point A to point B, the result was not of sufficient quality to handle the bombing side of the equation. That demanded a much higher level of navigational accuracy—the exact same set of conditions, in fact, that had existed during the European war when Gee yielded to Oboe. Let's return to our Black Holers to see how the B-52 handled this bombing refinement.

The fellows had finished their pre–initial point work and were now beginning the Before IP checklist. As before, the navigator read the items off and the radar navigator took the action required. After working their way through a couple of the yellow pages, they came to the Bombing Data Check. At that point, both men forced themselves even more alert, determined to ensure the critical weapon ballistic inputs were set absolutely correctly. (One must remember that gravity-propelled nuclear weapons acted just like any other dropped "dumb" bomb.)

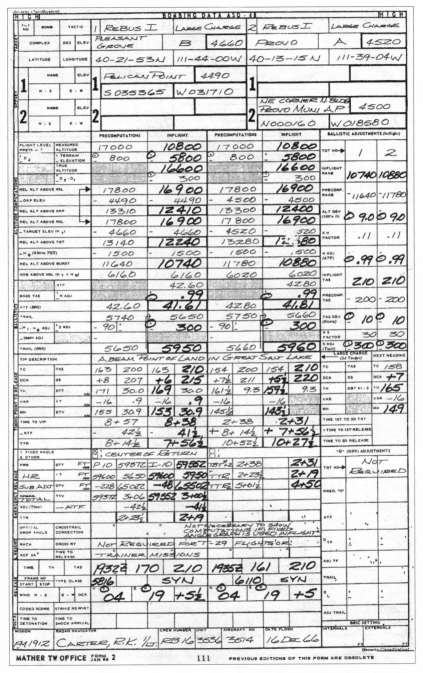

Fig. 12. The Bombing Data ASQ-48 form, more commonly known as the "ballistics," was used on all gravity weapon deliveries, including nuclear. (*Author's collection*)

NAV: "Bombing altitude?"

RN: "Reads as computed."

The bombing navigation system computers had to be told the absolute altitude—height above the terrain—the aircraft would be flying over the target. B-52 crews dealt with up to six "types" of altitude, which varied according to temperature, air density, altimeter setting, and inherent instrumentation errors. For example, when a pilot is getting ready to take off, he requests an "altimeter setting" from the tower, which is the same thing one's local TV weather forecaster calls a barometer reading, say 30.12. When that ready-to-take-off pilot sets 30.12 in the Kollsman Window of his altimeter, it then reads the same as the airport's elevation above mean sea level (this is called true altitude). Later, when the pilot (military or civilian) climbs through 18,000 feet, he did and still does reset his Kollsman Window to the standard datum plane setting of 29.92 (the altimeter then shows pressure altitude), a procedure that ensures all aircraft at high altitude are on the same page regardless of whatever the local barometer indicates below them.

NAV: "ATF and trail?"

RN: "Reads as computed."

These required geometric input numbers referred to the weapon's precomputed actual time of fall in seconds and the horizontal distance in feet the bomb would travel between the intended point of impact (i.e., when the aircraft would be directly over target) and a point directly beneath the bomber at the moment of ground impact (i.e., the number of feet the aircraft would then be downrange—the precomputed "trail" amount, which is the equivalent compensation necessary to account for the bomb's slower-than-the-aircraft's forward speed as a result wind, gravity, drag, etc.). So many different variables influenced these computations that it is difficult to offer a meaningful example. A very simplistic illustration might serve to at least give an idea: A standard-issue, conventional bomb dropped from an airplane traveling at 200 knots true airspeed at a height of 10,000 feet above the ground would have an ATF of roughly fifty seconds and a Trail of about 13,000 feet.

NAV: "Offset One?"

The B-52 BNS had a very useful feature called offset aiming, which allowed the bombardier to lay his electronic crosshairs on a "show" return while actually bombing a nearby "no-show" target. During the offset aiming point (OAP) checks, as are being conducted here, the radar navigator would carefully read back the two sets of numerics he had previously loaded in while the nav listened to make sure it was correct. Each of the two sets of OAP data was six digits long, expressed in feet; each bore a cardinal direction designator—north, south, east, or west. To repeat, these values were the precise angular distance separating what the RN would aim at and the actual target; that is, the linear number of feet the offset aiming technique was going to "fool" the bombing computer during the bomb run.

RN: "Offset One reads 123456N and 654321E."

NAV: "Roger, readback correct. Offset Two?" The second offset would almost always be the final aiming point—the "drop numbers."

The RN dutifully recited the data for OAP Two.

After the nav rogered this readback, the two men cleaned up the balance of their Before IP check and the navigator turned his full attention back to navigation. He would be determined to give his RN a perfect entry into and departure from the initial point, a procedure SAC called a "precision turn." In an aircraft moving at nearly the speed of sound, a pilot could not wait until actually crossing the turn point before starting a turn; a B-52 making a 90-degree course alteration had to begin the activity approximately eight

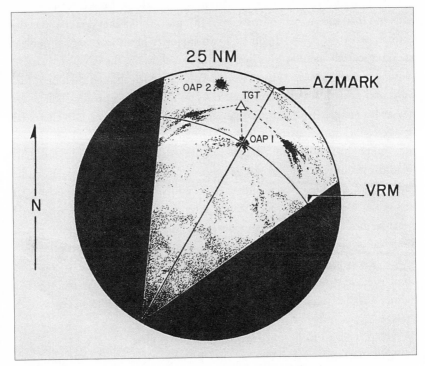

Fig. 13. A hand-drawn "radar scope prediction" of a B-52 bomb run, in sector-scan mode. AZMARK refers to the azimuth; VRM means variable range mark. (*USAF, Mather AFB NBT Student Study Guide, "Basic Operations" Workbook, 1967*)

nautical miles back from the actual turn point on the chart in order to roll out precisely on the bomb run course.[8]

With the ship IP inbound, the tempo picked up. Pilots sat straighter in their seats, the EWO cranked up his oscilloscopes and jammers, and the gunner made ready his Quad Fifties. Down in the Black Hole, the naviga-tor-bombardiers had flipped their yellow checklist pages to Bomb Run (Syn-chronous). The BNS heading was again verified against the other compasses (accurate headings were crucial; even the smallest error could result in a "bad bomb"). One last time all circuit breakers and switches were confirmed set and in the correct position. At the proper moment, the radar navigator switched his scope from an omni-like, full-scan presentation into a pie-shaped sector-scan, with the aircraft's nose now at the pivot of a fast-sweeping V. Sector-scan magnified images in the direction of travel and eliminated extraneous returns off to the sides, making it easier for the radar navigator to identify his bomb aiming points.

Once the BNS stabilizer unit had adjusted to this new operating mode and the radar presentation settled down, the RN threw his electronic cross-hairs out into the vicinity of the target. If it looked like they'd fallen into the correct "return" neighborhood (the vast majority of all real targets, nuclear or conventional, were nearly always radar "no-shows"), the RN proceeded to switch the hairs over to Offset Aiming Point One. Both men then bent for-ward and peered intently into their screens—the RN at his ten-incher, the nav at his smaller five-inch repeater—to make absolutely certain the radar nav had placed his crosshairs in the right spot. The RN controlled most of the tuning controls for both scopes and he would twirl his knobs and dials to adjust his broadcasting strength and antenna tilt until he was satisfied he had isolated the OAP "paint" to as small and sharp a return as possible. If he were to use the wrong range marker settings, for example, the OAP would either be too big or too small. A too low video gain setting and the point would disappear off the screen; too high and the OAP would bloom. As with the B-17 optical bombardier and his Norden, a B-52 radar navigator on a synchronous bomb run had to have a deft touch, an indefinable something that for a very few moments transformed him from a highly skilled technician into an artist.

RN: "Nav, confirm I am on Offset One."

NAV: "Roger, I have your crosshairs on Offset One."

With the target and OAP One now both "acquired," the RN contacted the aircraft commander. The moment was significant, in that it represented that instant in the mission the AC would yield his supreme authority over to the radar navigator. Crews could sense when this transition occurred; the RN's voice took on a new, authoritative timbre, while the pilot became deferential, ready to follow instructions.[9]

"Pilot, this is radar. Say PDI." Before doing anything else, the RN wanted a cross-check between his equipment and the pilot's deflection indicator, the needle that indicated where the crosshairs were relative to the B-52's nose.

"Two degrees left" would have been a positive response from the pilot. That meant the IP-inbound heading was pretty good and that the RN had probably laid his crosshairs in the correct place. If the pilot had said "twenty left," something was wrong.

"Roger," the RN would say, "switching to OAP Two."

OAP One was farther out and could be acquired sooner than Two, which was the final aiming point. Two was always nearer the target and bore a much smaller angle between it and the aircraft's nose, minimizing lateral aiming error.

"Navigator, radar," the RN said over the interphone, though the two were sitting just a couple of feet apart, "I show a good OAP cross-check, my crosshairs are now on OAP Two."

"Roger," the nav said, "I confirm you are on OAP Two."

The RN cycled his crosshairs back to the target for another check, making sure they still landed in the right vicinity. Even though the target itself might be a "no-show," a good radar man could always tell if his hairs weren't falling where the objective was supposed to be, invisible or not.

If everything still looked good, the RN permanently switched back to the second OAP. The next thing heard would be: "Pilot, radar. Target acquisition confirmed and we are synchronizing on OAP Two. Center the PDI and keep it centered."

"Roger," the pilot immediately responded. "Centering the PDI."

World War II movies usually portray this particular exchange in more stirring fashion. The scene plays out something like this: "Pilot to bombardier, you have control of the aircraft," which is followed by a mysterious jiggling of the aircraft and dramatic music, further followed by, "Bombardier to pilot, roger, I have the airplane." What they were doing, though one doubts the actors or directors in those pictures fully understood this, was slaving the Norden or H2S bombing system to the Flying Fortress C-1 Autopilot, enabling the bombardier to then control the airplane from his position in the nose. The B-52 had this feature as well, but SAC found that bombing accuracy was improved by using the skills of the pilot to keep the PDI centered (it was first called a PDI in the B-17), rather than turning the work over to "George."

At about the 240-second mark on the To Go meter, the final portion of the bomb run checklist was performed—the Release Configuration Check.

NAV: "Release circuits disconnect?"

RN: "Connected, light on."

NAV: "BRIC?"

RN: "Selected position, light on, light dim."

The bomb release interval control (BRIC) provided many dropping options when used with long strings of conventional weapons, and a fuller discussion of that process will follow in a later chapter. On this checklist, the BRIC didn't have much to do; the B-52 carried a maximum of four internal nuclear weapons.

NAV: "Master Bomb Control Switch?"

RN: "On, light on."

NAV: "Bombing System Switch?"

RN: "Automatic."

NAV: "Bomb Door Control Valve Lights?"

RN: "Off."

All the while, the radar navigator continued synchronizing on OAP Two. As the airplane got in closer, the radar presentation would often change, sometimes significantly. If a crosshair adjustment had to be made (a layperson might not even see the movement), the RN alerted the pilot he was making a move.

RN: "Refining aim to the left."

PILOT: "Roger, turning left one degree . . . PDI recentered."

When the nav announced "thirty seconds TG" over the intercom, he also started a stopwatch, to be used as a last resort to manually drop the bomb if for any reason the BNS suddenly broke down before the bomb release line was reached.

From here on, if everything was working properly, things happened automatically. The bomb doors were ordered open by the BNS and when the TG meter ran down to zero, out the nuclear weapon went. This is how that moment was to be handled as per the yellow checklist: Bomb release monitored—"Bomb away"(RN/P).

According to doctrine, immediately after "Bomb away" (the RN always said those words over the interphone, in keeping with the no-assumption, positive confirmation nature of all bomb run procedures) the B-52 went into a combat breakaway maneuver that was designed to get the bomber as far away from the blast as was possible. While still in that steep turn, the Black Holers would be closing the bomb bay doors and conducting their postrelease checklist. Once the airplane was straightened out and the cockpit had been cleaned up, it was either on to the next target or the next segment of the mission.

Obviously, when practicing nuclear attacks over friendly territory, one does not actually drop objects from the aircraft. To assess bombing accuracy, SAC established a nationwide network of radar bomb scoring (RBS) sites to score the runs. A steady electronic tone was used; the RN turned it on at twenty seconds TG, and it went off automatically at bomb release. The RBS monitoring site then determined where in the sky the bomb had been released and then further calculated where it would have actually hit on the ground. The RN/bombardier's goal was always a "shack," a direct hit with no measurable error. An acceptable margin of "circular error," or CE, on radar synchronous nuclear bomb runs was generally considered to be around five hundred feet, though the error criteria used for crews to remain "reliable" seemed to fluctuate a bit over the years. This may well have had something to do with the capability of the different B-52s; the Gs and Hs, for example, were superior bombing platforms to the models that came before them. Such variability was most clearly demonstrated by B-52D conventional bombing results in Southeast Asia, which appeared to deteriorate as the years went by. By 1972 and the Linebacker campaigns, the aging bomber's actual CE results were coming in at closer to one thousand feet, and sometimes even greater. To be fair, it was much easier to RBS-score a single, relatively large (and hypothetical) nuclear bomb than it was to evaluate the accuracy of an actual three-kilometer-long string of conventional weapons, which often contained bomb mixes that had inherently different ballistic qualities. Also, one other scoring factor should be mentioned regards the nuclear RBS releases—there was bound to be a greater margin of error when gravity weapons were dropped from very high altitudes versus those let go from, say, five hundred feet off the deck.

Once our almost-Ready rookie crew had successfully flown the required number of practice sorties and negotiated all the other Positive Control–related ground issues, they were ready for their final check ride with one of the wing's Standardization and Evaluation crews. When that had been satisfactorily completed, there was but one last step to being qualified to join the force as a Combat Ready Crew able to stand Pad or fly Airborne Alert—their Single Integrated Operations Plan certification. During that SIOP briefing to the wing or air division commander, where the crew's competence to successfully strike the specific nuclear target assigned by the president had to be thoroughly demonstrated, it was the bombing and navigation team that did most of the talking.

"Sir," the radar navigator would say to the general, near the end of a long and detailed recitation about what the Black Holers would be doing during every minute of the mission, "we will cross the initial point near Dubna at four hundred feet and turn right to a heading of one-seven-zero." His pointer indicated the track on the projection screen. "The bomb run will take eight minutes. As soon as the aircraft completes the IP turn and is straight and level, I will seek out OAP One, the center of the airport at Sheremetyevo. While I am refining my crosshair placement, the nav will update his position counters one last time using the airport as a fixing GPI point. OAP Two is a late showing return; we expect it to emerge at three and a half minutes TG, and I will switch over to it at that point."

"What is the target and weapon?" the general asked abruptly, in a deliberate attempt to upset the RN's presentation and throw him off stride. Part of the certification drill was to see if the crew could handle surprises under pressure and to make sure they understood the mission in all its dimensions.

"Sir, the target is a hardened ICBM complex. It is heavily protected and will require several direct hits. We have been informed on a need-to-know basis that our mission against this target is the seventeenth strike scheduled."

"Seventeenth against Moscow?" queried the general, interrupting the briefing's rhythm once again.

"No, sir, we do not have a need to know regarding the exact number of sorties against the entire city. This will be the seventeenth strike against the missile complex."

The RN paused for a respectful moment before addressing the other part of the general's question. "The weapon assigned is a Mark-28, set for a 1.1 megaton yield. It will be parachute retarded and fused for a delayed burst."

"Thank you, please continue."

The slide changed. "OAP Two is located in the North Centrum of Moscow, Tverskaya Area. We have it here on a close-up image."

Beginning in the early 1960s, hypersecret CORONA spy satellites (their existence has only recently been declassified) began taking stereoscopic, three-dimensional pictures of the Soviet Union from 100 miles up, with resolution accurate enough to pick out individual automobiles.

"We anticipate a sharply defined radar return," the radar navigator continued, tapping his pointer at it, "coming off a large building at the intersection of Leningradski Prospect and the Garden Ring."

The general affected a skeptical look. "Are you certain you can identify this return? I assume you are about to tell me this will be your final aiming point."

"Yes, sir, on both counts. I have studied this building carefully, both from satellite imagery and our simulations of what the target environment is expected to look like on mapping radar. It is constructed of brick and reinforced concrete, its long side perpendicular to incoming track. From our attack angle, it offers a very distinct and reliable paint." The RN rested the tip of his pointer next to an extremely small spot on the screen. "At the bomb release line, my crosshairs will be laid here—'tap-tap'—directly on top the northwest corner of the building."

The two-star nodded at the conceit the RN could refine his aim to that degree, on something that looked like nothing more than a tiny dot, though probably not surprised; highly confident radar navs weren't a rare breed. "Tell me, captain," the general said to the RN, unable to resist asking the question and curious how this fellow would answer, "just exactly how is it you will be able to separate out this building's northwest corner from, say, its southeast corner?"

The RN responded instantly, ready for the question. "Sir, by adjusting my antenna tilt four degrees down at 30 TG and carefully refining the video gain at precisely 15 TG, it will be possible to pull the northwest corner from out of the clutter. Imagery suggests that portion of the facade is twenty feet higher than the southeast corner, hence the opportunity for differentiation and breakout of the slightly brighter return."

The division commander smiled appreciatively at the delicately controlled performance, while nearby his horse holders could only blink their eyes and rub their noses. "Well, gentlemen," the general said to everybody in the room but with a twinkle in his eye only the RN could see, "it appears we are in good hands."

And it was true; the nation was in good hands, for no one took the nuclear war business more seriously than the men who would be asked to fight it. No one was more determined than they to successfully fulfill their mission; knowing that public knowledge of such determination would more than anything else prevent it from ever actually happening. At the same time, nobody on earth—not the war protesters, not the college professors, not the politicians, not the philosophers, not even, dare we say, a saintly Nobel Peace Prize winner—was more frightened of nuclear weapons nor understood the threat they posed to humanity more profoundly than the combat crewmen of the American Strategic Air Command.

Until 1965 this was the essence of SAC. Up to that point, its only mission had been strategic nuclear deterrence; its primary weapons platform the mighty Boeing B-52 Stratofortress. By the mid-1960s, the command had reached its apex, thought by many to be militarily invincible. Both friend and foe, either admiringly or grudgingly, fully understood and had to deal with the fact that SAC's KC-135/B-52 combination was the world's only independently operating, unlimited range weapon system capable of massive, consistently accurate, all-weather, day or night, nuclear bombardment.

Very shortly, however, the planet's geopolitical center of gravity was to experience a tectonic shift, and the game would change. Tensions that had been building in Southeast Asia for years were boiling over. Months earlier, in August 1964, naval forces from the United States and North Vietnam engaged one another in the Gulf of Tonkin. By the end of that year, 23,000 U.S. sailors and ground troops were stationed in South Vietnam. In February 1965, the Viet Cong (VC), the "indigenous resistance" to the American-supported South Vietnamese government, attacked the U.S. base at Pleiku. The very next day, American and South Vietnamese air forces attacked targets in North Vietnam, whose government had made no secret of their direct military support of the VC. On February 10th, the Viet Cong struck back against a barracks at Qui Nhon, killing twenty-three American soldiers. On March 2, the American Tactical Air Command (TAC) launched Operation Rolling Thunder in an escalating tit-for-tat against North Vietnam's military infrastructure. And with that, the American/Vietnamese war was off and running.

After a great deal of foot dragging by the bigwigs in Omaha regarding getting sucked into this very untidy, nothing-in-it-for-us fracas (the formal argument was "We need all our bombers for nuclear defense!"), SAC reluctantly agreed to demands by the White House and Pentagon to get on board the Vietnam bandwagon. The crews' first inkling of this development came in early 1965 when a new wrinkle was added to B-52 training sorties. Several squadrons were asked to load up MB-4 practice bombs (containing ten-pound black powder charges) and haul them down to Matagorda Island Bomb Range off the Texas coast, where they were dropped on remote targets in lieu of an RBS scoring tone. These "iron bomb" practice runs (something most Buf crews had never before experienced) began occurring with greater and greater frequency, especially in the F model wings. The rumor mill was finally sated in late winter 1965, when thirty B-52Fs were sent to Guam and ordered to make preparations to "carpet bomb" targets in South Vietnam. The aircraft sent to Andersen AFB were supplied by the 7th Bomb Wing at Carswell (which also was assigned a D squadron in 1969) and the 320th Bomb Wing from Mather (a busy place in those days).

All of this was prelude to one of the great ironies in air combat history.

Tactical Air Command was about to use its pinpoint, though scantily loaded fighter/bombers to execute Operation Rolling Thunder, a strategic bombing campaign against the supply, command, and control structure at the enemy's heart in North Vietnam, while Strategic Air Command would soon be directed to use its heavy, big-impact bombers in close tactical support of friendly ground troops in South Vietnam, under a program designated Operation Arc Light.

CHAPTER TEN

Turning on the Arc Light

I t apparently was a randomly selected name, the next available in the Joint Chiefs of Staff codebook. If at that same moment in early 1965 an emergency airlift had been mounted to rescue imperiled soldiers at a winter-darkened Arctic Circle station, it would probably have received the designation. But that didn't happen, and now, of course, one can't imagine any name other than Operation Arc Light for the eight-year Stratofortress campaign in Southeast Asia.

The B-52's first combat action under Arc Light auspices occurred on June 18, 1965, and it wasn't pretty. Thirty B-52Fs were loaded with conventional bombs and launched westwardly out of Guam, in what became known as the "Arc Light One" mission. It was about three thousand miles from Andersen AFB to Vietnam—across a wide stretch of the western Pacific to the Philippines, then a jog to the north of that huge island nation, followed by another leg over the South China Sea—about five and a half hours of flying. An hour or so in-country and five and a half back to Guam brought it to a twelve-hour sortie, which meant the bombers would need an aerial refueling somewhere on the outbound route. An area off the northern coast of Luzon, the Philippines' main island, was chosen for the activity. Besides being far enough along in the mission for a good bit of fuel to have been burned off, it was located over international waters and within relatively easy reach of the KC-135 Stratotankers stationed to the north at Kadena AFB, Okinawa.

Arc Light One was perking right along until just before reaching the refueling area when everything went to hell in a handbasket. The airplanes had been grouped into ten three-ship cells spaced only a few minutes apart, a configuration none of the participants had ever flown before. The first cell arrived early at the tanker rendezvous and, for reasons unknown, decided on their own to establish a circling pattern to kill off the extra time. In so doing, they flew right through the second cell. Two ships collided and eight of the twelve crewmen were killed. During the subsequent refueling, one of the Fs ran into trouble getting its gas and had to break off for Kadena. Shaken, the force managed to pull itself together and go on to bomb its South Vietnam targets. Unfortunately, the strikes proved to be ineffective, almost embarrassingly so. Then, on the way home, another bomber ran into electrical problems and had to divert to Clark AFB, the Philippines. The remaining twenty-six ships limped back to Guam.

The next few weeks brought considerable harrumphing and finger pointing, but in the end a lot of good was salvaged from the Mission One fiasco. Most notably, revisions in formation flying and air refueling procedures were put into place, better target identification protocols were established by ground commanders, the air/ground chain of command and communication was improved, and weapon mixes underwent a thorough review. By the time the strikes resumed in July, things had improved considerably; within a few months, Arc Light was running on all cylinders.

Andersen operated two squadrons of Fs until mid-1966, when the newly modified "Big Belly" Ds began replacing them. Even at that early date, it had already become clear that a lot more B-52s, armed with much bigger payloads, were going to be needed to fulfill the Pentagon's expectations in the rapidly widening war. Although the original Fs would wind up flying only 1 percent of all Arc Light sorties, they did achieve two important things: 1) the implementation of the basic Arc Light operating procedures SAC would use over the next seven and one-half years, and 2) the establishment of the B-52 as a dominant ground support instrument that could not only inflict tremendous damage but was also highly effective as a morale-busting "terror weapon."

It was the arrival of the D model B-52 that brought Arc Light to maturation. Almost overnight, Gen. Curtis LeMay's bomber became the most powerful piece of artillery any battlefield had ever seen. By late 1966 both friendlies and the enemy no longer needed convincing that the most fearsome event they were ever likely to witness was an up-close and personal massed Stratofortress attack. The D's new paint scheme—pitch black on the bottom and sides, mottled tan and green on top—added to the airplane's growing "meanest mother in the valley" reputation.[1] When configured in the standard three-ship cell pioneered by the Fs, with bomber number 2 positioned one nautical mile in trail and staggered to the right of lead, and number 3 two miles back and staggered to the left, the B-52Ds combined cell loads of 252 500-pound and 72

750-pound HE bombs could utterly decimate a "kill box" measured one kilometer wide and three kilometers long ("1 klik by 3").

Arc Light conventional weapons were delivered two ways: 1) the already discussed radar synchronous bomb run, and 2) ground-directed Combat Sky Spot, which was introduced in 1966. As mentioned in the previous chapter, nuclear bomb aiming accuracy was determined by transmitting an electronic "tone" to SAC-owned RBS sites. Imagine, then, Combat Sky Spot as RBS in reverse; a radar/computer package that instead of tracking the accuracy of a bomb run, guided the aircraft to the bomb release line. The procedure was straightforward—after the bombers departed the IP at the preplanned heading, altitude, and airspeed, Vietnam-based Sky Spot controllers radioed the lead bomber heading corrections and a countdown to release, with the other two bombers in the cell dropping off number one.[2]

At the heart of the Sky Spot bombing system was a sophisticated apparatus derived from equipment the RBS people had long used for their scoring work, which SAC had originally dubbed the MSQ-77 radar. Because of the in-house nature of that nomenclature, Arc Light staff and crews almost always referred to the RBS/Sky Spot sorties as "MSQ missions," pronounced "Mis-cue" (though most of the military world continued to use the more generic "Sky Spot" term). The new system proved out immediately and was soon made available to other Allied combat units. Tactical Air Command (TAC), in particular, used the MSQ radar network for many of their fighter/bomber drops.

In early 1968 U.S. Military Assistance Command–Vietnam (MACV) made it known that, though enthusiastic about Sky Spot, it expected Arc Light to provide even greater flexibility in dealing with fast-breaking ground combat situations. "Mac-Vee" was headquartered in Saigon and controlled all U.S. armed forces engaged in the Vietnam War, which meant it usually got its way. Combat Sky Spot/MSQ was therefore further refined into what was called Bugle Note, where B-52 cells arrived at a prebriefed IP as before but would then be directed by the MSQ controller to a target of opportunity. This near real-time capability, also characterized in some quarters as the "Quick Reaction Force," was tremendously successful, and by the middle of 1968, 80 percent of Arc Light sorties were operating under Bugle Note parameters.

There was another plus to the Sky Spot system. Bomb damage assessment (BDA) comparisons between radar synchronous and MSQ/Bugle Note drops revealed the latter procedure was more consistently accurate, for the same reasons Oboe radio beams could place bombs more precisely than a Norden optical delivery. Radio-ranging measurement was not only less susceptible to inherent equipment errors, it also wasn't affected by darkness, bad weather, or imprecise human aiming. It did have two significant limitations, however. Sky Spot/MSQ/Bugle Note was limited to line-of-sight (LOS) distances, which meant the radar could not see the bombers over the horizon, and by definition the transmitters had also to be situated on turf controlled by the United States or its allies. It was therefore restricted to use only in South Vietnam and certain adjacent areas.

By early 1967 both Sky Spot and the B-52Ds were veterans of the conflict, with standardized operations that could lay out and successfully execute large numbers of combat missions on a daily basis. This had become possible not only because of SAC's outstanding ability to systematize procedures but also because of the relatively static nature of the fight. Already, the Vietnam conflict had taken on a World War I cast—there was no discernible end in sight, the "lines" were unchanging, the same operating bases remained in place for years, and fighting strategies revolved around personnel attrition. Everyone close to the war sensed it would be a prolonged fight, with little prospect for a single, defining engagement (e.g., a Normandy landing). Accordingly, the SAC Arc Light bomber force at Andersen settled into what became an almost permanent "temporary" routine.

For those just-arriving cadre Big Belly D wings, it was, at least at the beginning of the war, an exciting time. Although few admitted it, nearly all of the bomber crewmen were looking forward to some REAL ACTION. They would have arrived at The Rock in one of two ways; either the airmen flew one of their own squadron bombers across the pond to relieve another D model going home or they "cattle-carred" it on a SAC tanker along with several other crews. It was a long flight to Andersen from just about anywhere in the continental United States, so official policy dictated that the first twenty-four hours after landing were devoted to crew rest. As all involved would soon discover, there would be precious little of that commodity in the future—to paraphrase an old Marine Corps drill instructor refrain, crewmen's souls may have belonged to God, but their rear ends were now owned by Arc Light.

The first combat mission was designated an over-the-shoulder flight, whereby an experienced Arc Light aircraft commander and radar navigator flew with a rookie crew "looking over their shoulder" to make sure they understood all the conventional bombing procedures and to answer questions. While the men couldn't know it, the routines they would establish on this initial Arc Light sortie would vary little from all the others yet to come.

At the appointed hour, a bus picked each aircrew up at their quarters[3] and delivered them to Andersen's new Arc Light briefing center, a large, white, solidly built structure that seemed the embodiment of what was shaping up to be a very long-haul war. After grabbing a cup of vile-tasting joe, the men filed into the building's main room and settled into their designated seats. What followed was not unlike the way World War II movies portray air combat mission briefings, though the Arc Light versions lacked the snappy dialogue and statuesque leadership provided by the silver screen's Gregory Pecks. Crews were grouped together in rows with a center aisle left open for comings and goings. A raised-platform stage in front of the theater supported a lectern, and the obligatory projector and screen stood ready to flash images of the mission routes, targets, bomb loads, intelligence reports, air refueling times, weather, and recovery alternates—plus a few risqué cartoon slides sprinkled in for levity.[4]

Fig. 14. Arc Light premission briefing. Note how the two "Black Holers" (middle, glasses) are working diligently while the others are jaw-boning or taking a nap. (*306th Bomb Wing photo album; author's collection*)

Following the time hack, the mission briefer, intelligence officer, and weather forecaster conducted their presentations, and then the wing commander stepped to the podium to offer a few words of encouragement. After the chaplain mopped up, the crews were dismissed to their individual specialty briefings. The pilots waded through the usual mountain of forms ("SAC takeoffs are not approved until the weight of the paper equals the weight of the aircraft"), with special attention given to routes, clearances, fuel management, and the aircraft weight and balance calculations. The gunners and EWOs broke off to study the ins and outs of bomber defense for the particular mission being flown. If the target was down in the Mekong Delta, with virtually no threats at high altitude, there wasn't a lot to do. If, however, the mission was farther north, say along the Demilitarized Zone (DMZ); Ho Chi Minh Trail; or, until October of 1968, into the southern portions of North Vietnam, then considerable attention was given to MiG fighter or SAM threats.

Meanwhile, the navigator-bombardiers had adjourned to the target study rooms. If the mission was a radar synchronous run, the session would be intense. After the chief of bomb-nav specified in detail the target and off-set aiming points, along with any additional related information, the room would quiet as the two-man teams turned on their light projectors and slowly scrolled through the recon photos and/or radar mapping simulations of the target environment. If, however, the sortie was to be a ground-directed MSQ/Bugle Note drop, the discussions would be more abbreviated—with timing issues to the IP especially critical. There was zero room for error in this work; perhaps the greatest fear a Vietnam War bombardier had—even more than the threat to his own life—was that he might somehow make a mistake and kill friendly troops.

After the specialty briefings concluded, it was time to reboard another bus. The first stop was the in-flight kitchen, where crewmen selected box lunches of fried chicken or roast beef/ham and cheese sandwiches, supplemented with raw carrots, celery, oranges, apples, cookies, and individual-sized cartons of milk. The food was not something even a high school cafeteria would brag about, but then again it wasn't the canned rations the poor grunts in Vietnam foxholes were eating either. Each crew received a jug of cold water and a large urn of coffee, to be strapped against the lower compartment fuselage just above the honey bucket and adjacent to the relief tank. The crews considered the very close proximity of this in-go/out-go paraphernalia as fully in keeping with Air Force crew-comfort design philosophy.

Next came the life support center to pick up a large metal "chap kit" box housing the crew's survival equipment. Therein were six individual issues of a direction-finding beacon, two-way radio, dehydrated food, flashlight, flares, shark repellant, first-aid articles, twenty rounds of .38-caliber cartridges, and a Combat Masterpiece revolver—all of which were prestuffed into a many-pocketed nylon garment worn round the torso and thighs in the manner of cowboy chaps. Many first mission crew members had not handled a gun since their training days and were often a little nervous about the way some of the other fellows bandied about their Smith & Wessons. Everyone made an effort to be grimly nonchalant, as if they were hardened deputies forming a posse in Marshal Dillon's office.

At last, the men arrived at their airplanes. New aircrew just stepping off the bus generally had a similar first impression—OK, so they were in the war now, but the Andersen flight line really didn't look all that much different from the one back home. The parking revetments, taxiways, and runways were made of the same asphalt and concrete as in the States, and the same blue maintenance trucks busily darted here and there. Identical yellow MD-3 External Power Unit carts, necessary for both keeping the ships alive while sitting on the parking ramp and starting the engines, littered the tarmac, their familiar umbilical cords plugged into the big black bombers. As always, wheeled vehicles scurried here and there, engines were continuously starting up or shutting down, and flying machines noisily taxied to and fro. Except for the overall larger size of the flight line and much greater numbers of airplanes, the scene had a customary look, sound, and feel.

A closer examination, however, revealed Andersen's differences. Heavily armed soldiers stood constant guard at each airplane (only nuke-loaded Alert birds got that at home) and along every road and checkpoint. The maintenance personnel that serviced the warships were considerably more tense and somber. And unlike the secret dark-of-the-night movement of nuclear bombs on a Stateside base, weapons on Guam were delivered openly and around-the-clock. First-time crews were especially fascinated by the long ammunition trains being tractored in from Andersen's jungle bomb dump. Scores of Munitions Maintenance Service (MMS) "jammer crews" quickly unloaded this rolling stock, inserting the preassembled twenty-eight-bomb clip-ins into the weapons bay (three per plane) and fastening individual blivets on the wing pylons. Also noteworthy was the activity around the tail stinger. The new guys watched, some for the first time, the careful loading of bandoliers of armor-piercing .50-caliber incendiary cartridges into each Quad Fifty pod.

Fig. 15. Internal clip-in assemblies ready for bomb bay installation. U-Tapao revetments, 1968. (*Author's collection*)

After forcing themselves away from this "show," the rookie Arc Light airmen would begin their preflight by gathering around the bomber's crew chief to go over the Form 781, the aircraft's maintenance log.[5] Within the looseleaf pages of that thick notebook—recorded on an unexplainably poor grade of white paper—were all the ship's aches and pains, marked with a comment or red-penciled symbol to denote their seriousness. The aircraft commander took several minutes to carefully peruse the form, sharing any and all relevant information with the affected crew members.

Three types of maintenance write-up symbols could be found inside the 781: an informational, a general remark about something that could be lived with; a Red Slash (diagonal line), indicating a problem that might turn serious or disable a critical piece of equipment, though not sufficient to stop the music; and a prominently displayed Red X, highlighting either a safety or flight issue or a glitch that could result in an unsuccessful mission and/or lost aircraft—no one can fly the bird until fixed. An example of each follows:

Informational

PILOT: (Scratching chin while pointing at the write-up) "What's with the pee can?"

CHIEF: (Clearing throat) "It leaks."

PILOT: "Yeah?"

CHIEF: (Following up) "Bottom's rusted out. No time to replace it."

PILOT: "Yeah?"

CHIEF: (Averting eye contact) "It'll get messy if you use it, Sir."

PILOT: (Feigning indifference) "Hey, no sweat. We'll just hold it. The trip only lasts twelve hours."

Red/(Diagonal)

PILOT: (Turning to the senior navigator-bombardier) "Hey, Radar, a couple of your Black Hole watchamacallits are cocked up."

CHIEF: (Turns to address RN, eyes rolling as pilot moves away to check something else) "Sir, the MADREC diagnostic check showed a couple of weak vacuum tubes. We haven't got the minutes to install new ones."[6]

RN: "No problem. Give the new tubes to the nav. He can stick 'em in on the way over."

PILOT: (A few minutes later, returning to the problem with worried expression) "Hey, Radar, we gonna have to abort?"

RN: "Negatory. Once again your illustrious bombing and navigation team has Saved The World For Democracy."

Red X

PILOT: (Looking around) "What's with all the maintenance guys?"

CHIEF: (Blinking rapidly) "Sir, it looks like we got a pretty good leak in the number eight hydraulic pack."

PILOT: (Staring at a huge, growing pool of red fluid under his right wing) "Right."

CHIEF: (Voice lacking conviction, while meanwhile another blue bread truck pulls up and a half-dozen more green-fatigues pile out and sprint toward the aircraft, tool boxes banging against their thighs) "They think they'll have it fixed before engine start time."

PILOT: (Eyes glazing over) "Right."

After dealing with the various maintenance issues (and there were ALWAYS a lot of them),[7] the new crew began its preflight. While the nav team tentatively introduced themselves to conventional bombs and the EWO to his specialized ECM antennas and chaff dispensers, the pilots proceeded to the walk-around inspection. For most first-timers, it was more a tip-toe-around. Despite the men's long intimacy with the aircraft type, the Arc Light B-52Ds, all decked out in war paint and bombs hanging from them like Christmas tree orna-ments, somehow looked very different. Cautiously running their hands along the fuselage and idly kicking the tires—a reflexive, possibly congenital pilot idiosyncrasy—the drivers would slowly begin to see the airplane in a different light, a feeling not unlike discovering an entirely new and exotic side to an old girlfriend.

Fig. 16. Author preflighting/prearming 750s on a "stub pylon." *(Author's collection)*

Here the thing was, this giant warbird at once so familiar and so alien. A total of 185 feet wide and 156 feet long, it would depart the earth this day carrying thirty tons of bombs, with its total gross weight approaching a half-million pounds. Bearing that enormous load were four clusters of twin-truck five-foot-high wheels (eight altogether), configured in tandem fashion under the fuselage (plus one small wheel under each wing tip). This quadricycle landing gear also featured a unique crosswind crab capability, which is to say the wheel groups were designed so that during landings and takeoffs the fuselage could be kept pointed into the wind by swiveling the undercarriage left or right, thereby enabling the gear itself to track straight down the runway. No other airplane in the world shared this control advantage. No other airplane needed it.

Getting that massive contraption into the air wasn't easy. The D model B-52 had eight Pratt & Whitney J-57-P turbojet engines, each rated at a normal thrust of 9,000 pounds. Now that was certainly a great deal of push (in comparison, TAC's largest Vietnam fighter/bomber, the supersonic F-105F Thunderchief, had a single 26,000-pound thrust engine), but when the aircraft was loaded to maximum Arc Light gross weights, it wasn't quite enough to get the Dog model Buf solidly airborne. To boost takeoff engine power and solve that unstick problem, a procedure called "water injection" was used.

At first blush, the concept of mixing water with fuel sounds absurd. But, not to worry, the Stratofortress pocket-protector gang had the physics figured out. Here's the way it worked: When the throttles on a D model were advanced for takeoff, that action also opened an injection valve, which began spraying water into the air inlet of each engine. The H_2O instantly vaporized, increasing the density of the incoming air. Hence, more oxygen (aka fuel) became available to the engines, resulting in increased thrust. Before every mission, a water tank in each wing was filled to a combined capacity of 300 gallons, enough for 12,100 pounds of wet-rated thrust for approximately 110 seconds ("dry" takeoff thrust was rated at 10,500 pounds). Bottom line: A "wet" takeoff gave a max gross-weight Arc Light B-52D enough extra shove to get it safely up to about 1,000 feet and moving forward at well above stall speed.

After our rookie crew had finished their external look-see, they briefly entered the aircraft to check out parachutes and ejection seats, plus throw a few assorted preliminary switches. Everybody then exited the plane to get out of the stifling heat and stretch their legs for a few last minutes before scheduled engine start.

This was usually about the time when the Red Slashes and Xs on the Form 781 had either been resolved or reached crisis point. If the write-ups had been fixed, that was that, and everybody proceeded forward. If, however, a Red X was still unresolved, it was now time (probably past time) to get on the horn and call Charlie Tower, Arc Light's version of *911*. Located directly adjacent to the airport control tower, Charlie Tower housed the Lords of the

Fig. 17. McCoy Crew E-30 taking a few minutes in the shade after the preflight and prestart checks and before lighting the fires for another 1968 mission out of U-T. Author in front, instructing the crew chief to wait for that taxiing B-52 to come into view before taking the picture. *(Author's collection)*

Launch. Its omnipotent leader was a carefully selected, highly experienced B-52 instructor pilot whom everyone referred to by his radio name, "Charlie." At Charlie's elbow, beck, and call were a cluster of experts in ground traffic control, air operations, maintenance, and munitions, along with direct phone lines to the command post and Boeing (in Seattle) in case of changes in orders and/or emergency consultations.[8] He needed all that support to go with his responsibilities, for it was always one of the several rotating Charlies—not the squadron commander, not the wing commander, not even the Third Air Division three-star general—who bossed Arc Light launches and recoveries.

The best way to show how Charlie functioned is to offer a typical scenario. The drill begins with a standard launch of six bombers in two cells (let's designate them Red and Blue, spaced ten minutes apart), with Red One the lead cell and wave leader. It is five minutes after engine start and ten minutes before taxi time:

"Charlie, this is Red One."

"Red One, go."

"Rog, negative number eight hydraulic pack. They thought they had it fixed, but she just blew another gasket."

"Red One, roger. Stand by one. Break-break. Red Two, this is Charlie, say status."

"Charlie, Red Two is in the green."

Charlie would then ask Red Three the same question. He would also be simultaneously checking the qualifications of all the crews, especially Red Two's ability to assume the cell/wave lead position. By this time, all six crews in the wave had read between the lines and knew the score; the boys in Red One were packing their bags as fast as they could.

"Red One, Charlie. Uncle Ned confirms your aircraft is an abort. Bag drag to Spare One."

"Roger, Red One shutting down and in a bag drag. Out."

The Red One crew now made a prison-break move to get themselves and all their equipment out of Red One and into the Spare One aircraft, which in anticipation of exactly this kind of situation had already been preflighted and its engines started by the Spare One flight crew. All of this was a blur to the men in Red One: It is impossible to imagine how twenty minutes worth of high-stakes, hyperintensive human activity can be squeezed even further into five until one has experienced something like an Arc Light Bag Drag.

"Charlie, this is Spare One." The transmission was usually accompanied by labored breathing. "We are in the green and beginning our taxi." The old Red One crew was now in place inside a healthy Spare One airplane and on the move. The Spare One crew, having previously found themselves in the same predicament, had done everything possible to ensure a smooth turnover and a ready-to-go aircraft.

"Roger, Spare One, I copy. Break-break. Red Cell, Red Cell, this is Charlie. Be advised, old Red Two is now Red One, the cell leader. Red One you are now also the airborne commander and wave leader. Old Red Three is now Red Two. Spare One is now Red Three. Adjust your taxis accordingly. Acknowledge."

"Red One."

"Red Two."

"Red Three, roger. We are in passing gear about a thousand meters behind Two, should catch up to him at the hammerhead."

And the launch would proceed as scheduled.

When the hated bag drag wasn't necessary (and, thankfully, most of the time it wasn't), the regular routines could be observed. A few minutes before fire-lighting time, the crews in our example Red and Blue cells would finish up their short break and clamber back up the hatch steps and settle into their seats. Helmets went on, oxygen masks were clipped tight, and parachute shoulder straps were securely fastened. Quick glances also confirmed the parachute zero delay lanyards were looped through fastened lap belts, the former handy devices designed to instantly pop the chutes open should it become necessary to eject immediately after takeoff. At precisely the scheduled moment (counted down by the navigator), the pilot twirled a raised forefinger and he and the copilot brought their Buf to life.

B-52 engines were conventionally numbered from left to right, as observed from inside the cockpit. The far-left-hand outboard engine was #1, its mate #2; #3 and #4 were housed in the left inboard pod; #5 and #6 were inboard right; and #7 and #8 in the far-right-hand engine pod. The J-57, like all jet engines, was actually a type of internal combustion engine, though more efficient and with far fewer moving parts than the old reciprocators. Instead of a mechanical system based on cams, lifters, and pistons, jets draw oxygen into their combustion chambers via rotating compressor blades positioned just behind the engine intake. When a certain pressure is reached inside those chambers, fuel is added and the mixture ignited. The exploding gases become extremely hot and expand, whereby they are allowed to blow out the back of the turbine, producing thrust. These induction, compression, ignition, expansion, and exhaust processes all pretty much take place simultaneously; to make the engine run faster, just keep adding more air and JP-4 fuel (essentially kerosene). B-52 turbojets were not especially complicated in theory—making them work well, however, was altogether another matter.

To start a J-57, it's first necessary to get the compressor blades moving fast enough for sufficient pressure in the combustion chamber to allow the fire to light. SAC used two methods: 1) a "cartridge start" for quick-reaction pad Alert aircraft, where black powder canisters were inserted into the #2 and #8 engine nacelles and ignited on signal, instantly getting those two turbines spinning rapidly and then using that power surge to start the other engines; and 2) the "everyday" method, which provided a more orderly (though slower) way of initiating the combustion process by using the MD-3 External Power Unit.

The Dash One Manual explained how the latter MD-3 pneumatic start was performed:

> Pilot announces "Starting No. 4." Co-pilot positions No. 4 starter switch to START. At a minimum of 15% rpm on the turbine [thanks to the MD-3 Power Cart jump-start], pilot advances No. 4 throttle to 90%. As No. 4 engine reaches 45% rpm, co-pilot places No. 4 starter switch to OFF. As No. 4 accelerates through IDLE rpm, co-pilot places all remaining starter switches to START. As the engines reach a mini-

mum of 15% rpm, pilot advances throttles No. 1, 2, and 3 and co-pilot advances throttles 5, 6, 7, and 8 to IDLE. As the engines reach 45% rpm, co-pilot places [remaining] starter switches to OFF.

Once the beast's engines were up and running, the MD-3 was disconnected and all the aircraft's systems were shifted to internal power. While the pilots made ready for taxi and takeoff, the navigator-bombardier's ran their own pretakeoff checklists down in the Black Hole, including securing both the main entry hatch and pressure bulkhead door to the bomb bay, turning on the radar sets, and cranking up the BNS, Doppler, and astrocompass.

A crew's first mission was usually flown in the tail-end Charlie position, the last airplane in the standard six-ship wave format discussed earlier—hence our rookies would be in that scenario now known as Blue Three. With Reds One, Two, and Three already airborne (about ten minutes earlier), Blue cell lined up at the hammerhead, its three Bufs nose to tail. The Blue Three pilots would be completing the last of their pretakeoff checks—all four alternators started and checked; all ten hydraulic packs on, pressures checked; air-conditioning master switch on; hatches and bomb doors confirmed closed; gear crosswind crab adjusted for prevailing wind; control columns checked for free movement; seat and rudder pedals adjusted; flight instruments set; water injection pumps on; stabilizer trim in takeoff setting; wing flaps 100 percent, lever down; fuel switches 9, 12, 13, 14, 15, and 16 on, initial transfer started; and decision speed times reviewed.

"Crew," the aircraft commander said, as he released the brakes on the nav's countdown, "prepare for takeoff."

Even during the most routine of missions, there were always hundreds of onlookers watching an Arc Light launch. No matter it rain or shine, first time or the hundredth, they would invariably look up from their work, peer through fences, scurry to the top of a building, or even stand on their vehicles to get a glimpse of yet another big black bomber thundering down Andersen's saddle-back runway.[9] There was, and still is, near unanimous agreement by aviators and groundlings alike that the maximum-weight Arc Light D models, with eight screaming water-injected turbojet engines and billowing clouds of thick, dark smoke pouring out behind them, generated the most spectacular of all B-52 takeoffs. Not only did the whirling exhaust and black/camo paint jobs make the Bufs look like the baddest boys in town, but the things sounded, especially as they took off one after the other, like something straight out of Hades. Part of it had to do with the aural characteristics of the J-57s, part with the water injection process used during takeoff to thicken the intake air, and part, perhaps, was owing to the acoustical nature of the Asian bases themselves. Whatever the reasons, the combination resulted in a spine-chilling, two-mile-long takeoff run that produced a hideous, almost other-worldly shrieking, something one aircraft commander likened to "a thousand squirrels being ground up feet first." The frightful din would spill off the runway and roll across all of Andersen, not dampening until the echoes had traveled deep into the Guamian jungle.

All of this was but moments away for our rookie Blue Three crew. After one last quick traffic scan out the cockpit windows and a nod from the over-the-shoulder pilot, who was sitting on the instructor pilot jump seat a little behind and between the two pilots, the AC nudged the throttles forward and the Buf rolled onto the runway.

CHAPTER ELEVEN

First Combat Mission

"**P**ilot, this is nav. Fifteen point six seconds, NOW!"

"Committed."

After passing "S1" decision speed, Blue Three had no other choice but to continue, no matter even if the engines started falling off. Their best chance—probably *only* chance—to survive a serious emergency was to get the thing at least far enough into the air to eject. For Black Holers, the prospect of an "early departure from the aircraft" jacked the pucker factor up even higher; while the pilots, EWO, and gunner ejected upward (D gunners jumped out of the tail), the nav-bomb team's downward firing seats would drill them straight into the ground.

As the Buf slowly gathered takeoff speed, the pilot concentrated on runway directional control while the copilot kept his left hand pressed against the throttles to ensure none of them inadvertently retarded. Twenty seconds into the launch, the airplane rolled through the dip in the middle of Runway 06R and started up the backside. With the nose now pointed slightly upward, the pilots could see only blue sky ahead and Pacific Ocean on the sides; another mile of ground roll and they would be on the edge of Pati Point's 600-foot cliff.

The seconds slowly ticked by. Just before encountering the overrun and five knots away from "S2"—between 135 and 140 knots—the copilot keyed his mike.

"Coming up on unstick . . . NOW!"

The airplane's wheels separated from the concrete, however grudgingly.

Almost immediately, the ship was caught in Blue One and Two's not yet fully dissipated wake turbulence. The pilot kept both gloved hands welded to the control column, which seemed to be fighting back with everything it had. Despite his struggle, the AC remembered to tap the toe brakes and stop eight under-fuselage wheels from spinning. Off to his left, just beyond the three-mile national sovereignty limit, he caught a glimpse of the ever-present Soviet spy trawler. Within minutes, its sailors would send out an intelligence report stating that six B-52s were airborne.[1]

"Gear up!" the pilot commanded.

The copilot raised the gear handle and seven seconds later said, "Six are up . . . and in the green." That would be four sets of dual wheels fully retracted, plus two wing-tip outrigger gear.

The copilot was the only one looking at those green bulbs; the aircraft commander had his hands completely filled with converting "20,000 aluminum garbage cans flying in loose formation" into a functioning aerospace vehicle. The D model did not have the advanced "power steering" features of the later-built G and H models, using instead the long-proven, though by then outdated, World War II pulley-and-wire servo technology. It was therefore often necessary just after takeoff, when low speed and jet wash caused instability along the lifting and control surfaces and the big fella had to be handled like a rodeo bronc, to use full left and right throws on the yoke. This was a highly disconcerting exhibition when observed from the instructor pilot's jump seat, one that left the vague impression the airplane was somehow in the clutches of Stan Laurel and Oliver Hardy. Steady foot pressure was also necessary on the Bunyan-sized rudder pedals in order to maintain coordinated movement through the air and to minimize the effects of any adverse, side-to-side yaw.

After passing 180 knots indicated air speed, the pilot ordered, "Flaps!"

"Coming up," the copilot responded.

The pilot immediately began making stabilizer trim adjustments with a thumb button on his control column to compensate for the loss of lift/wing configuration changes. He would be looking to marry the changing flap and constant climb power settings with a trim that yielded an upward vertical velocity of about a thousand feet a minute, while simultaneously eliminating as much excessive fore and aft control column force as possible.

"Flaps at fifty percent," the copilot reported.

The pilot's airspeed meter slipped past 190 knots. The manual trim wheel by the throttles was too slow to accommodate the aircraft's abrupt aerodynamic changes, and using it would also mean the AC taking his hands off the wheel, so . . . more click, click with the electric trim thumb button on the right-hand side of the control column.

"Flaps at thirty percent."

Airspeed between 200 and 210 knots. Click, click.

"Flaps full up."

Airspeed steady at 220 knots. Click, click, and click—fore and aft control forces now neutralized, meaning the nose wouldn't rear up or dip down dangerously if the pilot should momentarily relax his grip on the yoke.

A few minutes later, with the airplane now safely airborne, the AC nodded at his copilot to take over.

"I got it," the copilot announced firmly, as he seized the column.

The right-seater got the feel of the Buf for a moment or two before settling back into the climb, perhaps deciding on a few minor throttle adjustments— "eight pipes in the organ and it takes a mighty wide hand to play them." In addition to being big and clumsy, the B-52 Stratofortress was also a "flat flier," meaning it moved vertically through the atmosphere in a near-level attitude, unlike nearly all other aircraft that climbed and descended nose first. This unusual aerodynamic characteristic stemmed largely from the huge shoulder-mounted wing attached to the top of the fuselage, which was a necessary design feature owing to the ship being wider than it was long. Even with the high wing configuration, tiny landing gear still had to be installed under the far wing edges to keep them from tipping into the mud. The rest of the crew impudently referred to this outrigger gear as the "pilot training wheels."

That huge airfoil was surprisingly limber, causing many an eyebrow to raise when the airplane encountered restless air. Built with an eighteen-foot arc of dihedral flexibility, the Buf's wings would often flap in the breeze, sometimes giving the perception the airplane was a giant bird of prey hunting for its supper. While no doubt important in mitigating aerodynamic stresses, that bit of engineering did absolutely nothing to improve a crewman's peace of mind, especially on certain occasions—say a lonely, bumpy, pitch-dark night over the ocean at 40,000 feet while poking through the tops of a nasty line of thunderstorms.

This wing-flapping dynamic was also contributing to growing problems with the D model's thin metal covering. Like aging dowagers, their epidermal paint jobs were no longer able to cover the many chips and dents, not to mention the heavy wrinkling that was taking place along the fuselage and under the wings. All those skin folds, creases, and ripples were becoming increasingly disturbing to the crews, in that it did not take an M.I.T. graduate to understand whatever was going on underneath could not possibly be good.

"Passing through 18,000 feet," the nav announced.

"Roger," the pilot acknowledged. "Crew, reset altimeters to two-niner-niner-two."

Red and Blue cells would continue clawing their way into the stratosphere until they reached the assigned en route cruise altitudes. Blue One, situated about eighty miles behind Red Three, leveled off at 33,000 feet; Blue Two nosed over at 33,500 and one nautical mile in trail; and Blue Three stabilized at 34,000 and two miles behind the leader—the 500-foot separation between aircraft a safety precaution. The cell pilots switched fuel tanks (a constant process to keep the ships in balance), set their throttles for 440 knots true airspeed and settled up on a heading of 290 degrees magnetic, though Two and Three would be required throughout the mission to use the white vapor trails in front of them as their primary directional reference. The wind was relatively calm, as it often was at this altitude and in this part of the ocean—evidence of why the great water body below them had originally been deemed "pacific," though the airmen in Blue cell, like sailors for hundreds of years before, well understood the capricious nature of equatorial climates.

The Blue Three Black Hole guys immediately settled down to the business of navigating their airplane across the western Pacific. After shedding cumbersome helmets and unshackling themselves from parachutes, the two slipped on lightweight gray-colored headsets and rolled up their sleeves.[2] The RN

Fig. 18. B-52D radar navigator station. Tracking handle just to front of the RN's right hand. Photo taken on a deadhead back to Andersen. *(Author's collection)*

got the big radar set perking the way he wanted it, while the nav unfolded his black-and-white strip chart. There wasn't room to accommodate large, unabridged maps on the navigator's small worktable, and the nearly blank, accordion-folded strips, displaying little more than a course line drawn across empty squares of latitude and longitude, also ensured the least amount of sensitive data was carried aloft.

An Arc Light navigator usually made a bit of a fuss about arranging his charts and tools just so—yellow checklist to desk left, so it almost rubbed up against the radar navigator's right forearm when the RN had hold of his tracking handle; three or four presharpened #2 lead pencils jammed into tiny receptacles sewn on the upper left arm of his flight suit; a compact rechargeable Sanyo flashlight stowed in a zippered pocket beneath the pencils; the aforementioned strip chart laid flat across the narrow table; flight log sheet positioned table right, partially covering the chart; and plotter, dividers, and the indispensable MB-4 circular slide rule at stage front.

Before leaving the immediate vicinity of Guam and the Marianas, the Blue Three RN used his radar to give the navigator one last good set of GPI fix coordinates, which the young man both recorded on his chart and installed in the Doppler-driven lat/long counters. By using that final known land position as an "anchor," the nav had a good starting point for tracking the Buf's progress to the Point Golf air refueling rendezvous above the Philippines. He would have only celestial navigation to actually "fix" the aircraft's position over the water (the accuracy of the counters slowly deteriorated without regular fix updates).

Interestingly, in the B-52, the electronic warfare officer made the actual heavenly observations. It made good sense to do it that way; the EWO was a rated navigator, had the time to assist the busy nav, and was physically close to the Periscopic Sextant, a basic sextant modified with a long-necked periscope that was inserted through a special port in the top of the fuselage (eliminating the need for a drag-inducing observation dome). The navigator did the precomputations and radioed up the preliminaries; the E-Dub found the bodies, did the two-minute shoot on each, and then radioed down the readings to the navigator, who converted those numbers to a fix on the black and white chart. This buddy system worked quite effectively, though SAC's division of labor rankled the Black Hole right-seater a little; not only did the EWO get all the fun while he was stuck with the dirty work, the upper-decker eventually became the better celestial navigator.

From a practical standpoint, it was not necessary for all three navigation teams in an Arc Light bomber cell to engage in full-scale celestial position finding—they were, after all, only one or two miles apart. The primary responsibility for the cell's navigation, which at this point in the mission boiled down to being on the correct heading and exactly on time, fell to the leader, though his work was continually monitored by the two navigators behind him. If the lead nav did run into trouble, say in the event there were unforecasted heavy winds, or navigation system malfunctions, or airplane mechanical glitches, or even a brain short circuit (it happened), the Black Holers were allowed to use the ship-to-ship command radios to discuss their problems. In the real world, however, that didn't happen too often, at least in terms of a direct and frank exchange—and for a very human reason. Navigators may confess to one another that they are temporarily disoriented, but would rather be burned at the stake than broadcast that compromising detail to the rest of the planet. If a situation did develop, more subtle methods were used to handle it.

"Blue One nav, this is Blue Two nav. Hey, that's a hell of a south wind, isn't it?"

A few seconds on the old Seiko would tick by while the Blue One nav digested the transmission.

"Two nav, this is One nav, roger." Sometimes the lead magellan would forget to unkey his mike and you would catch him nervously clearing his throat. "Yeah, sure is," the fellow would then suddenly say in a stronger voice, the light bulb finally coming on. "I've been evaluating it for a while now."

Liar, liar, pants on fire. He'd been sitting there fat, dumb, and happy—maybe not bothering to get that one extra celestial fix and for sure not knowing his counters and Doppler had gone haywire. His equipment and DR showed him on course, but the winds had blown the cell well to the north.

"Roger, roger, One, this is Two again. Thought you'd like to match our counter readings with yours before finalizing the alter heading."

"Yeah, you must have read our minds. We were just thinking it'd be a good idea to get a cross-check. Ready to copy." Numbnuts One would now find out where his cell was.

Another, rather tentative voice might chime in about this time. "Uhh, Blue One, this is Blue Three nav . . . yeah, uhhh, Two's counter readings are pretty close to mine, within a few miles." A Gold Star for the rookie.

With the other two ships reporting coordinates that close to each other, the lead nav could be fairly assured they were correct. Based on the radioed data, he would furiously compute a new heading to the next point, maybe adding an airspeed adjustment to compensate for having been wandering all over the sky. The cell pilots would be expecting a correction, by virtue of having over-heard the entire exchange between the three navigators.

"Blue Cell, this is Blue One." By unspoken agreement, the lead pilot had taken back his command radio. "Stand by for alter heading due to heavy winds."

"Two."

"Three."

All six Black Holers would be hoping the lead aircraft commander had bought the double shuffle; nobody wanted the Blue One nav to look bad, especially in front of the man he worked for. Everyone knew their own turn in the "whereinhellami" barrel would eventually come.

A couple of minutes later, with his cell now properly forewarned, the leader radioed the official order.

"Blue Cell, this is Blue One. Turn left ten degrees, new heading 280 degrees magnetic. Maintain 440 knots true." The lead nav had determined the little bit of time he had lost could be made up with some maneuvering work just before the air refueling—better that way than screwing around with the more complicated and less fuel-efficient throttle jockeying.

"Two."

"Three."

And then the human voices quieted, and for a long time all that could be heard in Blue cell's crew compartments were humming black boxes, whining gyros, the whistling slipstream, and screaming engines. The aluminum-wrap skin that separated the men from the stratosphere and J-57s was surprisingly thin—if the aircrews hadn't had on helmets or headsets, earplugs would have been necessary to protect their hearing. Trapped as they were in the lower com-partment, the navigator-bombardiers were subject to an even more intense level of sensory overload. For it was down in the cockpit's underbelly that the Buf's heavy scent settled and ripened; where sickening kerosene smells, engine-heated cabin air, vague suggestions of overwarm wiring, greasy-metallic odors thrown off by black-box electronic glow, and the ever-delightful fragrance emanating from the relief tank all blended together into one devastating bouquet. Such peculiar charms were further augmented by a claustrophobic lack of space, spa-tial disorientation caused by fuselage oscillations, cumulative psychological wear and tear encouraged by lack of windows,[3] and the constant, stomach-churning turbulence. The combined experience had long ago convinced other rated Air Force officers, indeed other Buf crew, that only brain-dead lunatics with cast-iron digestion could or would put up with the Stratofortress Black Hole.

The Buf's radar navigator and navigator took perverse pride in that reputation. As repulsive as the lower compartment could be, it was to them a special place. The Black Hole was their office, their control room, their sanctum sanctorum; the central nervous system of a highly complicated war machine that could be effectively operated by only a handful of human beings. Strategic Air Command's operating doctrine had recognized this from the very beginning; if something didn't work for them, that is if there was anything that hindered the Black Hole's ability to successfully bomb the assigned target, then it simply didn't work for anybody. While the pilot was the ship's commander, the man charged with the ultimate responsibility for the aircraft and its objectives, it was the navigator-bombardiers who were key to a successful B-52 strike.

After a thousand miles of empty ocean had passed under Blue Three's wings, the advisory over-the-shoulder radar navigator, who since takeoff had been sitting quietly at the instructor navigator's position near the bulkhead door to the bomb bay, stepped up to the nav, pulled the right side of the rook's headset to one side, and started yelling into his ear. Although it was very difficult to understand the fellow because of the terrible racket inside the nonsoundproofed compartment, the young navigator nodded, getting the message. He keyed his floor mike switch.

"Radar, I show us two hundred nautical miles east of Point Escarpada."

Having been attentive during the premission specialty briefing, the RN caught the action cue. "Roger, nav. Be advised, Blue One and Two are stable at our twelve o'clock, and I am switching out of station keeping mode into full scan mapping."

In addition to all its other features, the B-52 bombing and navigation system radar provided for a formation flying format that eliminated ground clutter and painted only nearby aircraft. While the lead RN in Blue One kept his radar in the full scan mapping and weather-avoidance format throughout the mission, Two and Three were better served by using the "station keeping" mode, enabling them to maintain constant contact with the other aircraft. This was particularly important at night and/or in the soup, when the bombers might inadvertently get too close to one another.

At this point in the flight, however, with a land feature once again approaching (the radar set had a maximum mapping range of two hundred nautical miles), the Blue Three bomb/nav team would be anxious to update the hours-old running dead-reckoning position showing on the nav's counters with their own hard radar fix.

"I'm painting Escarpada," the radar nav said, "coming up on the zero-six-eight degree radial at one-niner-five nautical miles . . . ready, ready, NOW!"

It was a rare Arc Light RN who didn't take advantage of Point Escarpada, a nicely contrasting land/water feature located on the northeast tip of Luzon, the Philippines. The extreme distance had ruled out using the radar crosshairs to get a GPI fix, but, as discussed earlier, an aircraft's position could also be determined by taking a radar range and bearing off a known point.

Less than a minute after the RN said NOW, the nav had plotted the range and bearing, penciled in a fix triangle symbol over the pinhole his dividers made on the white strip chart, and noted the time next to it. After picking the new fix's latitude and longitude off the chart, he twirled the knobs on the control panel in front of him and updated his counters.

All three of Blue cell's nav/bomb teams would be working Escarpada over, as well as computing new ETAs and headings to the Arc Light air refueling "timing triangle," a preplanned dogleg that supplied the necessary means for the bombers to arrive at the Point Golf refueling rendezvous exactly on schedule. Depending on whether the B-52s were early or late, they could either cut off or extend the dogleg accordingly. This timing triangle procedure had been so named because all the optional course lines on the chart (dotted lines as opposed to the normally solid) appeared as a series of triangles.

It was crucial the B-52s arrived at 20 degrees 20 minutes North Latitude and 122 degrees 50 minutes East Longitude (i.e., Point Golf) precisely on schedule—and we are talking here plus or minus seconds. Cell lead navigators became nervous if they missed hitting it by more than a quarter of a minute. Why so uptight? Because at that assigned moment three KC-135 tankers would come screaming out of the north, whistle past the point on a predesignated heading, and be gone in an eye blink. Everybody was going 600 miles an hour, and if the weather was bad, or it was a murky night, or the rendezvous radar wasn't working properly, and then a fellow compounded the problem through poor rendezvous timing resulting in the cell missing their tanks—well, young man, you just done screwed the pooch.

The life-giving KC-135s were lovely to behold when they appeared over that imaginary X in the ocean just east of the Batan Islands.[4] Oddly enough, the shared joy of Strato tankers and Strato fortressess coming together in the air was somewhat at odds with the rather arms-length, diffident relationship the two types of crews had on the ground. As a matter-of-fact, face-to-face exchanges between "bomber pukes" and "tanker toads," either professional or social, were relatively rare—the bulk of the bomber-servicing tanker squadrons were based on Kadena AFB, Okinawa, while most of the Bufs lived at

Andersen and U-Tapao, Thailand. And even when the airmen found themselves assigned to the same base, they didn't mix much. Same Air Force, same SAC wing, same fundamental mission, yet different airplanes, different duties, different world views. SAC tanker and bomber crews were the true odd couples—almost strangers on a personal level yet completely joined at the hip professionally. Tankers lived to service bombers; bombers couldn't survive without tankers.

Perhaps this seemingly unnatural detachment can at least partially be explained by a bald truism in military aviation—the sexy frontline warplanes always get the glory. Tanker units were among those that were involved in "support," which in the U.S. armed forces meant any airplane that didn't carry guns or bombs. Somehow, the "support role" insinuated a certain candy-assness toward those so engaged, no matter how preposterous such an idea clearly was. Little is served by wallowing in Freudian mumbo jumbo over the meaning of this collective personality disorder, one often shared by the support troops themselves; it was and still is simply the way red-blooded American soldiers perceive each other in a wartime context.

Such thinking was not confined to the military community; it was highly unlikely, for example, that any Vietnam-era Stateside newspaper editor ever wrote a headline like this:

CRITICAL KC-135 STRATOTANKER REFUELING ALLOWS
B-52 BOMBERS TO SUCCESSFULLY STRIKE OBJECTIVES IN
HANOI AND HAIPHONG AND RETURN SAFELY HOME

Nope, what the folks back home got every time was this:

GIANT B-52 BOMBERS SMASH ENEMY TARGETS
IN HANOI AND HAIPHONG

Like SAC's loyal and vastly underappreciated ground maintenance and munitions troops, the tanker crewmen gracefully accepted their obscurity. Rarely did they allow resentments to show, preferring instead to let their work do the talking. And those actions spoke volumes; few in the general public are aware that Strategic Air Command's fleet of KC-135s touched nearly all of American military aviation in Southeast Asia, refueling not just bombers but helicopters, fighters, fighter/bombers, and recon aircraft as well.

The two most important responsibilities SAC's Stratotankers had during the Vietnam War were: 1) supporting Tactical Air Command's fighter/bomb-ers and other aircraft in all Southeast Asian theaters—a program designated Operation Young Tiger, and 2) refueling B-52 Arc Light sorties operating out of Guam. The KC-135s at Kadena were involved in both operations, though Arc Light formed the bulk of their work. It was also the most familiar; in Young Tiger operations, tanker aircrews were faced with unprecedented demands—flying near or sometimes over hostile territory, refueling fight-ers very low on juice or with difficulties just before going in or coming out of battle, improvising spur-of-the-moment rendezvous points, and making crucial "them-or-us" decisions when both tankers and receivers were bounc-ing on empty. Conversely, gassing up B-52 bombers at designated points on preplanned routes was something the 135 boys did every day—to the point that experienced Young Tiger tank crews came to view the Arc Light Point Golf rendezvous as old hat. It never quite got that way for the bombers, probably because the Bufs had so much more at stake. B-52 lead crews who missed Point Golf lost their jobs; they would fly their next mission near the back of the wave along with the rest of the great unwashed.

Fortunately for the rookie crew in Blue Three, they weren't facing that kind of responsibility this first time out. That was in Blue One's lap, most particularly with the fellows down in its Black Hole. And now, with the tim-ing triangle maneuvering completed, Blue One turned the cell westbound and was calling for a slow descent to refueling altitude. Blue One would level off at 27,000 feet, Two at 27,500, and Three at 28,000. B-52/KC-135 air-to-air refuelings were almost always done in lower-altitude blocks, because the denser air significantly improved the receiver aircraft's aerody-namic controllability, a very important consideration when two heavy, fast-moving airplanes are operating within a few feet of each another.

At about this point, the over-the-shoulder radar navigator in Blue Three again unbuckled himself from the IN seat and shuffled up to a spot between the RN and nav's ejection seats. Yelling terse monosyllables and gesturing animatedly in navigator-bombardier sign language, he outlined in detail their specific rendezvous/refueling duties. The three men could have made the com-munication process a lot easier by speaking over the ship's interphone, but Black Holers detested using the radio for anything other than necessary busi-ness, sensing not without some cause that impromptu technical discussions might suggest to other crew the downstairs people were uncertain of their work, and that, of course, was something to be altogether avoided.

Arc Light's Point Golf bomber/tanker electronic rendezvous was a carefully orchestrated event. The first thing Blue cell's RNs did was clean up their radar screens by switching out of mapping/weather format and into station-keeping mode, enabling them to detect the unique radar-paintable identifiers each of the three approaching KC-135s were squawking on their AN/APN-69 Radar Beacon Transponders. As soon as each radar nav had picked out his designated tanker, he and his pilot began working together to line up behind it. The procedure took place without benefit of spoken word between the two aircraft, under what Strategic Air Command called "silent refueling." This wasn't as difficult or dangerous as it might sound; the technique had long been practiced as part of the nuclear SIOP, the Single Integrated Operations Plan. Such a security precaution was equally valid during Operation Arc Light; eavesdropping anti-B-52 Soviet trawlers lurked in every corner of the Pacific.

After finishing his instructions, the over-the-shoulder radar nav returned to the IN station near the rear bulkhead door and strapped in. The crew RN set his jaw, leaned in very close to the radar scope, and got down to cases.

"Pilot, this is radar. Our tanker is at fourteen miles, twelve o'clock." Both airplanes had hit the timing just right and were tracking along the same course.

Hiss, hiss.

The aircraft commander had clicked his mike switch twice in acknowledgment of the RN's call, sending an electrically charged "hiss-hiss" through the intercom. B-52 crews had developed a communications short-hand that reduced much of the "pilot-to-nav" type dialogue; extended in-flight technical conversations between fellows who ate, slept, and flew together for months and even years on end were often superfluous and always undesirable. One hiss, not often used because it was more ambiguous, meant a question or suggested something negative. Two hisses indicated yes, roger, or simply, I understand.

"Pilot, radar. Tanker is at seven miles and we are steadily closing." The 135s did most of the initial rendezvous maneuvering, in deference to the less-agile, higher-priority Bufs.

"Roger," the pilot said, "I have a talley-ho." The AC had the tank visually, though per established procedures the rendezvous would continue electronically no matter the good visibility (visual flight rules [VFR] rendezvous minimums were five nautical miles; instrument flight rules [IFR] minimums using the rendezvous radar were two nautical miles). Even during a VFR rendezvous, the pilot was always glad to have the radar's cross-check—sometimes it wasn't that easy to eyeball exact distances.

The copilot now initiated the refueling checklist, items that included cleaning up the cockpit, turning off all unnecessary electrical equipment, engaging various refueling control switches, making sure everyone had strapped in, and otherwise preparing for first contact.

"Pilot, radar. Four nautical miles."

Hiss-hiss.

Shortly thereafter came, "Pilot, three miles."

"Roger," the pilot said, "and, man, is that sun ever tough!"

Military aviators are often hard on ground-pounding mission planners, and this was another example of why. While the refueling track above the Philippines met every operational necessity, it failed to account for one very prosaic, yet potentially quite dangerous circumstance. Late afternoon arrivals at Point Golf directly faced a setting sun. On certain occasions during high-altitude flight, it is almost impossible to look even in the general direction of Earth's star, creating the kind of hazard American auto commuters heading home to western suburbs have long contended with. As luck would have it, the rookie Blue Three crew would get to face this bazillion watt lamp (perhaps the real Arc Light?!) for the first time on their first mission.

"Take it a minute, copilot," the AC said, blinking away the tears. "I'm gonna adjust my seat."

Buf drivers were wily fellows—they didn't get the job because they were slow on the draw—and all of them had their own tricks for dealing with this kind of problem. The Blue Three pilot used a technique common to many; he flipped down his helmet visor and lowered his ejection seat as far as it would go, using a narrow shadow cast by one of the forward window partitions to mask his eyes from the worst of the glare. The KC-135 pilots were usually sensitive to the situation as well and would sometimes alter their refueling headings just a tad in an attempt to help out.

"Better," the AC said, after settling in. He grasped the yoke and jiggled it slightly, an indication to the copilot he was reassuming control of the ship.

"One mile," the RN said.

Hiss-hiss.

Even in broad daylight, the Blue Three pilots could clearly see the tanker's red and white rotating beacons, which loomed larger and brighter as their Buf closed in. The AC had fine-tuned the throttles to a speed ever so slightly greater than the Stratotanker's, his creeping approach by the book—"below, behind, and directly in trail." The emphasis here was on below. It was extremely important the pilot not allow the bomber to be caught in the wake turbulence of the 320,000-pound KC-135, a very sizable aircraft in its own right.

"Pilot, radar. One-quarter mile and it's all yours."

His rendezvous work completed, the RN secured himself and his equipment, taking care to place the BNS radar antenna in a full negative tilt position so as not to fry the 135's boom operator. The Buf drifted closer and closer in.

"We are at precontact position," the copilot reported.

The B-52 was now stabilized fifty feet behind and ten feet below the tanker. Both aircraft remained motionless relative to one another, while cockpit instrument scans were made to ensure all systems were operating normally. Once satisfied, the Buf pilot caressed his throttles and started the ship forward again, literally inch by inch. The Blue Three rookies were enjoying one piece of good fortune; the air was smooth.

"Contact position."

At this juncture during a routine Stateside refueling, if the pilots were pleased with their approach to the tank and feeling loosey-goosey, there might have been a little unauthorized ship-to-ship chatter:

Buf copilot: "Fill 'er up and check the tires."

Boom operator: "Roger, sir, and how 'bout a windshield wash?"

The Blue Three crew had themselves engaged in similar banter back home, but during this, their initial Arc Light refueling on the way to actually kill people, such a frivolous act would have been unthinkable.

There was now less than a "first and ten" between the Blue Three pilots and the man in charge of transferring the fuel, a noncommisioned officer known as the "boomer." He could be plainly seen on the other side of a windowed fairing below the 135's tail, facing the B-52 in a prone position and wearing a very serious expression. While the Buf aircraft commander held his ship in the contact position with rocklike steadiness, the boom operator slowly telescoped the thirty-foot-long boom down to the refueling door located above and slightly behind the bomber pilots' heads. As long as Blue Three stayed within the boom's "envelope limits"—a miserly window roughly equivalent to one square yard—the fueling could safely commence. The Buf pilot would be aided by the receiver's director lights located on the bottom of the tanker's fuselage; the electronic display of red and green lamps—green for "you are in the profile," red for "approaching outer limits"—gave him specific feedback for making corrections forward, back, down, up, right, or left. All this is easy enough said, but make no mistake, air refueling was *the* single most difficult skill, including landings, for a B-52 pilot to acquire. Men who could not master it, in any weather, with or without autopilot assistance, did not stay aircraft commanders for very long.

"Slipway doors open and ready for contact light is on."

The ships were ready to mate. A moment later Blue Three's crew heard and felt the solid thunk of the boom seating itself in the refueling receptacle.

"Taking fuel," the copilot said in a near whisper. Precious JP-4 flowed into the bomber at a rate of 6,000 pounds per minute.

Fig. 19. "Contact!" Just downrange from the Point Golf air refueling rendezvous. *(306th Bomb Wing photo album, "Arc Light—1968–69"; author's collection)*

Down in the Black Hole, repository of all things olfactive in the bomber cockpit, the nav/bomb team immediately caught the scent of fresh kerosene. Anyone sitting in the instructor pilot jumpseat behind the pilots, or the bunk position just aft of it, would also hear the distinct sounds of fuel rushing through an exposed pipe in the ceiling, from where the copilot was distributing it to the aircraft's twelve fuel tanks. All activity and conversation in the ship ceased while the AC was on the boom—for the same reasons a golf gallery remains motionless and hushed while critical putting is under way. Out beyond the front windshield were two additional pairs of copulating aircraft, all soundlessly engaged in similar off- and on-loading.

After fourteen minutes and thirty seconds of continuous lock-on, Blue Three had its scheduled 87,000 pounds.

"Disconnect," the copilot reported. The boomer retracted his boom, the KC-135 pilot advanced his throttles as the Buf pilot pulled eight back, and the two airplanes quickly separated. The tankers nosed northward, back to Kadena, while the three bombers swung around to the southwest and the South China Sea. The Bufs climbed back to their cruise altitudes and settled down for another ocean crossing; the Vietnamese coast was still a couple of hours away.

Much to the surprise of the sweaty-palmed crew in Blue Three, entering hostile territory wound up being not that much different from flying into controlled airspace back in the States. Everybody—no matter whether they were transports, recon, tankers, fighters, or bombers—had to get permission from Ground Control Intercept (GCI) to enter Vietnam, a kind of "go-to-war clearance." A commonly used coast-in point for B-52 Arc Light strikes was in a region to the north of Cam Ranh Bay, a piece of Allied geography controlled by a GCI entity known as Bongo.

"Bongo, Bongo, this is Red One." The wave leader and his cell, still ten minutes ahead of Blue cell, could be heard hailing GCI as the bombers prepared to penetrate the Vietnamese air defense identification zone.

"Red One, this is Bongo, reading you five-by. Squawk standby for ident."

After it had been established the ground controller and Red cell leader could hear each other loud and clear, a brief IFF transponder ritual ensued whereby the Buf's identity was confirmed and that he was indeed where he was supposed to be. Ten minutes later, hot on the heels of Red cell, Blue One made the same call and received the same interrogation. Once those formalities were successfully concluded, the wave of six bombers was cleared to its initial point.

Blue Three's first mission would likely have been a Sky Spot/MSQ/Bugle Note strike, perhaps on a truck park/troop concentration in the always troublesome "Parrot's Beak" region, an area adjacent to a jutting chunk of ostensibly neutral Cambodia that arrowed directly at Saigon, less than forty miles away. The Cambodian side of the Parrot's Beak was the southern end of the Ho Chi Minh Trail, a notorious sanctuary from where Viet Cong and North Vietnamese Regulars staged attacks against the capital city almost at will.

Blue Three's crew now got down to the Before Sky Spot tactic and Pre-IP procedurals. The men were very familiar with most of the activities on those checklists, all necessary features of any type bomb run. The new action items, specific only to MSQ/Bugle Note, were naturally handled more deliberately.

When the three airplanes arrived over the IP, they turned inbound and steadied up on their assigned altitudes, airspeed, and heading. The bomb release line could be expected in another ten minutes.

"Pilot," Blue Three's radar navigator said over ship's intercom, "You are two and a quarter miles behind Blue One."

"Rog, closing it up."

Because of the cell's release timing requirements, Blue Three had to be precisely one nautical mile behind Two and two nautical miles behind One.

"Range is now one and two miles," the RN affirmed. "Echelon at this time."

The Blue Three pilot had made up the necessary ground and was now required to move slightly to the left of leader, while Two moved a little to the right. This echeloning was needed to spread the cell's 324 bombs equally over the entire target box.

While that was going on, the Blue One copilot established positive radio contact with Sky Spot. After yet another transponder authentication, Blue cell received its first bomb run call from the MSQ controller.

"Blue One, this is Sky Spot. Turn right two degrees, and you are six minutes and twenty seconds from release." Blue One turned, Two and Three silently followed.

Blue leader would have rogered only that first transmission; there were to be no further acknowledgements to the controller. Nobody wanted any more radio chatter than necessary; Vietnam radio voices were constantly "walking over" one another as it was. Furthermore, why supply the enemy with additional "incoming" intelligence? The Sky Spot radar would instantly inform the controller if the cell leader hadn't turned to a new heading.

MSQ could only "see," and therefore guide, the cell leader; the controllers operated under the assumption the other two bombers would be carefully shadowing One. Blue leader alone would release on that very carefully used countdown-ending word—HACK! When it came (and bombardiers had to hear THAT EXACT WORD before they were allowed to drop), the lead bombardier mashed his thumb on the release button, while each of the trailing navigators started a stopwatch and counted down the timing delay seconds to their own bombardiers.

"Nav," the Blue Three RN said, "start the bomb run checklist."

"We are a Mis-Que release," the nav sang out. "The cell will drop on their countdown." He flipped a yellow page and called out the next item.

"Bomb release interval control switch?"

"BRIC set on TRAIN."

One of the biggest differences between a conventional "iron bomb" run and a nuclear release was the multiple settings in the bomb release interval control, or BRIC unit. Dropping a single bomb was relatively straightforward; releasing eighty-four from the bomb bay and another twenty-four from two separate wings in EXACTLY THE CORRECT SEQUENCE was a good deal more complicated. It wouldn't do at all, for instance, to let go of internal bomb #54 until #49 located just below it had already departed.

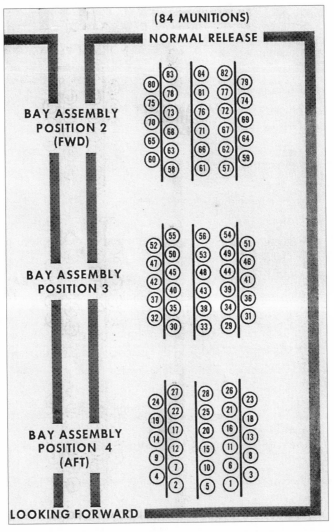

Fig. 20. B-52D bomb bay release sequence, 1 through 84, using 500-pound Mark-82s. *(USAF, ACM Delivery Manual, T.O. 1B-52C-34-2-1, 1969)*

"BRIC counter?"

"Set as briefed."

"BRIC light?"

"On, light dim."

"BRIC Interval."

"Set as briefed, it'll be a nine-point-eight-second string."

In this case, the bombs would systematically fall away from the airplane for nearly ten seconds.

"Master bomb control switch?"

"On, light on."

"Bombing system switch?"

"Manual."

"External arming switch?"

"Armed."

"External release power switch?"

"On."

"Bomb door control valve lights?"

"Off."

One more extremely important bit of business for Those Who Followed was left to verify.

"Radar, this is the nav. Confirm my computation of seventeen point five seconds Time Delay to release after Blue One's drop."

"I concur, seventeen point five seconds Time Delay."

"Roger, and crew, we are standing by bomb doors at Sky Spot's one hundred and twenty-seconds To Go call."

During the exchanges, Sky Spot had continued to give heading changes to Blue leader. A sudden wind shift was threatening to complicate things.

"Blue One, this is Sky Spot. Turn right another five degrees. Coming up on one hundred and twenty seconds TG, now."

"Radar," the Blue Three nav said, "open bomb bay doors."

"Coming open."

A groan could be heard amidships; the airplane shuddered from the airflow disruption.

"Turn right two degrees, track is stabilizing," Sky Spot crackled. If the wind didn't change again, they were probably OK. "Sixty seconds to go."

The ship roared on, the edgy crew dead silent.

"Twenty seconds, maintain heading."

The nav gripped his stopwatch. The radar navigator picked up his D-2 "pickle switch"—a black, push-button actuator about the size and shape of a "C" battery that was attached to a cord connecting it to the release system—and held it in his right hand. Both men cocked their thumbs.

"Blue One, this is Skyspot. Ready, ready . . . five, four, three, two, one, HACK!"

At that instant, Blue One dropped its bombs and the Blue Three navigator punched his stopwatch stem. The seconds ticked by; at around eight elapsed seconds, Blue Two would have released. At about that same moment, the Blue Three nav stepped on his floor mike switch.

"Radar, stand by count. Five, four, three, two, one, HACK!"

The Blue Three bombardier lowered his thumb on the D-2 switch and pickled out the eggs, announcing, "Bombs away!"[5]

The airplane rose buoyantly; in just a few seconds it would completely disgorge 60,000 pounds of dead weight. While the pilots immediately began retrimming the beast, the RN positioned his left hand next to the emergency armed release (EAR) switch while simultaneously watching the amber-colored BRIC lights blink sequentially away. The EAR mechanism was originally intended for use in a crisis, but it had also been found handy for cleaning out any stray iron bombs still left in the bay after a release sequence had cycled complete. The navigator continued to keep his eyes glued to the stopwatch.

"Coming up on EAR time, NOW!"

The RN toggled the EAR switch, precisely nine point eight seconds after he had mashed the pickle switch.

"Pilot, nav. Break right, NOW!"

A standard Combat Breakaway Maneuver after the bomb drop was mandatory on every Arc Light mission, never mind there was no thermonuclear blast to run away from. Nevertheless, official SAC policy called for it, and therefore it had to be done. While the crews often found such bureaucratic dogma inconvenient—sometimes even humorous—this particular example of Omaha's doctrinaire thinking was to have tragically fatal consequences during Operation Linebacker Two.

The Blue Three AC bent the Buf into a fifty-degree angle of bank and held it there until the ship had completed a 180-degree turn. Down in the Black Hole, with the bomber still in the turn, the radar navigator hunkered over the obsolete, but still functioning optical bombsight between his knees and aimed the six-power instrument at the ground impact point. Seconds later, Blue One's exploding bombs walked their way across the field of view, followed on the right by Two, and then on the left by his own payload. All three strings had arrived parallel to one another, forming a nicely balanced Roman Numeral III. The radar navigator twisted in his ejection seat harness to flash an excited thumbs-up to the over-the-shoulder RN cooling his heels in the instructor navigator seat. The veteran smiled indulgingly, then rested his head back against the bulkhead door and reclosed his eyes.

As one might suspect, MSQ/Bugle Note missions didn't always run as smoothly as this one. The author has it on exceptionally good authority the

Fig. 21. An Arc Light bomb damage assessment photo taken by a B-52 vertical camera. Note the Roman numeral III strike pattern. Although bomber #5679 appears "out of the box," the symmetry of the three-ship drop strongly suggests there was no crew error. *(USAF BDA strike photo; author's collection)*

following incident is true:

MSQ controller: "Blue One, stand by for release countdown."

Unexpected long pause. Command radio transmits sounds of a mike keying and rekeying.

MSQ controller: "FivefourthreetwooneHACK!"

Although seriously startled by the abrupt count, Blue One RN obediently pickles out weapons. Halfway through his release cycle, a strange, new MSQ voice comes on the air:

"Negative, negative Blue One! Disregard that last! Coming up on your bomb release . . . ready, ready, HACK!"

Dumbfounded Blue One bombardier desperately scours BRIC panel for his "Anti-Grav Bomb Retrieval Switch." A few seconds later, the original controller comes back on the air, yelling hysterically:

"NO! NO! USE THE FIRST ONE!"

Later on the way home, when the rookie Blue Three bombardier was filling out his BDA form, he would record six secondary explosions coming as a result of the cell's strike. Blue Two, during an independently held debrief, would claim four solid hits. The most experienced of the three men, the Blue One RN, informed Intelligence there were two medium-sized flashy-red secondaries spuming black smoke (probably petroleum dumps) and two late-arriving "flyers" (released bombs that either broke a fin or otherwise got goofed up on the way down and didn't fly ballistically). Which of these reports finally got bubbled up to the top brass the author cannot say, but his impression at the time was that the most optimistic of a cell's BDA analyses usually received the warmest welcome.

While Blue Three's crew conducted their postrelease checks, its aircraft commander re-formed on the other two ships. Blue leader steadied the cell up on a heading of east and out over the South China Sea. The trip back to Guam would be anticlimactic in the extreme.[6] On the way over, the adrenaline had flowed pretty freely and time passed quickly, but the deadhead home was going to be excruciatingly long and boring. Within an hour, a deep fatigue had set in and everybody fought to stay awake. Trips to the pee can and coffeepot started up on a regular basis. Box lunches were opened and picked at; the Blue Three guys would discover the fried chicken held up the best. Some of the fellows tried to nap a little, in between filling out the endless paperwork every SAC crewman contended with on every sortie, war or peace.

Some early white-scarf wag defined flying as: "Hours and hours of sheer boredom—punctuated by moments of stark terror." There was a great deal of truth to the axiom, though thankfully those "moments" were rare when an airplane was just cruising along. Still, things did go wrong even in routine situations, especially with older, complicated war machines like the B-52D. Also, there were always the gremlins to contend with, ever alert to such choice opportunities as long, sleepy deadhead legs—all the better if it was at night and over the ocean. Rookie Arc Light crews were particularly vulnerable.

"Uh, pilot, this is the copilot."

"Yeah?" The Blue Three AC had been dozing in his seat and was groggy.

"EGT has pegged on number five." The exhaust gas temperature on that engine was indicating an unacceptably high 580 degrees Fahrenheit.

"Bad gauge?" Rule number one: First blame the messenger.

The co shook his head. "Don't think so." He paused for another instrument scan on all things related to engine number five. "Oil pressure is dropping fast too. No other warning lights or malfunctions that I can see."

"Think we should keep it burning?" the pilot said, in the midst of a mighty yawn. Despite the seriousness of the indications, he was beat and couldn't shake himself fully alert.

The copilot shrugged his shoulders, either not sure how to answer or not willing to take a stand. But that was fine; he had already done his job bringing the problem to the immediate attention of the aircraft commander, who got paid to do the heavy lifting. And it wasn't a "stark terror" moment, at least not yet, though it certainly had the potential to become one. Continuing to run an improperly operating jet engine was no trifling matter—lots of things could happen and almost none of them pleasant. The Buf was rated to fly safely on as few as six engines (and could stay in the air with only four in certain circumstances), especially if it was at altitude and running light, but the loss of an engine would almost certainly disrupt routines and cause them to slow down. Fortunately, cell integrity and timing issues were no longer of concern; the only important objective remaining was to get the crew and airplane safely back to Andersen. In the end, the AC correctly decided there was no percentage in adding unnecessary risk.

"Shut it down and advise Blue One."

Great, thought the Black Holers, let's pile on the agony to this already rear-end numbing marathon. The two were far enough removed from the problem to seriously resent the pilots for taking the action, though they probably wouldn't have been quite so disdainful if at that moment they'd known Act Two was very shortly to follow.

"Uhh, pilot, this is the copilot."

"Yeah, yeah," the AC said irritably, as he stared at the number six engine EGT gauge, "I see it."

Five and six were clustered together next to the fuselage on the right wing. Five was already out for the count, cold as a cucumber. Now number six had contracted the same disease.

"Something funny is going on in that nacelle," the copilot remarked needlessly.

The pilot sighed deeply and slashed his right forefinger across his throat. The copilot did the dirty deed and notified the leader. The RN volunteered that Blue One and Two appeared to already be pulling away.

"That spread is going to get bigger," the pilot grumbled back. "As a precaution, I'm going to continue to hold normal power settings on the remaining six. Better sharpen up your navigation the rest of the way home."

The Buf's crew lapsed into that certain wary discontent common to a flight when it starts to turn sour. Meanwhile, their crippled Stratofortress lumbered on, still grinding out the miles; nearly a thousand more would have to pass before it could settle back into its nest. After the nav and EWO took a celestial observation, the ship again fell silent, save as always for the whistling/screeching engine and slipstream noises. In an attempt to get comfortable enough to doze, the nav unbuckled his seat belt and slithered down low in his ejection seat, stretching his legs full out in an attempt to rest both boot heels on the stabilizer unit behind his desk and below the forward instrument panel. A few minutes later, however, he was sitting bolt upright and shivering, arms folded across his chest.

"Hey, copilot," the young man whined over the intercom, "it's colder than a hag's breast down here. How about some heat?" The upstairs right-seater controlled the ship's crude and extremely temperamental cockpit heating system.

"You know once I try cranking it up," the co said wearily, "you'll bitch it's too hot."

The navigator sighed. They'd had this exchange so many times, it had become a cliché. The Black Holer remembered in the nick of time to move his head slightly to the left just before a filthy stream of engine-heated hot air came blasting out of the overhead duct. Almost instantly, sweat poured from his face, while his feet, far away from the heat and nearer the cold underbelly of the airplane, continued to freeze. Groaning in resignation, he took up what would become his standard Arc Light back-haul configuration—wrapped in an Arctic survival suit below the belt, stripped to a T-shirt from the waist up.

Some time later, the Buf hit a patch of turbulence, bouncing the radar navigator's head hard off the optical bombsight, where he had been resting it. After a full cycle of juicy curses frustratingly masked by the constant cockpit racket and a half-hearted attempt at massaging out the fresh red spot on his forehead, he glanced at his watch. It was still a good thirty minutes before the penetration let-down into Andersen.

Restless, the radar navigator decided to stretch his legs before the descent. After asking the AC's permission to leave the bombardier station and safing his ejection seat, the RN unharnessed himself and crawled out. While flexing his arms behind the navigator's position, the only place a man could stand up straight in a B-52D, he also threw in a few deep knee bends to help restore feeling below the waist. Suddenly curious about life outside the lower com-partment, the RN stepped over to the upper-deck ladder and climbed up high enough to peek out the small starboard-side window ("mid-body day/night indicator"). It was the first time he'd glimpsed the outside world since strap-ping the thing to his butt nearly twelve hours earlier.

Buf Black Holers had few chances to lollygag and so it was always a treat whenever a fast look-see could be squeezed in. SAC was grimly determined no one should have any fun while riding in their noble bomber, and that went double for the no-window guys trapped downstairs. At least out here on Arc Light, Blue Three's RN reasoned (hoped), Big Brother might not be quite as rigid or ubiquitous.

The RN raised himself up another step for a better view. Darkness fell heavily and quickly in the tropics, and the horizon line separating the sea from the sky had become almost imperceptible. Looking out into the black, he found it difficult to maintain his internal "gyroscopic" bearings; one could no longer tell where the firmament ended and the ether began. Because of his lofty perch, he was able to look down "over the horizon" and see stars,[7] adding further to the illusion he had somehow "slipped the surly bonds of earth," as John Gillespie Magee, the World War II Spitfire pilot and poet, had put it. Above the ship, the saucer-shaped star-cloud called the Milky Way dominated the heavens, its brilliance stunningly undiminished for those fortunate few who could observe it from beyond the planet's troposphere.[8] Jupiter glistened above the gently flapping right wing, while the moon shone earnestly off to one side. Sirius, the brightest of all the stars, held forth with its usual luminos-ity, despite having yielded its distinct singularity to a thousand other pricks of light. Far below the airplane, underneath the benign-looking, yet still dead, inboard engine pod, he could just make out a few moon-reflecting clouds topping the dark blanket of the Pacific Ocean, like dollops of whipped cream on pudding. With up and down and earth and space nearly indistinguishable, it was easy for the radar navigator to take the next step and imagine himself a lonely voyager afloat in the cosmos, perhaps on a journey to yonder moon, as other men not terribly unlike him were actually doing a half a world away. He pressed his nose against the cold window and let his mind swirl with images of all that had brought him to where he was at that moment.

Blue Three trembled. The aircraft commander had disengaged the autopilot and was beginning the penetration into Andersen Field. The RN tore himself away from the window, scurried down the ladder, and strapped himself into his ejection seat. Within moments, the engine noise had fallen off markedly and the altimeter began to steadily unwind. The two navigators carefully monitored the descent with regular altitude calls (as they were required to do) until the airplane reached breathable air at 10,000 feet, where it leveled off.

"Nav, this is the pilot. Cabin is depressurized, and you are cleared for the bomb bay check."

It is probably safe to say the most unpleasant of all Arc Light prelanding duties was the "bomb bay check," a task that fell to the Black Hole and by further extension, the navigator, its most junior occupant. SAC mandated that before a poststrike bomber was allowed to land, a visual inspection of the bomb bay was required to ensure there were no "hangers," still-shackled bombs that failed to release; or the even more dangerous "resters," released blivets either wedged atop another hanger or lying naked on the bomb bay doors. Resters were, of course, no longer "safed" by their anchored arming wires, and it therefore had also to be assumed their now free-turning vanes would have spun the required three hundred revolutions necessary to fully arm them. The real kicker here was that, no matter if one of those little nitroglycerine-filled puppies was back there or not, the bomber *still* had to land. What set a hanger or (especially) a rester landing apart from routine arrivals was 1) the extremely careful manner in which the pilot attempted to set the beast down, 2) the firetrucks and rescue wagons standing by in case of pyrotechnics, and 3) the size of the subsequent underwear and flight suit laundry bills.

The navigator crawled out of his ejection seat and quickly readied himself. He couldn't wear his parachute; there simply wasn't enough room for both it and him to squeeze through the narrow passageways leading to the bomb bay. He donned his gray headset (for noise suppression) and slipped on a pair of leather gloves, then withdrew his trusty Sanyo flashlight from its shoulder pocket. After clumsily edging past the over-the-shoulder RN at the IN/honey bucket station, the young man switched on the Sanyo and twisted the pressure bulkhead door handle open. There was a sudden, screechy-woosh caused by the slight pressure differential between the crew cabin and the atmosphere at 10,000 feet, and he involuntarily jumped back. After a couple of deep breaths and a few seconds to become accustomed to the even louder racket, the navigator leaned forward and giant stepped through the opening.

He was now on the alternator deck, the fuselage compartment that housed the ship's electric current producers. His feet were perched precariously atop a catwalk made of weight-saving perforated metal no more than six inches wide; a very narrow walkway that was also perpetually greasy from leaky machinery oils. It was quite difficult to stay balanced on the tiny ledge, particularly once a man started forward in the standard bomb bay check "duck-waddle." The shuffling gait was made necessary because the crawlway and its immediate surrounds were both too small and too hot to move across either by walking upright or on hands and knees.

Getting through the alternator deck was a real challenge, especially with regard to the enormous physical effort the duck-walk mode of locomotion required. One can imagine performing this circus trick while the ship relentlessly bored on, a fellow bouncing around like a cork on the ocean and desperately trying not to topple off the tiny crawlway. The nav had to further endure the unavoidable burns and cuts from the surrounding hot, sharp-edged machinery encountered en route, as well as not allow himself to overreact to those injuries and lose his balance. Meanwhile, and despite the headset, the noise level remained so incredibly loud it was painful. Inevitably in such circumstances, one's thoughts were filled with images of his own extreme vulnerability should anything go suddenly wrong with the airplane.

After traversing the alternator deck (about ten feet), the nav arrived at a second bulkhead door. After some difficulty in opening it (he'd never done it before), the rookie passed into the forward wheel well, a compartment even scarier and noisier than the alternator deck. The great fear on this leg was not just slipping off the catwalk, but falling into the dark abyss below, a place no navigator had any confidence he could ever escape from—aside of course from the pilot lowering the landing gear and dumping him. Blotting out even the suggestion of that scenario, and after scrunching along for an additional sixteen to eighteen feet, the nav at last arrived at another bulkhead door, the one that opened into the bomb bay.

With heart pounding and his hands and shoulders aching from the several injuries he had sustained (he would soon learn how to avoid the worst hazards), the young man swung the door open and flashed his light around the cavernous, empty bay. Following a quick look—too quick, he later admitted to himself; in the future he would spend a few more seconds vetting it properly—he slammed the hatch closed and hurried back as fast as he could to what now seemed like the quiet, comfortable, and spacious accommodations of the Black Hole. The over-the-shoulder radar navigator graciously closed the cabin bulkhead door behind him, while the nav flashed a thumbs-up to his RN, who radioed the good news to the pilot.

On a first mission, it sometimes happened the seasoned over-the-shoulder guy and the hard-breathing rookie would at this moment lock eyes, with the former offering a knowing nod and a tight smile.[9] It was a small but important gesture, acknowledging the young navigator's initial bomb bay ordeal and, even more important, granting him membership into the ranks of a tiny fraternity that was completely unknown outside the American Air Force—experienced B-52D Iron Bomb Artillerymen. "Yesterday, I didn't know what it was," went an old military saying, "and now I are one."

The pilots began their landing checks as soon as the nav was strapped back into his ejection seat:

"Altimeter setting?" the copilot queried.

"Local Andersen barometric pressure set," the AC responded.

"Fuel panel?"

"Checked. Crossfeed valve switches 9 and 12 positioned opened."

"Best flare speed computed and checked?" This exchange occurred between the copilot and the nav. "And nav," the co continued, "entering arguments are Flaps 100 percent Down, Air Brakes No. 4, and a landing gross weight of 245,000 pounds."

"Roger, copilot," the nav came right back, reading from a table in his yellow checklist, "that computes to 129 knots, best flare landing speed."

"Roger, copy best flare 129 knots."

At this point the aircraft commander interrupted the usual routine by firmly reminding the crew they were landing with two dead engines on the right side and that the emergency procedure, Landing with One or More Engines Inoperative, was in effect. The entire crew was to review their emergency Dash-One directives for this approach and landing and take all appropriate action. He informed the copilot they would follow the normal landing procedure except for the different rudder trim adjustments necessary to compensate for the reduced and unequal (asymmetrical) engine thrust. Finally, he confirmed, the desired best flare speed would remain at 129 knots.

"Standby pump switches?" The copilot was again addressing the pilot.

"All on."

"Autopilot?"

"Disengaged."

"Throttles?"

"Set."

"Airbrakes?"

"Set, No. 4."

The two pilots maintained their usual, and constant, instrument panel scans throughout the approach, giving special attention to the critical engine gauges of the six remaining J-57s.

"Crew," the pilot said, "cross-check zero delay parachute lanyards hooked."

Moments later, Blue Three turned final and was cleared to land.

"Crosswind Crab?" the copilot queried.

"Set, knob down." The landing gear angle selected would compensate for a ten knot crosswind from the left.

Blue Three would be alighting on Andersen's Runway Zero Six Right, the same strip of concrete it had departed from a half day earlier.

"Landing gear lever?"

"Gear down, six down, in the green."

"Wing flaps?"

"100 percent, lever down."

The pilot had to maintain a firm grip on the yoke as the increasingly sluggish beast neared the runway—applying just the right amount of pressure to the left rudder pedal all the way in to correct for the asymmetrical thrust. He properly touched the rear gear first, almost exactly on centerline. The ship hit the pavement firmly—the AC had decided to carry a little plus speed on final ("a couple of extra knots for the wife"), that being by far the lesser of two evils between a slightly hard/long landing or a fatal approach stall. Airbrakes Six were applied, the drag chute deployed, and the Buf began its customary "driving over a corduroy road" landing roll.

"Good chute!" the tail gunner called out, as the forty-eight-foot-wide white nylon bag blossomed. The drag chute served to both slow the bomber down and save wear and tear on the brakes, though the thing would still need three-fourths of the runway before it could safely swing off the active.

"Charlie" in his tower (a different colonel than the one who had presided over their takeoff) advised Blue Three of the taxi route to their parking revetment, adding an "attaboy" for handling the two-engine-out emergency so capably. After deplaning, the very fatigued crew was met by a blue bus and transported to the Arc Light Center building, where they faced yet another couple of hours of maintenance and bomb damage assessment debriefings. Just after they entered the building, as had been the custom since early in the European war with just-landed B-17 and B-24 crews, they were greeted by the chaplain with an offer of a shot of rye whiskey. This official "medicine" was dubbed Old Methuselah by the crews, no matter what the bottle label might actually have read. First-time crews invariably took the chaplain up on his offer, and almost as invariably never did it again—the whiskey was just awful (probably on purpose).

For Blue Three's six newly popped cherries, their postflight thoughts were a

Fig. 22. Postmission beer and hot dogs at Andersen's "Gilligan's Island." *(306th Bomb Wing photo album; author's collection)*

mixed bag. Although the Parrot's Beak milk run had wound up being no more dangerous than an occasional nuclear practice sortie back in the States, they had nevertheless for the first time in their lives dropped live weapons in anger and killed other human beings. That was a sobering realization, but yet—the whole Arc Light package hadn't quite turned out to be what they'd expected. Was this really war? At the moment, all they could say for certain was that they were in it up to their eyeballs, whatever it turned out to be. To a man, they sensed their young navigator caught the essence of what the future held with a comment he made while the crew inhaled postdebrief hot dogs and beer under the palm trees at "Gilligan's Island."

"Well, that was fun, boss," the young man had said sarcastically to his aircraft commander. "When can we do it again?"

The answer came a couple of brews later. Bus time for mission two was forty-four hours away.

CHAPTER TWELVE

The Southeast Asian War Games

rc Light flew its first B-52 combat mission on June 18, 1965, its last on August 15, 1973—more than eight years, 125,000 sorties, and 10 million bombs later. Although the Stratofortresses had been engaged in what was universally billed as the "Vietnam War," it was, in fact, a region-wide conflict. This often overlooked but important aspect of the fighting can be quickly grasped by noting the geographic location of the B-52s' targets: 55 percent were in South Vietnam, 27 percent in Laos, 12 percent in Cambodia, and 6 percent in North Vietnam.

In 1966, Arc Light's first full year of operations during the Southeast Asian war, Andersen mustered 5,000 missions, triple the number from the previous year. The sortie rate doubled to 10,000 annually beginning in April 1967, when U-Tapao Royal Thai Naval Air Base, located on the Gulf of Siam eighty miles south of Bangkok, was opened up to the B-52s. U-T dramatically increased SAC's ability to prosecute the growing list of targets coming out of Saigon's MACV. Then, in February 1968, following the Pueblo Crisis in the waters off Korea,[1] Kadena AFB in Okinawa was incorporated into the operation, becoming the third and final Southeast Asian Stratofortress base.

From the beginning, the Arc Light flying routine had revolved around a standard format of several regularly scheduled daily launches. As discussed earlier, and except for special ops or large gaggle raids, these missions were made up of two three-ship cells launched ten minutes apart, for a total of six aircraft in the wave. It had been found early on that this was the optimum number of Stratoforts for a ground support strike. Any more and bombs, crews, time, and money were wasted; any less and the target didn't receive the necessary attention. A typical day at, say Andersen, saw four launches spaced about six hours apart. Each bore its own formal, and informal, mis-

Fig. 23. Circa 1968–69. What has become an iconic Vietnam War photo—Arc Light's B-52D 55-0100, "Old 100." *(U.S. Naval Institiute Archive)*

sion-window imprint. For example, the two cells scheduled for the noon take-off (generating a bus time of around 7 am) were officially designated Red and Blue, but to those six Buf aircrews, they had "drawn the Breakfast Club." Conversely, the Black/Brown troops with bus times of oh-dark-thirty were "on the Graveyard Shift."

Arc Light waves were identified by their cell call signs, which were always based on a color—examples of the combinations used would include Red/Blue, Purple/Grape, Copper/Gold, Ivory/Walnut, Black/Brown, and so on. These labels were permanent, becoming so fixed in the crew's minds that the men had only to hear the cell color to know when the airplane had launched and if it had come from The Rock, Kadena, or U-T.

The missions from Andersen were the most fatiguing; they always involved an air refueling and typically ran twelve to thirteen hours round trip. Kadena missions did not require a tanker and were "only" eight to nine hours—maybe not so much shorter sounding to the layperson, but to an aircrewman flying the Buf day-in and day-out, it made all the difference in the world. U-Tapao sorties averaged four to five hours—even better yet, but they carried a serious drawback. Crews were scheduled to fly *every day* at U-T. During a six-month TDY tour, the men could expect to be cycled through all three bases, probably three or four times. Everyone literally lived out of their B-4 and duffel bags.

The Rock was hands down the least desirable in the rotation. The missions were miserably long and Andersen had little to offer the airmen during their off hours. Crew officers slept in a common room, barracks style, which afforded no privacy whatsoever. TDY personnel, as opposed to PCS folks, were second-class citizens on every Air Force base, and this was doubly true at housing-challenged Andersen. Meals were usually taken at either an open cafeteria known as the "Rice Palace" or at the Officers' Club. The gunners, as enlisted men, were toted off in a bus after the postflight beer and hot dog BS session at Gilligan's Island to separate NCO (noncommissioned officer) quarters, where several of them roomed and messed together.

Preferences for Kadena over U-T, or vice versa, depended on the individual tastes of each man. Although the missions were longer from Kadena, the climate was more comfortable, the food and quarters better (two men to a room), and there was a lot of shopping and sightseeing to be had all over Okinawa. U-Tapao was a forward operating station, with the crews housed in temporary trailers (four men in two pairs, sharing a common bathroom in the middle of the trailer). By far the most relaxed militarily of all the bases (and the most un-SAC-like), just about anything went at the Thai base, as long as a man didn't hurt himself or anybody else and showed up sober for each of his daily missions. The bachelors, both the official and unofficial, liked U-T the best of the three, for all the usual reasons.

The combination of the three Arc Light bases allowed the B-52 iron-bomb sortie rate to peak in 1968 and 1969, with each of those years contributing about 20,000 missions. Not coincidentally, this was also the time when the greatest number of men on both sides were shooting at each other. By 1970, however, the intensity of the conflict had fallen off dramatically, caused mostly by increasing American domestic unrest and waning political support. Accordingly, the B-52 sortie rate also began declining, not rising again until the Linebacker campaigns in 1972.

By September 1970 Army and Marine tacair (tactical air) strike requests had dropped so significantly it was determined that both the Andersen and Kadena Arc Light operations could be shut down.[2] The entire program was consolidated at U-Tapao, which, in any event, had always been a much more efficient facility than the other two. The Thai base offered huge advantages: U-T was just two and a half hours flying time from every potential Southeast Asian target; the overall theater bomber force could be cut back without affecting its productivity; Kadena's political problems were greatly eased; and Andersen's onerous air-refueling requirement was eliminated altogether. And so it came to pass—a relatively compact force of forty-five to fifty U-Tapao-based B-52Ds were effectively able to handle all of MACV's 1971 air support requests. Arc Light's operations continued to be conducted solely out of Thailand until early 1972, when North Vietnam launched another massive invasion of South Vietnam and Andersen had to be reopened.

In the early years of 1965 and 1966, the B-52s were used mostly against enemy targets in South Vietnam, particularly in the Mekong Delta and in the areas adjacent to Saigon, where the big bombers conducted daily raids on Viet Cong base camps, supply caches, and troop concentrations. Arc Light's chief role, then and later, was to provide allied ground forces with immediate and very heavy artillery on demand—anywhere, anytime. As previously mentioned, the B-52 not only carried the largest payload of any warplane, but it also was the primary U.S. bombing platform equipped with full all-weather, day or night strike capability.[3]

It was in October of 1965 that the Bufs found themselves engaged in a large battle for the first time, providing direct support to the First Cavalry Division (Airmobile) at Ia Drang, an action that also featured the earliest large-scale use of the helicopter (the beginning of the "Huey" legend). In December of that year, Arc Light was able to lend a hand to the 3rd Marine Division's Operation Harvest Moon in the Que Son Valley. Both of those actions occurred at a time when the B-52 and the phrase "saturation bombing" were becoming inextricably linked. These were wide-area, blunt-instrument attacks; it was hoped that by dropping large, almost indiscriminate quantities of "aerial artillery," the terrorized Viet Cong would be driven back into their jungle hideaways, perhaps even cowered into permanent submission.

Unfortunately, the VC had no intention of giving up so easily. Furthermore, their North Vietnamese associates were becoming increasingly determined they should have continued access to enough war-making materiel to fight on indefinitely. That, of course, prompted the Bufs to shift much of their focus to the ever-growing enemy infiltration routes running north/south along the soon-to-become-infamous Ho Chi Minh Trail. The Trail originated in the western mountain ranges of North Vietnam just south of Vinh; worked its way down and along the borders separating Laos, Cambodia, and the Vietnams; and ended up at the notorious "Parrot's Beak" just above Saigon. It remained the backbone of the enemy's logistical framework throughout the entire Southeast Asian war.

The year 1967 arrived to rising Viet Cong activity across the board. Arc Light began mounting more and more daily sorties, especially into one particular hot spot called the "Iron Triangle." Located in the general vicinity of the Parrot's Beak, the fighting there became so intense that it finally evolved into a formal campaign called Operation Cedar Falls. As with all its assignments, the Buf's job in the Iron Triangle was to pound the hell out of *anything* the enemy could use to make war—troops, ammo stores, fuel dumps, communications equipment, trucks, cars, old recappable tires, you name it.

At the same time, air strikes along the Trail were continuing without letup. The Mu Gia Pass on the Laos/North Vietnam border, a funnel point that left enemy troops exposed to attack, became a favorite radar return to lay the old Q-48 BNS crosshairs on. By the end of 1967, Arc Light trips to the north around Mu Gia, Ban Karai Pass, Ban Laboy Ford, and selected other scenic mountain locations were becoming as routine as the air refuelings above the Philippines.

In January 1968 something not so routine occurred, an event that would mark a pivotal moment in the war—the Tet Offensive. The Viet Cong and North Vietnamese army had decided the time was ripe for a huge, surprise attack against all the major cities of South Vietnam, from Saigon in the south to the ancient capital of Hue in the north. Hanoi's primary Tet objectives were to 1) encourage a popular uprising in South Vietnam, 2) press for the collapse of the South Vietnamese army, and 3) dramatically increase war policy dissent back in America.

The first two goals failed; North Vietnam instead got a sound military thrashing. Although the three months of hard, bitter fighting cost the allied armies 5,000 dead and 16,000 wounded,[4] enemy forces were forced to withdraw from South Vietnam empty-handed while leaving behind 45,000 of their own men killed or captured. Unfortunately, even such large tactical victories did not equate to winning in this the strangest of all American wars to that date. The combination of the long Tet casualty lists, sometimes uninformed (often misleading) newspaper reports, and color television footage of the bloody carnage left American civilians with the distinct impression the battle had been *lost*. And that was the final straw in permanently altering the entire dynamic of the larger conflict. In a cruel twist, what North Vietnam was unable to win on the battlefield it was about to achieve (above objective 3) through a seismic shift in the political landscape.

On March 31, 1968, in response to the intense domestic and international hue and cry that followed Tet, President Lyndon Johnson hurled two thunderbolts. First, he extended an olive branch to North Vietnam ("Let us reason together") by ordering a bombing halt above the 20th Parallel (removing Tactical Air Command's juiciest targets in and around Hanoi, Haiphong Harbor, and the Red River valley), then announced that he had himself become a casualty: "I shall not seek, and I will not accept, the nomination of my party for another term as your president."

U.S. air combat tactics and objectives throughout all of Southeast Asia changed dramatically and overnight. Rather than continuing to take the fight directly into the North Vietnamese heartland, the United States had decided to pull its punches. Fearful of hostile press reports and international outrage over purported "massive civilian casualties" and "incinerated hospitals and orphanages," gravely concerned about provoking Red China or the Soviet Union by bombing their supply ships anchored in Haiphong Harbor, rattled over the steady erosion of domestic support (highly influential newscaster Walter Cronkite had just declared the war "unwinnable"), the Johnson administration came to the conclusion the Vietnam War could no longer be conducted in a conventional manner, nor was it possible to decide it solely through feat of arms.

Instead, the conflict had now to be reconciled through the new policies of aggressive diplomacy (Paris Peace Talks) and "pacification," the winning over of the "hearts and minds of the Vietnamese people." According to Washington's new way of thinking, by aggressively pursuing grassroots support in South Vietnam and at the same time keeping up steady military and political pressure on the North Vietnamese leaders, the tide could be favorably turned. Eventually, Uncle Ho (Ho Chi Minh) and his minions would come to see the folly in continuing a war against the great American superpower and sue for peace.

From the perspective of all the hard-pressed Americans in uniform slated to foot the bill for such convoluted reasoning, the sums added up much differently. What they saw on the bottom line was this: Rather than use one bomb to blow up a single boat filled with hundreds of tons of weapons in Haiphong Harbor, the U.S. government had now concluded it was better to use a hundred bombers to chase one truck down the Ho Chi Minh Trail. And that simply meant the war would continue to drag on . . . and on.

In any event, as far as those G.I.s and gyrenes stuck on the front lines when

LEAFLET TRANSLATION

LEAFLET THEME: B-52   LEAFLET NUMBER: 146-66-R

LANGUAGE: VIETNAMESE   SIZE: 6x3 (B&W)   PAPER WT: 20 lb

DISSEMINATION: VO-2.5; RT/TO-1.11

FRONT:

(Picture of B-52)

BACK:

THIS IS THE MIGHTY B-52

Now you have experienced the terrible rain of death and destruction its bombs have caused.

These planes come swiftly, strongly speaking as the voice of the government of Vietnam proclaiming its determination to eliminate the VC threat to peace.

Your area will be struck again and again, but you will not know when or where. The planes fly too high to be heard or seen. They will rain death upon you again without warning.

Leave this place to save your lives. Use this leaflet or the GVN National Safe Conduct Pass and rally to the nearest government outpost. The Republic of Vietnam soldiers and the people will happily welcome you.

(Picture of Safe Conduct Pass)

#146-66-R

ĐÂY PHÓNG PHÁO CƠ KHỔNG LỒ B.52

Các bạn đã trải qua những trận mưa bom khủng-khiếp gieo chết-chóc và tàn-phá. Vùng các bạn ở còn bị oanh-tạc nữa, nhưng các bạn sẽ không bao giờ được biết là vào lúc nào. Các phi-cơ sẽ bay thật cao, không thể nghe thấy và trông thấy được. Nó sẽ còn gieo chết-chóc cho các bạn mà không báo trước. Hãy rời-bỏ ngay khu-vực này để tự-cứu lấy tính-mạng. Hãy xử-dụng truyền đơn này hay Giấy Thông-Hành của Chính-Phủ quốc-gia để đến tiền đồn gần nhất của Chính-Phủ. Đồng-bào và quân-nhân của Chính-Phủ Việt-Nam Cộng-Hòa sẽ hân-hoan đón-tiếp các bạn.

Fig. 24. Bomb loads to South Vietnam, targeted at the indigenous Viet Cong, often carried one or two Mark 129 Leaflet Bombs. *(USAF, Air Weapons "SCAT HANDOUT," 1970)*

Tet hit in January 1968 were concerned, *nobody's* "long-range strategy" would have been worth spit—they were *right now* in a fight for their lives. This was especially the case along the Demilitarized Zone (DMZ), where one of the biggest battles of the entire war was about to get under way. It started with a surprise North Vietnamese army (NVA) attack on a U.S. Marine fire base located just a few miles south of the 17th Parallel. The American fortification had long been a thorn in the side of enemy troops assigned to defend the nearby Ho Chi Minh Trail. The initial clash quickly escalated into a bitterly contested seventy-seven day siege, with the Allies ultimately prevailing. Saigon's MACV assigned various aspects of the fight the usual series of operational code names; SAC's part was called Operation Niagara. To the average American, however, it would always be known as the Battle of Khe Sanh.

Even hardened Arc Light veterans were apprehensive when the word came down about the new type of very close-support bombing sorties (designated "Golf missions" by Eighth Air Force) they would be required to fly assisting the embattled, encircled Marines at Firebase Khe Sanh. Before then B-52 strikes had been conducted no closer than three kilometers from friendlies. At Khe Sanh, however, the high-flying Buf aircrewmen would have to unload their sometimes unpredictable weapons (e.g., flyers, hangers, and door resters) to within one kilometer, a thousand meters, of American boys. Now, to someone on the ground a thousand meters was a goodly distance, nearly two-thirds of a mile. To a Buf navigator, however, a thousand meters was but three or four seconds on his stopwatch. And to a Buf bombardier, a thousand meters was an almost imperceptible video distortion bloom on his radar screen.

It therefore came as a great relief after the first few sweaty-palm days to learn that the B-52 crews and Bugle Note controller teams were up to the task. Bombs were hitting right on target, with the enemy suffering heavy casualties. This helped boost the morale of the beleaguered Khe Sanh Marines and gave them some much-needed operating room for their resupply air drops. But just when the white hats thought they had gotten the black hats' number, the North Vietnamese army came up with a novel way to juke out the American flyers, and the sweat started flowing again.

As mentioned above, on the ground a thousand meters was nearly two-thirds of a mile. That's a bunch of territory to conceal a lot of folks in, especially when the people hiding figure out that one-thousand-meter stretch of ground they're squatting on is not "no-man's-land" at all, but is, in fact, a bomb-free zone. The closer the NVA got to the Marines, the safer they were.

While the Air Force brass and MACV stroked their chins and pondered

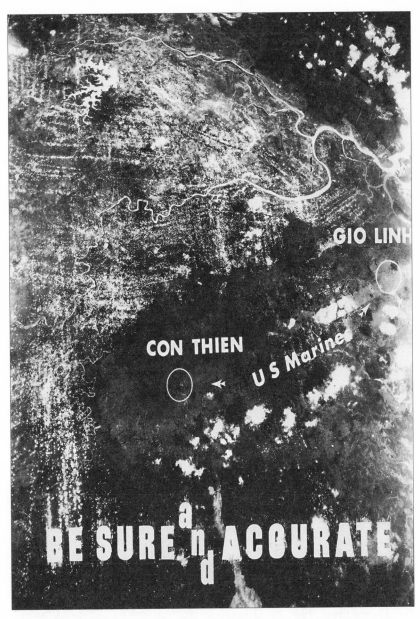

Fig. 25. Khe Sanh and Con Thien were two of the most heavily contested U.S. Marine firebases associated with the Tet Offensive and its aftermath. The B-52 chiefs of bomb nav handed this photo out to all their boys, emphasizing exactly what was at stake with *very* close-support bombing. *(Author's collection)*

the problem, the Leathernecks stuck on top of that bloody hill got busy and fixed it. They waited until the NVA settled in all nice and comfy and then, without bothering SAC, TAC, or the Marine Corps commandant over details, sent a misdirection play to the Bugle Note controllers guiding in the Bufs and fighter/bombers. This is kind of the way it worked out:

Bugle Note controller: "Hey, Marine, you sure those target coordinates you just gave me are no closer than a thousand meters from your position?"

Gyrene-in-charge at Khe Sanh: "No sweat, bring on the fireworks."

Gyrene-in-charge to buddy sitting in foxhole next to him after switching radio off: "Better get a grip on your tin pot. I'm dropping 500 meters off our nose, right on top of that rat's nest of Cong that's been giving us the finger for two days. We'll see if those Air Force pukes know what the hell they're doing."

During the Khe Sanh siege, B-52s flew over 2,500 sorties and dropped 60,000 tons of bombs against the North Vietnamese attackers, with Buf crews reporting over 1,400 secondary explosions. Along with Tactical Air Command and the combined air arms of the U.S. Army, Marine Corps, and U.S. Navy, American air power could claim a valuable assist at the Battle of Khe Sanh. All the same, the primary credit for the victory rested with the men who had to live on and hold that miserable hill for seventy-seven days—the United States Marines.

The fighting in Vietnam continued hot and heavy in the aftermath of Khe Sanh and Tet, though it became more a steady droning rather than repeats of the big, early 1968 clashes. The Viet Cong and North Vietnamese, content with their large propaganda victory, settled back into the static war that had preceded Tet, while the Bufs returned to bombing the Mekong Delta, Parrot's Beak, and Ho Chi Minh Trail. The year 1968 melted into 1969, with nothing truly remarkable occurring in the air combat department until the calendars at the Arc Light Command Posts at Andersen, Kadena, and U-Tapao read February 28, 1969.

The crews had no more than found their seats for that evening's mission briefing when it became clear something very big was going down just northwest of Saigon, around the "Fish Hook" region (the terms Parrot's Beak and Fish Hook were often used interchangeably to describe roughly the same geographic area). The enemy had moved four divisions of infantry plus equipment out of their Cambodian "sanctuary," so the intelligence briefer related, and was crossing the border into Vietnam, apparently heading for An Loc. The crews came alive; this was what everyone had been waiting for, a chance to get the NVA/Viet Cong out in the open. Sixty B-52Ds, carrying bomb loads equivalent to 720 B-17G Flying Fortresses, were launched against the freshly massed enemy formations. In a four-hour period during the night of February 28/March 1, 1969, the Bufs smashed a ten-square-mile target box whose extreme northerly edge was within a stone's throw of the Cambodian border. Outbound crews heading back to Guam in the early morning dark hours could still see the secondary explosions and fires burning behind them after they were well out into the South China Sea. The word the next day was that the enemy had been badly hurt and, even better, their offensive plans had been knocked into a cocked hat.

After that night's success, the Americans' appetite for more of the same was thoroughly whetted. Unbeknownst to all except the highest officials in the U.S. government and Pentagon, the White House had secretly decided there would be no more fooling around with Cambodian neutrality and the idea that the enemy could conduct the war with impunity and in safe haven from the other side of the South Vietnamese border. Operation Menu was clandestinely put into place,[5] which, among other things, authorized the B-52 force to bomb targets inside Cambodia itself.

Late in the day on March 17, 1969, minutes before the crew briefings were to begin, the Arc Light briefing theaters were cleared of everyone except each commanding officer, two or three key staffers, and the basic crews. Everyone else—wing staff, weathermen, intelligence officers, maintenance officers, chaplains, extra crew, slide projector operators, visitors—was ordered out of earshot and the rooms were sealed by guards. Each commander then took the podium and announced that, as on the February 28/March 1 mission, a total of sixty bombers would strike in the Fish Hook area. But this time they would be dropping inside Cambodia, on a very juicy target identified as Base Area 353, the combined NVA/Viet Cong nerve center, more generally known as the enemy's COSVN HQ (Central Office for South Vietnam–Headquarters). Bugle Note would direct the B-52s in, and the radar navigators were to drop on the controller's headings and countdown, no matter where he led the planes; there were to be no questions asked. Navigators were not to chart any position that might show the Stratofortresses on the wrong side of the border. Bombardiers were to ensure their bomb damage assessment (BDA) paperwork indicated the weapons had been dropped on the Vietnamese side.[6] The unspoken implication, of course, was that because Cambodia was technically a neutral nation (though not really in control of itself; the NVA ran the part of Cambodia bordering the Parrot's Beak/Fish Hook), the mission *might be* construed as an illegal act of war. How such a thing could possibly be kept permanently quiet did occur to the Buf crewmen,[7] but they had neither the time nor inclination to dwell on the matter. The only thing on their minds at that moment was, here's a chance to destroy the enemy's forward headquarters with a single blow. The NVA sanctuaries along the Cambodia/Vietnam border had long been ripe for the plucking, but North Vietnam had correctly believed (up to that point) that the Americans would not risk widening the war by dropping bombs inside Cambodia itself. In this, as they would again do in late 1972, they underestimated the resolve of Richard Nixon, the newly inaugurated American president.

And so the Bufs struck hard again. Crews reported tremendous damage to fuel and ammunition dumps (two war materiel items that instantly reveal themselves by way of immediate and powerful secondary explosions), though later reports indicated that while the enemy's COSVN headquarters had been hit, their command and control infrastructure was apparently not seriously compromised. Nonetheless, the physical damage wrought on this second sixty-ship gaggle was tremendous.

More heavy strikes into the same area followed in April, after which the Cambodian air campaign settled into a fairly regular, albeit still very secret, routine. It wasn't until April 1970, a full year later, when American and Army of the Republic of Vietnam (ARVN) ground troops commenced a ground invasion of Cambodia to once and for all clean out the border area, that the Cambodian air strikes were first acknowledged publicly. Ironically, Nixon ordered that highly controversial 1970 surface "incursion" at about the same time he announced he was withdrawing another 150,000 troops. The idea of the Cambodian ground initiative had been to protect the American flank while those troop withdrawals in South Vietnam were under way, but the folks back home weren't buying in. A nationwide protest ensued, culminating in the terrible Kent State, Ohio, incident on May 4th, when National Guard troops killed four and wounded nine students.

Pickett's Charge during the 1863 Battle of Gettysburg is often termed the "high water mark" of the South's cause in the American Civil War. The Cambodian air incursions beginning in March 1969, coupled with the carnage at Hamburger Hill in the A Shau Valley two months later,[8] could perhaps be regarded as the high water mark of the American war in Vietnam. By that summer of 1969, Vietnam had clearly become political poison in America, and Nixon was compelled to announce yet another new war strategy, a policy of "Vietnamization," by which he meant that from now on he wanted only

South Vietnamese boys to do the serious dying. The word quickly went out to U.S. Army and Marine Corps ground commanders; troops withdrawals were to begin at once. While this action did calm the home front to some degree, belligerents on all sides immediately understood the real implications—America intended to play defense for the rest of the war.

Meanwhile, the fighting continued. In early 1970, on the strategically important Plain of Jars in northern Laos, the long-running "secret war" between the communist Pathet Lao (aided by their allies, the NVA) and the American-backed Royal Lao Army (with the fiercely independent Hmong at its core) erupted into large-scale, open warfare. For the first time, the Bufs were allowed to intervene in their fight. This campaign was one of the few times during the Southeast Asian struggle that a pitched battle between conventional forces, including tanks, was conducted. Formations of B-52s struck at night and to great effect, including very many large and colorful secondary explosions, confirming at the very least that great quantities of *somebody's* war materiel was getting blown to bits. It is interesting to note these large 1970 battles on the Plain of Jars, indeed the entire Lao aspect of the war, are poorly documented in the history texts, a probable reflection of the very shadowy nature (think CIA and hired mercenary armies) of this chapter in the so-called "Vietnam" conflict.

Then, in early 1971, in an attempt to retake the initiative from the enemy and validate Nixon's policy of Vietnamizing the war, joint Allied forces attacked the NVA inside Laos in a very big action designated Operation Lam Son 719. The specific objectives were to blunt a possible new NVA attack and put a stranglehold on the Ho Chi Minh Trail supply routes. Hopes ran high early on that the Army of the Republic of Vietnam would be able to successfully conduct the ground operations on its own, aided of course by American air power. In fact, it was only the ARVN that was left to carry out an offensive surface fight; by this time the Americans were down to just 280,000 combatants in-country (with hundreds, if not thousands, more leaving weekly)—from a war-high strength of about 540,000 only a year and half earlier. Not only that, it was strictly understood that those U.S. soldiers who were still left in Vietnam could only be used for defensive purposes. But the American air forces remained available, including the B-52s, and they played a critical role in the Allied offensive. The Bufs would rack up many Lam Son sorties, especially in support of the ARVN's 1st Armored Brigade in its engagements near the Mu Gia Pass.

Unfortunately, it was all for naught; the South Vietnamese conducted the campaign so poorly that the long-term benefits of the operation were negligible. Indeed, had it not been for U.S. air support (especially U.S. Army helicopter forces), the operation might well have resulted in a disaster. Lam Son 719 made it abundantly clear to those in the know that Vietnamization was not going to work—the South Vietnamese military on its own was a mess; its only hope for long-term success completely hinged on the continued availability of massive American air power.

This fundamental weakness was not lost on North Vietnam. Sensing blood in the water, they launched their most powerful attack since Tet four years earlier. Dubbed the Easter Offensive by the Americans, the number one general in the north, Vo Nguyen Giap, bet the farm he could roll up all of South Vietnam with one throw of the dice. He kicked his invasion off on March 30, 1972, when over 120,000 NVA soldiers swarmed across the DMZ in Quang Tri Province and pushed south. This time the NVA pulled out all the stops, using weapons they had seldom if ever used before in South Vietnam, including Soviet T-34, T-54, and PT-76 tanks, the latest guided surface-to-air missiles, and 130-mm artillery pieces. For once, however, they were immediately and effectively confronted by several ARVN ground divisions, which had become emboldened by relentless American air support and bombardment. But the enemy's offensive was powerful, and they kept moving forward. In April the NVA launched heavy attacks against Kontum and An Loc. One more time the war turned white-hot.

In response to the invasion, the Arc Light force was immediately reorganized and reinforced under a program called Bullet Shot, which included reopening Andersen AFB on Guam and sending every available Stateside B-52D back to Asia. Several squadrons of B-52Gs were also dispatched, the first non-D models to be used in the war since 1966. By late spring, 1972, over 200 B-52D and G Stratofortresses were operating out of Andersen and U-Tapao. The overall code name SAC would assign their huge new offensive was Operation Linebacker.[9]

In early February 1972, the largest series of American air raids in over two years began along the South Vietnam/Laos border. On February 13, B-52s set a record for the largest number of theater-wide Buf sorties during one twenty-four-hour period. Then, in early April, fifteen B-52Ds raided the rail yards and oil storage facilities at Vinh, North Vietnam, the farthest north the Buf's had gone up to that date. A few days later, the airfields at Bai Thuong, North Vietnam were struck. On April 15–16, B-52s bombed targets near Hanoi and Haiphong, their first time ever in those neighborhoods. Air combat in North

Vietnam had suddenly reached a level not seen since Johnson's October 1968, bombing halt.

Just below the DMZ, in northern South Vietnam, a heavy American air interdiction campaign was taking a serious toll on the invading enemy troops and their supply lines. What's more, in a surprise to many, the South Vietnamese armed forces were putting up a spirited defense of their homeland. By early summer, the full weight of Allied resistance had become too much and the enemy's offensive withered to a halt. On May 30 the NVA withdrew from Kontum; on July 11 they left An Loc. In June the ARVN had launched a counteroffensive to good effect, recapturing Quang Tri in September. At that point, the North Vietnamese realized they had made a horrific miscalculation, a mistake that was to cost Comrade Giap his general's job. Actually, he got off easy—the Easter Offensive's real price came in human lives. By the time the leadership in Hanoi called the whole thing off, approximately 100,000 North Vietnamese and 40,000 South Vietnamese had been killed or wounded.

In early October 1972, things were looking up for the Americans. Owing mostly to the allies' favorable battlefield results, real progress was finally being made at the Paris Peace Talks. Both sides had agreed to a series of major concessions (excepting the South Vietnamese government, which was balking at every turn, fearing—not without cause—that they were being sold down the river). The National Security Council's Henry Kissinger reported back to Nixon, who was up for reelection in just a few weeks, that it looked like they had a done deal. Operation Linebacker (i.e., the renewed bombing of the North above the 20th Parallel) was terminated on October 22, and Stratofortress crews throughout the theater rejoiced—certain, like so very many other soldiers in so very many other conflicts, that "the war would be over by Christmas."

But the thing wasn't done at all. North Vietnam would suddenly get its second wind and the peace talks were destined to break down yet one more time, setting the stage for the drama's final act, to be finally played out that December.

CHAPTER THIRTEEN

Back to SAC

About a week before each six-month Arc Light TDY sentence was up, at least one member of the aircrew would arise from a night's slumber and loudly chirp that they had left just "six days and a wake-up!" The others would pick up the chant on the following mornings—five and a wake-up, four, three, two, one—until the dawn came on the final day, and a smiling AC said, "Pack your bags, fellas. We're headed home!"

Usually, the jumping-off point for this eagerly anticipated event was from Andersen. Some of the crews would drive squadron bombers back; the rest got the tank ride—the same drill as on the way over but in reverse. Those that were to ferry Bufs were careful they got aboard all their exotic purchases, most earmarked as gifts to sweethearts, wives, and children in tribute for all the hardships the loved ones had endured during the separation. D model "Big Belly" bomb bays and 47 Sections were stuffed hatch doors to airframe with teak bars and mahogany coffee tables from Hong Kong; bolts of silk, brassware, wood-carved figurines, and bundles of colorful temple rubbings (rice paper impressions taken off ancient Buddhist temple wall reliefs—a practice since outlawed) from Thailand; jade, ruby, opal, and blue star sapphire rings and broaches from the jewelers of Bangkok; Noritake table china, Mikimoto pearls, and Minolta 35-mm single lens reflex cameras from Tokyo; the very latest in Japanese "stereophonic sound" equipment from Okinawa, including Sansui receiver/amplifiers, free-standing Pioneer speakers, and Dual record turntables equipped with diamond-tipped Shure needle/cartridges; and, in whatever space remained, duty-free cases of $4-a-quart twelve-year-old Chivas Regal scotch. In keeping with the brotherly spirit of the moment, the plunder also included much of what belonged to squadron mates returning on the more crowded KC-135 tankers.

It was a good eighteen-to-twenty-hour nonstop haul back across the pond, depending on where in the States each crew and Buf called home. Deadheading a B-52 for so long a period was a sure guarantee it would be one very boring and fatiguing voyage. Only the basic crew was aboard, meaning no relief for the pilots or Black Holers in the flying and navigation, which typically included fourteen or fifteen celestial fixes and two aerial refuelings.

As each Buf landed in North America, one or two at a time, the tired but happy crews were greeted by their families and a small official party headed by the wing's rear echelon commander. That was it; no flag waving, no brass bands, no speeches—just a brief encounter with a sympathetic customs official, a cursory greeting from the commander, and then every crewdog promptly swept up his baggage and family and got away from the airplane, the base, and the other five guys as quickly as possible.

A personal aside: The author was a bachelor during his Air Force years, a condition that sometimes gave these homecomings a few extra wrinkles. For example, at the conclusion of his first tour, he and crew landed at Orlando (then just a sleepy southern town) in the early morning dark, an arrival time that winnowed down even further the already-sparse greeting delegation. Caught up in the delirious reunion of his crewmates and their families, our subject sat down on his B-4 bag to take it all in. A few minutes later, to his great surprise, he realized everyone had suddenly disappeared into the night, leaving him completely alone save a host of Florida's summer no-seeums and a couple of guards by the airplane. Another minute passed before it dawned on him he had no transportation to his off-base house. It'd been assumed all six men would be met by someone. A quick check with the guards further revealed the motor pool was buttoned up tight for the night. In short, one slightly bewildered first lieutenant navigator was stranded. Fortunately, one of the guards pointed out a pay telephone on the other side of the hangar. Our man bummed a U.S. dime off the guard and called his roommate, another Buf nav who had arrived home a few days earlier. Bleary-eyed, hungover, and extremely unhappy about being awakened in the middle of the night, the roommate reluctantly agreed to come out to the base and pick the orphan up. The two of them said not one word to each other on the drive home. Welcome back from the war, son.

Over the next several days of noncharged leave, the just-returned bomber crews basked in all the things they'd once taken for granted—a safe and open society; personal freedom of movement; really clean, nonmilitary clothes; showers and baths in fresh-smelling water; the company of "round-eyed women"; supermarkets; and home-cooked meals with plenty of butter, bread, milk, cake, pie, and ice cream.

Meanwhile, the B-52D wing staff members, who were already under tremendous pressure from CINCSAC (Commander in Chief—Strategic Air Command, pronounced "sink-sack") to restore their respective squadrons to nuclear Combat Ready status, were chafing at the bit for the crews to rise up off their butts and get back in the saddle. Each returning wing commander, who, like all their ilk, lived in perpetual fear of SAC HDQS anyway, barely had time to kiss the wife before the worry began over whether he could get his assigned quota of birds back on Alert by Omaha's deadline. For his part, CINCSAC lived in perpetual fear somebody—meaning the Soviets and/or the American Congress (not necessarily in that order)—was going to notice just how much the conventional war in Southeast Asia had compromised SAC's ability to adequately maintain America's nuclear shield.

All too soon the aircrew's short rest was over. Its end brought on a strong dose of world-weariness, that sort of nagging lassitude brought about by emotional stress and not sated by sleep. More than they ever would have imagined, the men resented having to transition back into Curtis LeMay's rigidly ruled Strategic Air Command after the looser flight operations, relaxed official atmosphere, and high adventure they'd just experienced in Asia. As the old saying went: "How you gonna keep 'em down on the farm after they've seen Paree?"

Nonetheless, after working their way through the requisite heavy sighing and bellyaching, the fellows took a deep breath and sucked it up. Closet doors flew open and stored 1505 khaki uniforms were pulled out and dusted off, while the threadbare and washed-out-to-gray "green bag" flight suits they'd been living in the past half year were exchanged for new issues. In quick succession came physical exams, a haircut, a trip to Personnel to make sure the transfer documents and payroll records had caught up, a quick couple of practice nuke sorties to knock the rust off, and an intensive review of the SIOP/Positive Control procedures. After all the squares had been filled, the men were officially recertified and declared available for Combat Ready Alert status.

Pad Alert, which is to say the notion of a bunch of bomber crews sitting around in a bunker next to their nuke-loaded airplanes waiting for the klaxon to sound, had been around since October 1, 1957,[1] when the fast-response ground alert system was first introduced. Within a year of that date, nearly all SAC bases had implemented "Alert," meaning roughly one-third of the crews

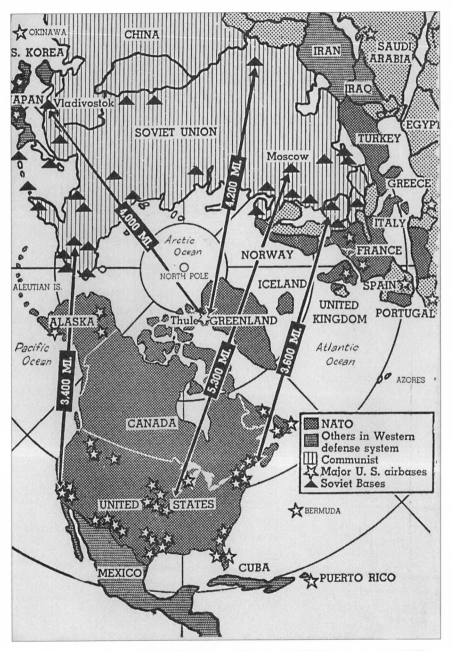

Fig. 26. The Cold War battlefield. *(The Air Force "Blue Book," USAF Yearbook, vol. 1, 1959)*

and airplanes from each station were ready twenty-four hours a day to respond within fifteen minutes to a surprise air or missile attack from the Soviets.[2]

Beginning in 1958, SAC came up with another program to further improve that reaction time—relocate a portion of its alert bombers closer to the Soviets. Accordingly, an operation called Reflex Action was introduced, calling for a certain number of B-47s and B-52s to stand Pad Alert at bases in Europe and North Africa. Several years later, Reflex inspired still another program that offered even greater dispersion and faster reaction time, an airborne alert operation dubbed Chrome Dome. In addition to the already in-place North American and European-based ground alert forces, Chrome Dome provided for a certain number of additional B-52s to continually orbit the polar regions (one route ran above Alaska, the other over Greenland) for up to twenty-four hours at a time.[3] Fully loaded with nukes, these airborne alert bombers were capable of penetrating Soviet airspace within one or two hours after receiving the Go Code.

In the mid-1960s, the Chrome Dome operation was further expanded to include orbiting alert routes over Europe. In this case, however, things did not go as planned. In 1966 a B-52 loaded with four Mark-28 nuclear weapons collided with a KC-135 tanker over Palomares, Spain, and crashed. All the weapons were finally recovered (the bombs were safed and did not detonate) but the incident resulted in a worldwide brouhaha. In 1968 another nuke-loaded B-52 crashed near Thule, Greenland. Again, the weapons were recovered, but that was the straw that broke the camel's back. Shortly thereafter, Chrome Dome and the entire idea of airborne nuclear alert was abandoned.[4]

Although the airborne alert operations garnered a lot of public attention during the 1960s, it was ground alert that took up the bulk of a Stateside SAC crew's time. That chore centered around the "Alert Shack," where the men worked and lived twenty-four hours a day over a fixed period that most often ran for one continuous week, immediately followed by three and a half days of post-alert combat crew rest and recuperation, or "C-Squared, R-Squared." Aircrew duties while standing Pad Alert included target/mission study, review of Positive Control procedures, daily testing on anything and everything, catching up on the latest flight advisories and regulations, occasional briefings by staff and/or distinguished visitors, and those inevitable make-work projects that seemed to appear with some regularity. At the conclusion of the week and following C-Squared came a ten-to-twelve day period filled with the planning and flying of two or three practice sorties. And then, for most of those crews assigned to short-handed D model wings, it was right back on Pad Alert. This schedule stayed in place almost without fail until it was time, once again, to rotate back to Southeast Asia.

The Alert Shack, also referred to as the "Mole Hole," was located near the entrance to the main runway. The nuclear-loaded alert bombers were parked on a very large ramp just beyond its several exit doors, arranged in a staggered/diagonal formation with a wide taxiway running between them that from the air suggested a "Christmas Tree." The entire Mole Hole and Christmas Tree complex was a very high-security area, surrounded by tall fences, concertina (razor) wire, and many heavily armed guards.

The Alert building proper was a no-frills, semisubterranean, two-level, concrete-block structure. There were living accommodations for eight to ten crews, plus additional space for other essential support personnel. The Mole Holes were climate controlled, with central heating and air conditioning. The crew quarters—bedrooms, restrooms, and showers—were on the lower level. The upper level housed the administrative offices, a briefing theater, target study rooms, a small library, a TV/game room/lounge, and a mess hall. The crews dressed in their best green flight suits, kept crisply ironed and appropriately decorated with the approved list of squadron patches, rank, name tag, and badges (as opposed to Southeast Asia, where the men wore only name and rank on their flight suits in case of enemy capture), and either a soft overseas cap or squadron baseball cap. If an important visitor was expected, or if the crew left the Alert Shack for a brief period, or if a man simply wanted to look sharp, he would wear an ascot (a tie-like scarf that could be fastened around the neck). The baseball cap and ascot always bore the semiofficial wing color (e.g., during the Arc Light years the 306th Bomb Wing at McCoy AFB, Orlando, Florida, was identified with the color red).

Alert crews did have limited freedom to move about the base, though they were never allowed farther away than a certain number of minutes from their bomber. They were required to travel together and in an assigned vehicle, usually an Air Force–blue pickup. The truck had a siren and flashing lights, and it was always given the right-of-way and preferential parking. The men enjoyed head-of-the-line privileges at the BX, movie theater, or anywhere else they went. Klaxons were positioned throughout the base to ensure aircrew were always within earshot and that all other base personnel could respond to the alert as they were required.

Passing personal down time was a never-ending challenge in the Mole Hole. Each man had his own way of dealing with it: Huddling around the always-on lounge TV, either watching the sporting event/program or arguing about the channel selection; playing Eight-Ball or Rotation on the nearby pool table (the TV/pool table area was always blue with cigarette smoke, tough to take even in that more tobacco-tolerant era); catching the evening movie in the briefing theater; reading in the cubby-hole library or downstairs in a bedroom (the author's favorite refuge); playing poker or bridge on empty mess tables; or just hanging around the hallways chewing the fat. Most everyone kept some kind of drinking mug in their hand, filled either with coffee (God help the mess hall attendant who let the coffee urn run dry) or "bug juice," a sugared, Kool-Aid-type soft drink whose colors and flavors changed daily. It probably should be stated for the record that under NO CIRCUMSTANCES was alcohol or drugs ever allowed in the Alert Shack, acts that would have been viewed by the men themselves as crimes akin to treason.[5]

Speaking of the mess hall, it was usually well run and the food good. SAC apparently believed in the same theory promulgated by America's submariner force, whereby it was deemed in the best interest of the U.S. Navy to provide sailors with the best possible chow when cooped up for months inside their underwater coffins. And so it was with SAC Alert crews. At the appointed times for breakfast, lunch, and dinner, chef-hatted servers stood poised while the fellows lined up cafeteria-style and picked out their favorite entree, side, and salad choices. Dishes could be ordered to personal preference (eggs "poached," steak "rare") and there was no size limit to the portions (inevitably causing weight problems with some of the older crewmen). Desserts of many choices were always available as well, a few presented with surprising flair. If our next meal was the last, so the men joked, then by God let it be a hearty one!

Just the same, and despite SAC's good-faith efforts to provide the amenities, Alert life was marginal at best. No matter how they sliced things, it was still seven days of closely monitored incarceration in a small and crowded facility. This generated a lot of human friction and many relationship issues; the married men were constantly mitigating domestic disputes and otherwise trying to keep their fragile families in one piece (efforts largely conducted on a single Mole Hole public telephone). Unfortunately, many of those personal problems were never fully resolved.[6]

Everyone shared in the already-mentioned, most persistent and vexing difficulty—spending one's free time. For sure, there was no way a fellow could watch TV, play cards, or shoot pool all evening long. Rather than bounce off the walls or fritter the clock away, many chose to extend daytime "office hours." After-supper activities—some requiring completion during that particular alert cycle, some oriented toward personal career growth, and some simply individual hobbies—might include such things as additional SIOP target study, further review of Positive Control procedures and SAC's "two-man, no-lone" rules,[7] preplanning the flight sortie that always followed C-Squared, professional advancement studies such as Squadron Officers School (SOS) correspondence courses, and model airplane building. Naturally, at any time day or night, the horn could go off, at which point everything was instantly dropped and the men raced for their airplanes.

Although a B-52 aircrewman knew in the back of his mind that whenever the klaxon sounded, there was always a possibility it signaled the real thing, the chances were pretty good (especially in the absence of any kind of international crisis) that it was just a drill. Just the same, the crews never took an alarm for granted nor failed to react each time as if it was indeed an actual SIOP launch. One moment a fellow might be lining up on the Fifteen and the next the cue stick was rolling across the velvet and through those balls still left on the table. The Mole Hole would go into an absolute uproar as scores of green bags flew out the quick-release exit doors located on both levels of the shack, while every khaki uniform and working fatigue in the building braced himself against the side of a wall or otherwise got immediately out of the way.

The boo-wahhhing would still be holding steady when the crews in the farthermost parked bombers arrived at their blue pickups—first guy to the truck took the wheel, the rest jumped into the cargo bed. As other crews streaked by on foot to the closer airplanes, the truck guys did a drag-race sprint the few hundred yards to their birds at the far end of the Christmas Tree. The vehicles were brought to a screeching halt in a designated spot where they would not interfere with taxiing bombers, and the men bolted for their airplanes. Each gunner made a beeline for the tail, while the two pilots, RN, and EWO raced up the entry hatch steps and into the cockpit. The navigator did not enter the airplane; donning ear protectors, he immediately put himself under the direction of the crew chief, and the two of them performed the external preparations for an Alert "cartridge start." (See engine start discussion in chapter 10.) The nav's yellow flight checklist under Ground Crew Scramble described his duties:

Man No. 2—Navigator

1. Remove front and rear engine plugs from engines 4, 3, 2, 1, in that order (crew chief is simultaneously doing same with engines5–8), and place clear of aircraft.

2. Remove left-side AGM-28 pitot cover (if so equipped, referring to

the underwing, nuclear-tipped Hound Dog air-to-ground missile—crew chief is doing same on the right side) and astrotracker cover. Covers and engine plugs placed clear of aircraft.

3. Cut off forward bay heater (used in freezing temperatures) and remove heater and ducting clear of left wing tip.

4. Remove forward ground wire (static electricity discharge). (At just about this point in the scramble, the pilot fired the two starting cartridges, beginning with engine #2. The nav monitored #2, the crew chief engine #8, each man with fire extinguisher in hand. The engines revved up very quickly).

5. Signal Man No.1(crew chief) when all equipment is clear and board the aircraft (the chief then buttoned up the hatch door behind the nav).

With the engines running, the bomber on internal power, and the full complement of crew aboard, prelaunch checklists were quickly completed and all systems gotten up and running. Meanwhile, two of the ship's officers had been carefully monitoring the radios, recording the command post's alert message and beginning the formal authentication process. According to Positive Control doctrine, it had to be at least two men. Because the pilots were very busy bringing the bird to life and the nav was assisting the crew chief, these duties usually fell to the electronic warfare officer and radar navigator.

It is perhaps worth pausing for a moment to speak briefly about Strategic Air Command's "Go Code" procedure, as it was handled during the Vietnam War era. Many Hollywood movies attempted to treat this subject, and none of them ever got it right. First and foremost, the picture people invariably insisted on making it too complicated, with too many gizmos involved. If ever someone wanted to make certain something went terribly wrong, it would've been to hand the "nuclear war on/off button" over to a mixed-bag of Rube Goldbergian toggle switches, tubes, transistors, flashing lights, bells, and whistles. The reality was much more straightforward—SAC's system of Positive Control strictly revolved around hands-on human procedures, and the only electronic device required was a ground-to-aircraft radio.[8]

Backing up just a bit: When a relieving Alert crew replaced those fellows currently on duty, the new men were required to conduct a meticulous procedure called "recocking the aircraft." This involved a complete all-crew aircraft preflight, followed by the navigator-bombardier's careful visual inspection and settings verification of the onboard thermonuclear devices. Once that work was completed, the relieving airmen loaded up personal flying kits and arranged their stations in a manner that anticipated a fast-response Alert departure. The Black Holers, for example, positioned checklists and dead-reckoning tools in their normal airborne locations near the tracking handle and on the nav table—and to expedite a quick strapping-in, they impaled their white helmets, with interphone and oh-two hoses already connected, on the downward ejection seat headrests. The crew also carefully stowed aboard whatever additional gear was required, including duffel bags filled with arctic survival clothing. All this paraphernalia stayed in the plane for the entire seven-day Alert cycle.

There was also one more piece of equipment hoisted through the entry hatch during the crew changeover, a sealed metal container known as the "Secrets Box." The pilot and the radar navigator each had separate locks to this box, and neither man knew the combination to the other. Both locks had to be opened for access to the highly classified strike folders, which contained all the data essential to flying the assigned routes and hitting the designated SIOP targets. (Conversely, without access to the box, the mission would be impossible to complete, probably breaking down very early on after missing the first air refueling rendezvous.) During the Vietnam era, SAC aircrewmen held three different levels of security clearance. Gunners had to be vetted at least through SECRET. The minimum level for electronic warfare officers, copilots, and navigators was TOP SECRET. The aircraft commander and the RN were held to a still higher standard, called TOP SECRET-CRYPTO. And it was just those two, acting in complete unison and only after an authenticated Go Code had been received, who were permitted to open the Secrets Box.

Returning now to our Alert scramble and the two officers copying down the command post's message, we find the transmission beginning with an encoded prefix, which indicated whether this was an exercise or operational launch (always good to know as quickly as possible). The CP then broadcasted a carefully enunciated burst of in-the-clear alpha numerics; that is, a series of spoken numbers and/or phonetic letters that might come out something like this: "One, Three, Five, Zulu, X-Ray, Whiskey, Six, Four, Two, and so forth." The two assigned crewmen carefully copied down and then authenticated these encoded transmissions by comparing the radioed data against the information on their own "break-open" plasticized cards, which aircrew referred to as either the "cookies" or "Go-To-War tickets." After the message had been received, decoded, and properly authenticated, the orders were, of course, immediately executed.[9] Keep in mind that during all this business, the pilots had been getting the aircraft physically fit to fly—experienced Alert crews were ready to taxi within three or four minutes of the first boot hitting the hatch steps.

There were several kinds of Alert messages. For example, the bombers could receive authorization to launch and fly to a point just short of Soviet airspace, a location known as the "H" Hour Control Line (HHCL), but not proceed any farther without an additional message and authentication. Then again, they could get the whole nine yards on the first message—that is all-out nuclear war had begun and you are to launch at once and strike your target as briefed. As might be expected, a number of subtle permutations were available that fell in between the two.

As we know today, of course, the real thing never happened. No actual Go Code was ever transmitted; no nuclear-weaponed Alert bombers were ever ordered to execute the SIOP war plan. This is not to say there weren't an almost infinite number of launch simulations from 1957 to 1991. No military unit believed in "practice makes perfect" more than SAC; whenever the klaxon went off, everyone on the base could expect at the very least some kind of exercise. These drills came in two essential forms:

> Bravo Exercise—Klaxon blows, crews run to airplanes, fire up engines and systems, and when everybody is ready to taxi, the times are noted. Results are reported to CP when each aircraft is subsequently polled. Aircraft are recocked and exercise ends.

> Coco Exercise—Same as Bravo, plus the airplanes initiate a taxi across the "Hold Line" and continue down the active runway (simulating a takeoff). Airplanes then return to the Christmas Tree via parallel taxiway. Bombers are polled and report engine start time, taxi time, and crossing "Hold Line" time. Aircraft reparked and recocked, and exercise ends.

The Strategic Air Command's degree of alertness, like the nation's ICBM arsenal and the Navy's nuclear-armed submarine force, pivoted around the nation's current Defense Readiness Condition, better known in the vernacular as the DEFCON level. There were five DEFCON stages of American armed force readiness, defined below in plain language:

DEFCON 5—Normal peacetime readiness;

DEFCON 4—Still "normal," but increased force alertness, something worrisome is going on;

DEFCON 3—A very serious event has or may happen. This level has only been invoked three times: The 1962 Cuban missile crisis, the 1973 Yom Kippur War, and on Sept 11th, 2001;

DEFCON 2—Deep trouble. Only been invoked one time, during the October 1962 Cuban crisis, the closest the world has come to thermonuclear war;

DEFCON 1—Officially described as "Maximum Force Readiness." It's actually more serious than that—war is now likely, probably even inevitable. This level has never been implemented.

Today, in the first decade of the twenty-first century, U.S. Defense Department's readiness conditions are organized under seven LERTCONS, broken down into the same five DEFCONs plus two additional EMERGCONs, or "Emergency Conditions," the latter pertaining specifically to an imminent or in-progress ICBM missile attack. Also, it is important to understand that these Defense Readiness Conditions apply only to the U.S. military, and are not to be confused with the new Homeland Security Advisory System (also with five levels), which uses the colors green, blue, yellow, orange, and red to indicate the degree of danger to the general public from a possible terrorist attack.

At just about the time all these nuclear war procedures had been thoroughly relearned and the combat crews were readjusted to Stateside/Alert life, the dreaded overseas Arc Light TDY orders would again come down. The wing immediately began scrambling to meet its deployment deadlines, individual aircrewmen plastic-wrapped their Class A Blues and 1505 Khakis and stuck them back in the closet, and Base Supply prepared for yet another major run on flying overalls. Overnight, SAC families turned grim, tempers flared more readily, conversations became increasingly clipped, and hastily scribbled to-do lists littered kitchen counters and coffee tables. Mom quietly steeled herself to take over command of the Home Front; the last twenty-four hours before departure were tearful and very hard on everyone.

CHAPTER FOURTEEN

Won't Somebody Please Turn Out
the Arc Light?

S o the story goes, a Buf copilot was returning to Andersen for his third
or fourth combat tour. After his just-arrived bomber had swung off
the active and was taxiing into a hardstand, and without his aircraft
commander noticing it, he switched the command radio over to Guard, an
emergency channel capable of simultaneously transmitting on all ultrahigh
frequencies (UHF). Turning his head away from the pilot, he surreptitiously
squeezed the control column mike switch and spoke into his still-attached
oxygen mask: "Oh God, won't somebody please turn out the Arc Light?"

That copilot was only echoing the anguished thoughts of nearly every B-52D
aircrewman. No matter how sick and tired a fellow got of the Stateside SAC
"Mickey Mouse" and constant Pad Alert, he was never really ready to go back to
the Orient. As the war dragged on year after year, with no prospect whatsoever
of any kind of resolution, those feelings intensified with each succeeding tour.
By 1970 morale among the D unit aircrews had sunk out of sight.

While no one could possibly have foreseen it at the beginning, Stratofortress operations during the Southeast Asian War were destined to last for a
stupefying eight-plus years—from 1965 until August of 1973, when the last
bombs were dropped against the Khmer Rouge in Cambodia.[1] During that
span the Bufs dropped nearly three million tons of bombs, a mind-boggling
number that dwarfed any single-aircraft campaign statistic from any previous
conflict. In comparison, Britain's premier World War II bomber, the four-
engine Lancaster, dropped a total of just 600,000 tons of bombs during the
entire global struggle. Toward the end of that war, in the well-known, mul-
tiraid battle over Dresden, Germany, in February 1945 (the "fire-bombing"
immortalized by Kurt Vonnegut in his book *Slaughterhouse Five*), "only"
3,900 tons of allied bombs were dropped. Even Curtis LeMay's Marianas-

based B-29s, in their final and successful 1944–45 assault against the Japanese homelands, released but 55,000 tons of high-explosive bombs and 109,000 tons of fire-making incendiaries. Armed with such statistics, the reader may wonder, and with perfectly good cause, how it was that the North Vietnamese and Viet Cong managed to stand up to the B-52 onslaught.

The answer is surprisingly simple: The lack of eligible, high-quality targets. Guerrilla wars (i.e., conflicts without lines fought by irregular bands of indigenous soldiers against a domestic or foreign set piece army), by their very nature, are initiated by people who possess very little in the way of large weapons stores, manufacturing capability, or municipal infrastructure. This was especially the case in the fight between the Americans and the Viet Cong/ North Vietnamese; while the United States possessed the most formidable economy (and arguably military) in the world, Vietnam had barely entered the Industrial Age. Even Hanoi was essentially a Third World city, with few modern facilities, services, and installations worth the attempt to cripple them. The lack of decent targets would have been bad enough, but America exacerbated the problem by electing to fight with one and sometimes both hands tied behind its back—when American battlefield commanders weren't dealing with bombing halts, untouchable enemy sanctuaries, and the restriction du jour, they still had constantly to contend with an incredible level of presidential and Defense Department interference and micromanagement.

The result was an epic tragicomedy. Even during the war considerable numbers of both ordinary and influential people, in and out of the military, had come to the conclusion that the conflict's "rules of aerial engagement" were worthy of their own chapter in Joseph Heller's famously absurd novel, *Catch-22*. To wit:

- Enemy air targets, as mediocre as they often were in the first place, could only be selected from a very carefully prevetted candidate list, and then only actually struck after meeting yet more parameters and conditions.

- For much of the war North Vietnamese airfields were off-limits to air strikes for fear Russian MiG fighter technicians might be injured.

- Enemy surface-to-air missile batteries could not be attacked unless they had fired the first shot, apparently to ensure American flyers did not appear overly provocative or perhaps so as not to upset equally touchy Russian missile technicians.

- A number of choice targets could not be approached from the most favorable angle because the attacking aircraft would overfly a hospital, orphanage, or some similarly "sensitive" installation, which presumably the enemy could hold up as the victim of an alleged "bombing atrocity."

- Most astoundingly, in a directive that would have made Heller beam, some targets were to be hit only one time and then only struck again if and when the North Vietnamese repaired them.

As for those few high-value targets that actually were eligible to be bombed or strafed, matters were made even worse for the B-52s, because during the greater part of the war they weren't allowed into the most target-lucrative (albeit most heavily defended) environment in the theater—the North Vietnamese heartland. From the outset of the air war, the American leadership had been loath to risk losing any of the nation's precious Stratofortresses to hostile fire—for three principle reasons: 1) loss of face, something the Eastern cultures did not have a monopoly on, 2) forfeiture of irreplaceable components in the nuclear defense triad, and 3) diminished perception in Soviet eyes of B-52 "invincibility."

This unwillingness to commit the B-52 to high-risk missions may have helped preserve the nuclear fleet, but it came with serious side effects. The most crucial of these was linked directly to the successful prosecution of the war itself. Holding back one of your most capable weapons because it could be damaged was comparable to a professional football team not playing its star quarterback in a big game on account of fears he might get hurt. The directive protects the asset all right, but the action is almost certain to cut down on offensive productivity and thereby put at risk the entire enterprise. Further, by taking out the star player, the defense no longer needs to concentrate on stopping that aspect of the offense and can focus more of its own assets on the remaining opponents.

There was another repercussion, maybe not quite as important in the larger view, but one that certainly held plenty of significance from the bomber men's viewpoint. A sizable percentage of Air Force fighter pilots regarded the Air Force's "let's not risk the B-52s" policy with great disdain, going so far as holding the decision personally against the Stratofortress aircrews. Sometimes the situation got a little nasty, with a few jocks very nearly accusing the SAC guys of cowardice for not venturing into what was known as "Route Package Six"—specifically, the very dangerous Red River Delta, Hanoi, and Haiphong Harbor region. An F-105 pilot named Jack Broughton, in his 1969 book *Thud*

Ridge, really roughed the boys up with comments like "I guess even our B-52 crews faced some problems, like stepping on each other's fingers reaching for the coffeepot and things like that." Such talk stung, never mind the basic fact that where the bombers went was completely out of the aircrew's control.

Also, the implication behind those kinds of statements tended to misrepresent the situation. Keeping the wide-ranging Bufs out of the Red River Valley did not mean they had been removed from harm's way. Over the years, the Stratoforts were to encounter any number of surface-to-air missile acquisition radars and, on a few occasions, tentative probing by MiGs, though thanks to combat crew professionalism, the tremendous amount of electronic jamming issuing from bunched up bombers, other ECM support aircraft, and, yes, the presence of many "little friends," no B-52 was seriously damaged in battle until late in the war. (Buf aircrew like to believe that wasn't just serendipity.) Six-ship bomber waves striking in the vicinity of Ban Loboy and the Mu Gia Pass, for instance, were never allowed to venture into that area without being accompanied by F-4 Phantoms on top to guard against enemy fighters (MiG CAP or Combat Air Patrol) and F-105 Thunderchiefs flying underneath the formations to protect the Buf's fragile bellies from SAMs. The combined impact of those comprehensive defensive packages were too much for the North Vietnamese army to handle, thankfully making serious MiG and missile challenges to the bomber waves rare events.

Other threats did remain, however. Occasionally B-52s drew small arms fire (e.g., during forced landings in South Vietnam) or took high-altitude flak, though happily almost all enemy Triple A arrived below the high-flying formations. Still, every now and then, the NVA gunners sprang a surprise. During one mission briefing preparatory to a sortie on the upper Ho Chi Minh Trail, a memorable exchange occurred between an inexperienced U-Tapao first lieutenant intelligence briefer and the wave lead pilot:

PILOT: "What about these new 105-millimeter antiaircraft guns we've been hearing about? How high up can they reach?"

1/LT: "No sweat, sir. Even if they are around your target environment, which we don't think is so, their effective elevation range is no higher than 32,000 feet, absolute tops. You'll be going in at 36 to 38. Piece of cake!"

Those words had no more than left the silver bar's mouth before the crews began hearing a little voice: "Calling Mr. Murphy; oh, Mr. Murphy, pick up on line one, please."

Sure enough, a few hours later and directly over the target, the bombers were met by a terrific barrage of technicolor flak—silver, orange, gray, and black. None of the Bufs were hit, but only because they had been lucky. At the next morning's briefing, the senior intelligence officer, his first lieutenant having mysteriously disappeared, explained what happened: "What we neglected to consider was that, yes, the one-oh-five mike-mike can only reach to about 32,000, but of course that is an absolute altitude, and it seems the NVA found a way to drag several of those big guns up to the top of a nearby 6,000-foot mountain peak." Roger, sir, and be advised that's a One-Oh-Eight on the Falcon Code.

But the central issue regarding B-52 exposure was this: No matter whether the Stratofortress faced hostile fire or not, flying the beast was just plain dangerous work. Throughout the Vietnam era, aircrews on the rapidly aging bombers had constantly to deal with engine fires, hydraulic failures, electrical shorts, jammed landing gear, stuck wing flaps, smoke/fire in the cockpit, and, the most feared event of all, because absolutely nothing could be done about it—structural failure. Most of those incidents turned out OK. Some of them didn't. Worldwide between 1965 and 1971, at least thirty Stratofortresses were lost to crack-ups and midair collisions. Many men had been killed in those crashes, and they were just as dead as soldiers who'd taken a bullet. The Buf airmen who had observed those bombers collide, or crash into takeoff barriers and blow sky high, or lose wings over the Andersen cliffs also paid a price—by the time the 1960s had yielded to the 1970s, not a few gray hairs were appearing on more and more twenty-five-year-old crewdog heads.[2]

Unfortunately for the tender egos of those who operated B-52s, and as Broughton indirectly pointed out, apples-to-apples comparisons between dying nobly in an air duel and becoming a charred corpse in a miserable smashup were not considered valid by those of the jock fraternity, who rightly considered their close-to-the-ground Red River Valley combat flying more hazardous than Arc Light, though whose work was the most productive was still another question. Still, one had to face the brutal truth. There was a difference between dying by accident or in the midst of combat—a manly one, fully shared by B-52 types themselves. (The Buf guys were getting a real taste of what "support" airmen regularly dined on.) Bomber crewdogs were not intellectuals or philosophers; they were men of action. Most perceived it more red blooded, more macho, to risk everything while someone was shooting back. Most had eagerly professed, or so the bar talk had long suggested at any rate, their aching desire to take the war "up north." It therefore became that much more painful having to wait for the terribly elusive "put up or shut up" moment to finally arrive.

But when it at last did come with the December 1972 "eleven-day war," those Buf crews still left standing were able to come away with a profound sense of relief and satisfaction in having both exorcised the macho demon and of seeing the damn war all the way through to a reasonable conclusion. That sense of vindication and accomplishment was made even sweeter by an equally profound event following the Paris Peace Accords—not only had Linebacker Two been the key to ending U.S. participation in the Southeast Asian War, but it was also instrumental in bringing the long-suffering American POWs home, including (not incidentally) many friends and associates of Thud pilot and B-52 arch-critic Broughton.

Yet the fact was that until early 1972, nearly all the heavy-bomber targets had originated farther down on the food chain than those allotted to F-105 drivers and the other allied fighter-bombers. As discussed earlier, SAC's interdiction and close-support targets were, by definition, tactical in nature, meaning the Buf's job was strictly to go after troops and war materiel undergoing direct distribution to or already in the field. For seven years that had been the work of the big bombers—hitting and rehitting enemy supply dumps, bridges, convoys, and troop concentrations. For the men of Arc Light, that meant there would be no striking deep in the North Vietnamese homeland, no taking out the NVA command and control structure, no stopping the manufacturing and/or importing of weapons, no bombing of supply ships in Haiphong Harbor, no destroying the enemy's will and capacity to resist—in short, no strategic bombing. It can well be imagined that for the men of the Strategic Air Command, those rules of engagement were incredibly frustrating.

Just how frustrating was it? Again, we offer another of our homely anecdotes. It was 1969, the height of the bomber war, if one measured "height" by the number of daily sorties flown, and aircrew attitudes (not the ones displayed on the pilot's instrument panel) were already well on their way to the crapper. There was one especially articulate electronic warfare officer—if a Buf crew possessed an egghead, it was the E-Dub—whose humorous musings during the postflight Happy Hour were always eagerly anticipated. No longer able to tolerate the insipid and nearly identical B-52 action summaries reported over and over in the *Stars & Stripes*,[3] this fellow appointed himself the "official Arc Light interpreter" of the newspaper, even going so far as to rewrite certain articles according to his own bent and disposition of the day. Often, after putting his pencil down, he would read aloud a "corrected version" of the S & S piece to his enthralled (OK, slightly inebriated) audience, an activity often accompanied by Peggy Lee chanting her black ballad, "Is

That All There Is?"[4] on the Andersen Officers' Club jukebox:

Original *Stars & Stripes* article: "UPI reported today that giant B-52 Stratofortresses struck enemy truck parks, troop concentrations, and storage depots in South Vietnam and along the Ho Chi Minh Trail."

E-Dub rewritten version: "The Rumor Mill reported today that for lack of any worthwhile targets, the Big Ugly Flukers landscaped shopping mall parking lots, manufactured several billion wooden matchsticks, and put into place an aggressive monkey birth-control campaign."

There were long periods from 1965 until early 1972 when it seemed like monkey mauling and matchstick making were indeed the B-52's chief role in life. Certainly, much useful interdiction of supplies and destruction of enemy troops did in fact occur as a result of Arc Light strikes, and no doubt the VC and NVA trembled whenever MACV wagged a flock of B-52s at them, and to be sure if the Marines or U.S. Army were in a bind, the Buf guys were more than ready to help out with close-support bombing. But there was always the elephant in the room—the lack of really good targets and a serious chance to finish off the bad guys. Even worse, everyone understood down to the very marrow of their bones that nothing was going to change for the better until the American leadership abandoned its Catch-22 manner of running the war.

Until that moment came, it was left only to endure. To not look ahead, but instead focus on a personal day-to-day strategy of moving one leg in front of the other, as does an infantryman embarking on a 30-mile forced march. The foot soldier does not think of the 30th mile, nor even the first, but only of his initial step, and then the one after that, and so on—for that is the only way he can get through what prima facie would be an impossible task. So it was with the B-52D cadre crew force throughout the endless Arc Light years.

Those first steps could be taken in different ways. Let us imagine for a moment how our hypothetical rookie Blue Three crew from earlier chapters might have gotten on their hiking boots, beginning perhaps in the Andersen O Club bar on the night before combat mission number one. They would have walked through the door with a certain swagger, trying very hard not to look like the fluking new guys (FNGs) they were. The place would have been jammed with drivers and bubble chasers, the bar lounge tables littered with a sea of blue and red baseball caps; dark blue for the 90th Bombardment Wing of Clinton-Sherman, Oklahoma, and barn red for the 306th at McCoy in Orlando, Florida. It would have been a boisterous evening—mouths running wide-open, juke blaring, and bottles and glasses continuously clinking.

After bellying up to the bar for their share of the victuals, the fellows would scramble for a table and sit themselves down.

"I suppose we ought to be thinking about crew rest," the copilot offered cautiously, "looks like an early morning wake-up."

The electronic warfare officer, an older man who had quickly gotten into the spirit of all things Arc Light, slammed his bottle of Olympia beer down on the tabletop and exclaimed, "Crew rest? Crew rest?" He eyed the copilot curiously. "Tell me, young man, is it possible the official interpretation of said somnolent condition could be subject to revision now that we six finely honed SAC-trained-killers have at last been unleashed against the evil Communist world?"

The copilot frowned. "According to regs, we have just enough time for one drink."

The EW brightened. "But of course, the regulations, my dear eaglet. Let me see now . . . hmmm . . . oh yes, now I remember. The eight-hour and fifty-foot rule." His voice turned stentorian. "NO SMOKING EIGHT HOURS BEFORE YOU FLY, NO DRINKING WITHIN FIFTY FEET OF THE AIRPLANE."

"It is good to know," the navigator said, after the chuckling had died down, "that our senior ranking officer is on top of things."

After a few minutes of innocuous small talk and another round of beer, the increasingly loquacious EW piped up with a comment that caught the rest by surprise.

"I am really looking forward to intercepting and analyzing some of those wonderful Russian SAM threat signals."

"What the hell do you mean 'wonderful'?" sneered the radar navigator.

"I mean they are works of pure beauty," the E-Dub said, "state of the art electronic enemy defenses in the flesh at last." He sounded as if he were about to tour the Louvre.

The copilot suddenly piped up, apparently catching a buzzword that stirred him alert. "Hey, I heard that Black/Brown hit North Vietnam last night, just above the DMZ. A guy said he was pretty sure more missions were headed that way. Shouldn't we be getting a little worried about SAMs and going up that far north?"

"Worried, young man?" the EW said. His teeth were showing, but he wasn't smiling. "Have we suddenly become aware of the possibility our precious hide might abruptly be returned to the primordial dust from whence it came?" He tsked, tsked, shaking his head in mock indignation.

"Jeez, I was just asking," the copilot said contritely. "A guy oughta at least know what he's up against."

Before the electronic warfare officer could pounce again, the aircraft commander leaned into the conversation. Cocking a slightly disapproving eye at the EW, he said, "You know, the co brings up a good point. Wouldn't hurt if maybe you took a minute and gave everybody an overall SAM-threat rundown. This is pretty much unknown territory for those of us who don't get our suntan from a cathode ray tube."

The EW looked a bit sheepish. "Yeah, guess you're right, boss," the major said to the captain who, in the air, outranked him, "I sometimes forget you guys don't deal with this stuff on a regular basis like I do." It was both an apology and a reminder that the crew too often took him for granted. The ins and outs of electronic defensive warfare was a mystery profession even to the spook's fellow navigators in the Black Hole.

The aircraft commander continued, "I personally would like to hear everything you can tell us about the enemy's antiaircraft guided projectiles."

"Right," said the EW, once again his confident old self. He shoved aside his Oly bottle, popped open an ever-present briefcase, and pulled out a grainy photo stamped SECRET NOFORN.

"Gentlemen, I give you the Soviet SA-2 Surface-to-Air Missile, one of the most formidable antiaircraft weapons ever developed. NATO refers to it as the Guideline—I don't know what the Russkis call it. It's a pretty compact item; only thirty-five feet long and less than a yard wide, it grosses out at two and a half tons and carries a high-explosive punch equivalent to one of our five-hundred pounders."

"What's the effective range, and how fast can they go?" the AC asked as he studied the photo.

"Hard to believe but they can reach out about thirty-five or forty kilometers and get up to sixty thousand feet. The bastards go like a bat out of hell, maybe Mach 4. The word is they're lethal if detonated within sixty-five meters of the quarry."

"I've never quite understood how they go about finding their targets," the radar nav commented.

"It's a one-two punch," the EW said. "I could go on for hours about the technical aspects, but it boils down to this: The enemy uses what we call their passive Spoon Rest radar for ranging and target acquisition, and when that's accomplished, they turn on a second, active radar, called Fan Song, for tracking and firing." The electronic warfare officer slowly rested his eyes on each man, taking them all in as a group. "You guys should know this whole Guideline system, everything together, was built by the Soviet Union specifically to kill B-52s." He let that sink in.

While the others had absently set their beers aside to concentrate on the lecture, Lt. Serioso Copilot continued to suck away on the suds. With his earlier worries over crew rest becoming increasingly dulled and a throaty girl singer crooning from inside the juke, he was starting to loosen up, his thoughts naturally turning to matters of the flesh.

"Hey, Mr. E-Double-U," the co blurted, with just the hint of a slur coming off the U, "just exactly what the hell is a Fan Song radar anyway?" He had spoken the words "fan song" in a suggestively sexy kind of way.

"My dear boy," the EW said wearily, "can it actually be true that all they teach you young men assigned to the forward observation deck is how to shift the gears?"

"Aw, cut with the crap, E-Dubs."

The radar navigator saw an opening and took it.

"Hey, Nav," the RN said to his Black Hole compadre, "that reminds me, better make sure that tomorrow we bring along the Turn Rock."

"Gee," the nav responded, taking a sip of brew, "you think we'll really need it?"

"Yep," the radar said, "things might get hairy, guys will have to be able to do a couple of things at the same time. We can't take any chances."

The AC rolled his eyes. The EW rubbed his chin thoughtfully, timing precisely the instant he was to recite his own designated line. "Say, Radar, just how does this Turn Rock work?"

"Well," the RN said, "it's quite simple actually, which of course is the fundamental idea. The rock is issued to the right-seat Banana Eater, I mean copilot—"

The co's lips curled.

"—along with the following placarded instructions: COPILOT IS TO HOLD ROCK FIRMLY IN BOTH HANDS AT ALL TIMES WHILE AIRCRAFT IS IN HOSTILE TERRITORY. TURNS TO STARBOARD ARE INITIATED BY THE FOLLOWING COMMAND: PILOT, TURN TOWARDS ROCK. TO PORT: PILOT, TURN AWAY FROM ROCK."

All three navigators sniggered at their wit.

"OK," the AC said in his command voice, "you rejects have had your fun." He had used the sensitive word "rejects" with just the right amount of edge—enough navigators had been pilot wannabes or washouts for him to score his own point. Nodding at the electronic warfare officer, he said, "Let's get back to the SAMs."

The EW didn't miss a beat, directing his gaze at the copilot. "A Fan Song is definitely not a cabaret tune sung by some young lovely, though it does make a funny little noise when it gets going that might explain the song part of the name. It's an integrated fire control and radar tracking weapon system; the fan-shaped scanning pattern makes it capable of identifying up to six targets at once. What's called the Spoon Rest system sorts through the clutter and isolates each painted target, then the Fan Song proceeds to gather up the pigeons, as it were, by locking on to their tail feathers and ramming the Guideline home."

"Hey, radar," the copilot said abruptly, unable to keep his mind on business once suggestive metaphors had been introduced into the discussion, "wasn't it you telling me about all that good-looking and available Okinawan poontang?"

"Yeah, and as the lone single fella on this crew, you're the only guy who can legally do anything about it. But one thing I've always wanted to know is, how come you always go after the big girls?"

"They remind me of a B-52."

The RN's Oly stopped just short of his lips. "You mean 'cause of their large size?"

The co grinned slyly. "Nah, because they're both good, stable bombing platforms."

The aircraft commander threw up his hands. The EW leaned back in his chair and chuckled for some time; for once the co had gotten off a good one.

The RN waited until everybody settled down before again turning the discussion back to surface-to-air missiles. "So, Mr. Electronic Warfare Officer, how are you going to keep those flying telephone poles off our back?"

"Through superior skill and cunning," the Old Crow said, carelessly tossing a wadded-up bar napkin on the lounge tabletop. "The SA-2s are fairly transportable and the enemy can and does move them around—all it takes is a dark night and a semitruck. Two or three hours after picking their new spot, the launch crews can be open for business. Our F-105 Wild Weasel fighter-bombers are always hunting for them, using the NVA's own Fan Song and Spoon Rest radars as reverse homing devices to jam an antimissile missile down their throats. That's all well and good, of course, but you can't get all the launchers with Thuds. The key is mutual ECM support—electronic noise up the kazoo coming from our own Buf formations and whatever additional jamming aircraft we can throw at them. If the bad guys burn through all that and are still able to get off a SAM launch, then yours truly has a few more tricks, including flares and chaff, to fool their acquisition radars." He shoved his chair back as they got up to leave, injecting one last note of rakish optimism into the evening's proceedings. "It's a constant game of cat and mouse, but fear not, my Hearties, for there is Super Raven to protect you!" And that's exactly what he and others like him did, reliably and skillfully, throughout the entire war.

Much, much later—after Blue Three and all the many hundreds of other bomber crews had metamorphosed into war-hardened veterans, finished the long fight, completed their post-Vietnam military careers, been restored to civilian life, embarked on new professions, and then finally graduated into retirement—the Arc Light/Linebacker veterans would come to look back on that first Andersen evening and coming initial mission, and all the days, months, and years that followed it, with profound nostalgia. Although by the new millennium their remembrances would become selective and the truly bad times mostly blotted out (a not uncommon occurrence in former combat soldiers), what did remain shined through with remarkable clarity. The vast majority of those memories turned on the bizarre happenings, the poignant episodes, the funny stuff, the so-called "good times," if you will—all of them recollections the men would carry to their graves:

> Attending that first briefing at Andersen's Arc Light Center building and reading SAC's official motto on a fancy banner above the door: PEACE IS OUR PROFESSION. And then catching a glimpse of a handwritten sign tacked up underneath it: War Is Just a Hobby.

> Walking the mile over to the Andersen O Club from crew quarters and stepping around the dung piles left by the washtub-size Guamanian toads, one of the most grotesque amphibians evolution has ever wrought. After dark, the guys on the way back to quarters after receiving their medication, using sharp sticks to torment said toads.

> U-Tapao in late '67 and early '68, when it was still tents, hooches, and dust, dust, and more dust. The so-called "Officers' Club" had been installed in the former Royal Thai Naval Officers' Riding Stable, complete with barn odors and a compacted dirt floor. During meals, resident geckoes were attracted to the tabletop, and sometimes, if certain lieutenant-type navigators played their cards right, a couple of the seemingly bloodless little lizards could be snapped in two and dropped into the AC's colorful garden salad without him being the wiser. (WARNING: Do not try this at home.) Later in the war, after the new, air-conditioned U-T club had been built, listening to a local band belt out "The Gleen Gleen Glass of Home."

Also at U-T, a visit to the nearby port of Sattahip and a little evening R&R. The fellows would climb aboard a "baht bus" (its namesake fare was equivalent to a nickel) and hold on for dear life as the virtually rudderless, tiny truck careened into town. Occasionally, a crewman who had already spent too much time at the O Club bar climbed on top the little vehicle's swaying roof and, while clinging precariously, would deign to stick his head upside-down over the open side and declaim to those below that: "The main thing to remember, boys, is that these here baht buses just ain't safe. No, sirree Bob! And that goes for B-52s, likewise, also, and too."

Taking off and landing at Kadena AFB, Okinawa, with tens of thousands of Japanese and native Ryukyuian protestors giving the Bufs the oriental equivalent of the finger. There was always the concern they might launch something a tad more sinister up a guy's way. After a couple of years, SAC tossed in the towel and pulled the B-52s off the island—the Japanese despised the big ugly feller even more than American fighter jocks.

Sneaking around Kadena at night to catch a glimpse of a Strategic Recon SR-71 Blackbird (nicknamed "Habu," or snake) taking off on a spy mission over Southeast Asia or Red China. Talking to Habu backseaters (navigator/observers) at the Kadena Club and finding out that whereas a Buf had to start a 90-degree precision turn eight miles back from the point, the SR-71 was going so fast it had to start 99 miles back in order to roll out on course. Checking out the sign over the Habu ops shack: YEA THOUGH I FLY THROUGH THE VALLEY OF DEATH I SHALL FEAR NO EVIL, FOR I AM AT 80,000 FEET AND CLIMBING.

Looking forward to an evening at Kenny's Place on Guam, the only decent restaurant on The Rock, and gorging on the all-you-can-eat $2.50 Surf and Turf (steak & shrimp) Combo. Ditto on the Kobe Beef available all over Okie-Knock-Knock.

The broken-down "Guam bombs," aged, rusty Studebakers, Plymouths, Chevies, and Fords that crews bought and sold to one another for about $100 to $300 a pop upon each Andersen arrival and departure. Plus, the too-rare trips in the old Studee or Fairlane to Guam's Tarague (pronounced Tah-rah-ghee) Beach, a chunk of real estate so close to an American's perception of an unspoiled "South Sea Island paradise" it could have been a Hollywood movie set.

Nights on Gate Two Street in Koza City, just outside Kadena Air Force Base. There was always a pungent odor blanketing the neighborhood, largely because of the adjacent "binjou" (open sewer) ditches. Anything one wished to buy was available on Gate Two Street, from street vendor snacks, to the latest Japanese transistor radios, to the favors promised by improbably named "night-club dancers" like Dawn Morning and Jade East.

The official Five-Day Rest & Recreation Trip (R&R travel was supplied by the Air Force, no regular leave charged) that came in the middle of each tour. Hong Kong and Tokyo were the favorite destinations.

After a rotation back Stateside, stopping by the home squadron ready room to clean out all the old paperwork that had accumulated in the crew locker. Then finding everybody's latest Air Medal Oak Leaf Cluster certificates at the bottom of the drawer, scrunched in between scraps of paper bearing such crucial reminders as: "Crew members will get fresh haircuts at least once every two weeks." In an apparent effort to save on the specially embossed certificates, two or more Oak Leaf Clusters were often combined on a single document. Before the Vietnam War, a single Air Medal award was so rare it called for a general officer presenter and a full parade and review.[5]

The simple pleasure in stopping at Andersen's "Gilligan's Island" after the bomb damage assessment and maintenance debriefings. Three or four palm trees anchored this "poo-poo hut" area located just a few steps from the Arc Light Center, and it was there the Roach Coach parked, bearing always ample supplies of beer, pop, and the standard green-hued Arc Light hot dogs. The missions always sounded more interesting and less harried when they were reflown while sitting on a shaded picnic table bolted to terra firma and with everybody slightly under the influence of the Olympia Brewing Company of Tumwater, Washington.

Speaking of hot dogs, who could ever forget those ultragreen babies that were served from a nook adjacent to the briefing room at U-T. The only bigger shock to the crew's digestive system came when it was discovered the little old mama san selling the damn things was a North Vietnamese spy. So the crew grapevine had it, she literally had an ear to the keyhole of the briefing room door, picked up what she could (understanding English MUCH better than she had ever let on), and sent the dope on to Hanoi. U-T hot dog sales dipped precipitously after her unmasking.

Checking in for the first time at a Bangkok hotel and having to throw out the teenaged girl who came, to one's great surprise, with the $5.00 room. Having the same lovely young lady, using perfectly serviceable English, profoundly cursing said scoundrel for his ungallant behavior while the manager, genuinely puzzled by the American's attitude, stood by nodding his head in approval.

Going to Christmas Eve midnight church services and weeping unashamedly.

Christmas mornings when "CARE packages" sent by the crew's families were opened. Inside could be found an artificial tree, decorations, and several boxes of small presents for all six men. Cookies were bonus gifts shared by whomever received them, even though they sometimes arrived in crumb form (wives and mothers quickly learned to send only soft cookies). For an hour, everybody was five years old again.

Later that same Christmas morning, and despite a twenty-four-hour VIET-NAM bombing halt, the rear echelon mortar forkers sending up a token six ships to unload bombs on an empty Lao mountaintop just because somebody wanted to justify "nonstop round-the-clock B-52 strikes." The author managed to draw this genuinely chicken-poop duty two Christmases in a row, and he has still not forgiven the Air Force for it.

Mail call, which always had a hard time catching up with the crew's base rotation schedule. It was not unusual to get a heavy batch all at once, some of it four-to-six-weeks old. Buf aircrewmen rarely had any other venue for regularly communicating with their Stateside families—in an emergency, the base MARS (Military Affiliated Radio System, a kind of ham radio setup) might be available to patch a fellow through to the North American telephone network.

Trips to Johny's Gems in Bangkok, as much for their free glasses of Singha beer as for the shopping. Thai beer was unencumbered by the lower alcoholic percentages American brewers were held to, and as a result the golden nectar went immediately to one's head (which of course was what "Johny" had in mind all along). More often than not, the fellows bought more rings, bracelets, necklaces, and brooches than they either needed or could afford, though these many years later the women in their lives are grateful for those imprudences.

Discussing another man's "figmosity," a condition that often showed up at about the same time as the "six days and a wake-up!" countdown. A fellow was assumed to be largely useless once he had "Gone Figmo," an acronym suggesting something like "Fooey, I Got My Orders, and, brother, am I ever out of this place!"

The always popular "Thai Bingo." The U-T base radio station would at regular intervals during the day broadcast (in the tone and cadence of a melancholy Bingo caller) the three digit numbers assigned to certain ladies employed at "New Land—Short Time 2 Dollar All Night 5 Dollar" who had that morning during their routine medical examination been found unfit for duty. New Land was located within walking distance of the base proper; a very seedy looking place in the daytime, at night the dim lights emanating from such establishments as the "Long Branch" and "Dry Gulch" saloons promoted the illusion it was a Wild West town. A personal memory: Getting nearly run down one day on the way into the orderly room when a young two-striper came blasting out the door in the middle of the Bingo announcements. As the fellow raced for the aid station, he kept shrieking, "OHH, NOOO!" over and over.

Watching the Thai base employees feed "Pete the Python" (he might have been a boa constrictor) after the U-T mission debriefings. Crews would saunter over to the big cage and take their positions while the snake slowly cornered, captured, and swallowed his live chicken dinner. Wagers were taken by the local entrepreneurs as to the exact moment the squawking cluck went down the hatch.

Arc Light aircrew's ideas of "rebellious" behavior, of which a few examples follow: Customized flight suits, some turning out so flamboyant the sun-glassed aviator looked like a tin-horn, Third World dictator; the navigators who took off their flight suit and ball cap name tags and substituted "Hey Nav"—a protest against the de facto loss of their personal identity ("Hey Nav, what's the new heading?"; "Hey Nav, how much longer before we can set this firetrap down?"); the "Snake Crew" from Clinton-Sherman, who became famous for carrying a pet habu in a wicker basket on thirty-three missions (for those who have always wondered, pilot Jim Hooppaw finally confessed—"Irving" was actually made of rubber); the anonymous aircrewman who clandestinely played the Patton tapes over the command radios during the Linebacker Two missions—"I'd be proud to lead you wonderful guys into battle any-time, anywhere." (He was RN Wilton Strickland.)

That memorable afternoon a McCoy crew demonstrated how hot 500-pound Mark-82s could be cooked without having them blow up. Minutes after taking off from U-Tapao, an engine heat manifold in the bomb bay ruptured, spewing incredibly hot air-bleed gases through-out the fuselage midsection. The fiery blast welded electrical wires together, burned up alternators and hydraulic pumps, and warmed the internal bombs to well past published limits. Black smoke poured out from behind the ship, engines began operating sporadically, red fuselage overheat warning lights flashed like lighthouse beacons, the gear and flaps cycled randomly, the bomb bay doors opened and closed without benefit of switch throwing, multiple voices from the command post and tower were screaming contradictory and useless instructions, and everybody on board the bomber had white-knuck-led grips on their trigger rings, moments away from performing a high dive into the Gulf of Siam. Of a sudden, the aircraft commander couldn't stand the chaos another second, yelling over Guard channel for everybody on the radio to "shut the fluke up" so he could collect himself. Just like that, all the ground-pounding armchair heroes fell pin-drop quiet. A few moments later, from out of that deep silence, a mike was keyed, with the AC saying in a preternaturally calm voice: "Copilot, if just one more thing goes wrong, we're going to have to think of something." They eventually landed safely, but Munitions Maintenance Service and the base laundry stayed busy well into the night disposing of half-melted bombs and cleaning up the residue from certain other actual detonations.

Dealing with the war protestors. Soldiers could and did put up with them back home—always painful to endure yet recognized, however grudgingly, as those folk's legitimate right under the U.S. political system. But when American prominente like singer Joan Baez, former U.S. attorney general Ramsey Clark, and Hanoi Jane Fonda made trips to North Vietnam and provided direct aid and comfort to an enemy at war with their country, most fighting men felt the treason line had been crossed. For a world-acclaimed celebrity like Fonda, in particular, to fly to Hanoi as a special guest of the North Vietnamese government, to call American soldiers "war criminals," to conduct Tokyo Rose–like radio broadcasts, and, worst of all, to don an enemy helmet and sit in an NVA antiaircraft gun battery chair as if poised to shoot down American flyers, represents one of the most egregious individual acts of the war. It continues to be a suppurating wound even into the new century, exacerbated by the subject's refusal to offer an authentic apology (a half-hearted, unsatisfactory mea culpa was issued some years ago) and to beg forgiveness for inflicting the gravest of all battle injuries—a knife to the heart.

The thrill of the first Bob Hope Christmas show. Followed by the disillusionment that set in while watching the second (or third), after realizing it was one slick operation, more a cue-carded/sound stage/movie set than something designed for the impromptu enjoyment of fighting men. Then hearing how financially successful those annual shows were back in the States on NBC-TV and wondering if it could be true there was more than an altruistic motive in the whole business. Contrasting the Hope Circuses with the unannounced, one-on-one, nonprofit United Service Organizations (USO) visits of other individuals who came without PR teams and TV cameras. Case in point: Two aircrewmen with the Christmas blues stopped at the U-Tapao USO Canteen for a cup of coffee and maybe a whiff of "the world." An unprepossessing, bearded man came over in greeting, spending the next twenty minutes trying to cheer them up. They had to be told by someone other than the fellow himself that he wasn't a USO employee at all but instead was a British actor traveling on his own and expecting nothing more in return than the satisfaction of having done a good deed. His name was Sebastian Cabot, "Professor Hyatt" on the old Checkmate TV series and "Mr. French" on the then popular Family Affair.

Bob Hope's redemption at his U-Tapao and Guam appearances during the dark days of the 1972 "Christmas War." His words and actions on that bleak night at U-T, in particular, were heartfelt and deeply moving. He gave all the Linebacker Two troops—staff, aircrew, crew chiefs, MMS, and ground maintainers—a real lift when they needed it most.

Listening over and over to what became the Linebacker Two theme songs: "I Wanna Go Home" and especially "Yellow River." Enjoying immensely the waves of irritation radiating from the permanent party Andersen AFB Officers' Wives Club when its members had to endure said tunes over and over. A portion of the lyrics from Yellow River follows:

> So long, boy, you can take my place
> I've got my papers, I've got my pay
> So pack my bags and I'll be on my way
> To Yellow River

> Put my gun down, the war is won
> Fill my glass high, the time has come
> I'm going back to the place I love
> Yellow River

> Yellow River
> Yellow River is in my mind and in my eyes
> Yellow River
> Yellow River is in my blood, it's the place I love

The entire B-52 crew that removed personal names from the back of their squadron baseball caps and had them replaced with "Yossarian." Not even the generals could make the fellows put their own names back on. They were our heroes.

By 1969 Joseph Heller's book had become an Arc Light institution—every Happy Hour could come up with at least one navigator-bombardier anxious to hold forth with selected readings from *Catch-22* (performed solemnly, as if it were biblical scripture). Reflecting the zany side of World War II air warfare from a B-25 Mitchell bombardier's viewpoint, the book's essential premise, the famous twenty-second catch, held that a concern for one's own life in the face of mortal danger was indicative of a sane mind; conversely, to allow one-self to be placed in a position flying life-threatening bombing missions would clearly be crazy. But if a man asked to be grounded because he might get killed while fighting in the air, that proved he wasn't crazy, and therefore he was still fit for duty and had to keep flying.

> Yossarian was moved very deeply by the absolute simplicity of this clause of Catch-22 and let out a respectful whistle. "That's some catch, that Catch-22," he observed. "It's the best there is," Doc Daneeka agreed.*

Those B-52 aircrew who first read Heller's book back when it initially came out in the early 1960s had at the time believed his story to be a ridiculous fabrication perpetrated by a reefer-happy beatnik. Now, however, based on their long experience with Arc Light and the Mad Hatter war they were caught up in, most men solemnly viewed the work as a documentary.

> "Bomb bay clear," Sergeant Knight in the back would announce.
> "Did we hit the bridge?" [pilot] McWatt would ask.
> "I couldn't see, sir, I kept getting bounced around back here pretty hard and I couldn't see. Everything's covered with smoke now and I can't see."
> "Hey Aarfy, did the bombs hit the target?"
> "What target?" Captain Aardvaark, Yossarian's plump, pipe-smoking navigator would say from the confusion of maps he had created at Yossarian's side in the nose of the ship. "I don't think we're at the target yet. Are we?"
> "Yossarian, did the bombs hit the target?"
> "What bombs?" answered Yossarian, whose only concern had been the flak.
> "Oh, well," McWatt would sing, "what the hell."*

CHAPTER FIFTEEN

December 18/19, 1972—
Linebacker Two's First Day

Bomber Assembly Point, Central Laos

O ver the course of the long night of December 18/19, 1972, 129 B-52
Stratofortresses from Andersen Air Force Base, Guam, and U-Tapao
Royal Thai Naval Air Base, Thailand, formed up along a track eighty
miles northeast of Vientiane, Laos. After organizing itself into three massive
waves spaced at four-hour intervals, with each three-ship cell lined up in single
file and compressed within the wave to only four minutes apart, the armada
proceeded toward the initial point.

Joining the seventy-five veteran D model bombers were fifty-four G models, the latter relatively new arrivals from the States. For this latest and, what
was hoped, last phase of the war, the military and political objectives were
deemed too ambitious for the Arc Light B-52Ds to handle alone, and it had
become necessary for SAC to call in reinforcements. Under the auspices of
Operation Bullet Shot (see chapter 12), there were now 206 B-52s stationed
at the two Asian bases,[1] more by far than there had ever been before, about
one-half of America's entire nuclear bomber force.

At a glance, the two now commingled B-52 types appeared quite similar,
with most of the staff leadership apparently assuming that whatever disparities
there might be between them would certainly be minor and could be quickly
ironed out. They could not have been more in error. In fact, the two Stratofortresses were so technologically incompatible, Ds and Gs could not even
be mixed together in the same three-ship conventional bombing cell. This
soon-to-be-discovered and rather unsettling circumstance proved to be only
the opening round of what would become a long laundry list of intrabomber
logistical difficulties.

As one would expect, the later-designed and built G benefited from more

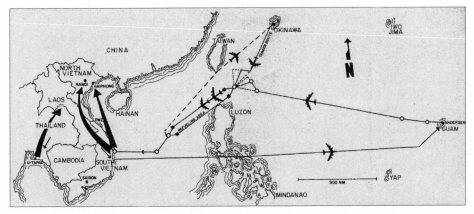

Fig. 27. The basic Arc Light and Linebacker inbound and outbound routes between the B-52/KC-135 bases and the Southeast Asian combat theater. *(USAF Monograph, Linebacker II: A View from The Rock, 1985; courtesy Air University Press, Maxwell AFB, AL)*

current design advances and a larger body of practical knowledge garnered from its predecessors' operational experience. This had clearly resulted in a better-engined, better-engineered Stratofort (as externally evidenced, for example, by the G's smaller, streamlined tip tanks and sawed-off rather than arrow-pointed tall tail), features that together greatly improved the bomber's aerodynamic efficiency and unrefueled range. Also, more sophisticated flight control and bombing navigation systems were introduced in the G, along with enhancements in cockpit layouts and even a few concessions to crew comfort (including ergonomic ejection seats and a decent heating system for the Black Holers). Additionally, the G gunner was moved into the forward compartment next to the EW, from where he operated his tail stinger by remote control, ostensibly bringing an improved cohesion to the defensive team. Nostalgia-minded airmen lamented this change, which permanently ended the long-standing tradition of manned gunnery positions on American bomber aircraft.

There were other dissimilarities. The G's paint job wasn't as sinister looking as the older birds' bearing a more Cold War–ish white on the fuselage bottom (for nuclear-blast reflection) mated to a light-green/tan pattern on top (to blend in with the earth during low-level attacks). And underwing weapon pylons were missing, there not having been sufficient time to modify the newer aircraft to accommodate the twenty-four external bombs routinely carried by the Ds. Neither did they have the Big Belly modification, and only twenty-seven 750 pounders could be loaded into the G's bomb bay. Nonetheless, and despite a vague uneasiness over that relatively weak punch, the G models gave every outward appearance of an imposing weapon system, and there was little doubt within the brass-hat community they would dramatically improve SAC's ability to prosecute the Southeast Asian air war.

Wrong.

To Buf crewdogs, the G's problems were conspicuous and abundant. The most serious was this seemingly glossed-over inability of the airplane to carry larger numbers of iron bombs, which meant it took three or four G model B-52s to equal the payload of a single D. That didn't sit at all well with the G aircrews; they were taking the same risks as the Dog model guys, but even their best efforts would only inflict a fraction of the damage done by the other. On top of that, the G's bomb-release mechanism didn't always work right, displaying a very unpleasant tendency to not let go of the weapons.

Electronic warfare officers were equally disturbed about the G's inadequate ECM suite and the bomber's corresponding exposure to the SA-2 Guideline surface-to-air missile. While the older D model fleet had clearly gone to seed, with increasingly serious maintenance issues showing up daily, the Air Force had nevertheless ensured that its regular Arc Light bombers were outfitted with the latest and most effective electronic countermeasures available. Regrettably, it had not been possible to similarly equip the Gs, for the same time-constraint reasons they hadn't received underwing weapon pylons or Big Belly–type modifications.

A few remarks about the D's ECM capability are in order. Between 1967 and 1969, following that same Big Belly overhaul, the Dog models also received updates under something called the "Phase V ECM refit." Installed at that time were the ALR-20 panoramic receiver set (the EW's primary search receiver, it had a small "TV" screen that visually displayed the entire military frequency spectrum), the high-powered APR-25 threat receiver (a warning system that used audio signals and a little round visual screen to instantly alert the crew when SAMs were in the air), ALE-20 flare dispensers (ninety-six flares, to be used against infrared, or heat-seeking missiles), ALE-24 chaff dispensers (1,125 bundles of aluminum foil radar decoys, called "window" during World War II), and state-of-the-art ALT-22 and ALT-32 high and low band (anti–Fan Song) pulse jammers.

So, while the Ds had been put in fairly good shape to fight over Hanoi, the conventionally ECM-fitted Gs were going in a day late and a dollar short. Actually, the latter had more trouble—two surprise Murphy pranks wouldn't get tripped until the fur started flying: 1) The B-52G's more sophisticated but heavily integrated flight control, fuel, hydraulic, and electrical systems gave it a much greater vulnerability to enemy fire, and 2) while the G gunner's new forward location may have helped defensive coordination, it also meant the crew had lost a valuable pair of eyeballs facing to the rear, a very important advantage when evaluating in-flight engine or flight control difficulties—to say nothing of assisting the pilots in evading SAMs and/or conducting hurry-up emergency bomb releases.

Our almost casual mention of that last rather provocative item begs a bit more comment. There were several emergency weapon drop schemes delineated in the navigator-bombardier's yellow checklists, and one of them (maybe the best) was a gunner-directed procedure called a Bonus Deal.[2] The technique had been used successfully in the D models throughout the war, on both radar synchronous and MSQ/Bugle Note drops. It worked thus: If one of the cell's B-52s lost its bombing radar, that airplane would line up behind another properly functioning Buf, approximately one mile in trail. With the aid of his fire-control radar, the gunner in the lead aircraft would then radio back range and center-line instructions to the pilots in the trailing bomber, keeping a very specific distance between the two aircraft. The Black Holers in the trailing bomber would use their ground speed to convert that fixed horizontal separation into seconds—exactly as the trailing aircraft did on MSQ/Bugle Note runs—and then wait for the bomb release call by the leading bombardier. The trailing navigator hit his stopwatch on that call and then directed *his* bombardier to drop their bombs a certain number of seconds later, theoretically in precisely the same point in space as had the leading bomber. Bonus Deal deliveries might not yield a perfect Roman numeral III impact pattern, but they almost always landed somewhere in the target box—an outcome infinitely preferred to either salvoing the blivets into the ocean or dragging them all the way back home for a typically hard, rough-rolling B-52 landing.

One can be certain, however, that those G model airmen approaching the IP on the evening of December 18th were not dwelling on Bonus Deal emergency releases—or for that matter, on any other of their aircraft's weaknesses. They, like the D crews, were mustering every ounce of their physical and mental strength to meet the technical demands of what was quickly shaping up to be the most momentous bombing mission of their lives.[3]

At about 7:30 PM North Vietnam local time (shortly after dark), the first wave of forty-eight Stratofortresses (thirty-three Ds and fifteen Gs) arrived at the IP and wheeled southeasterly toward Hanoi. With that turn, the stage was set for the biggest air battle since World War II. Seven targets were scheduled for the blitz—Phuc Yen Airfield, Kep Airfield, Hoa Lac Airfield, Kinh No vehicle repair facility, Yen Vien rail yards, Hanoi (Gia Lam) rail yard and repair facility, and the Hanoi Radio Station. The Bufs had their work cut out—historians would later declare that the Linebacker Two objectives were, collectively, the most formidably defended targets any bombing force had ever faced.

While the B-52s would be the centerpiece of the attack, they were by no means the solo act. Over one hundred other aircraft stood poised to support the heavies or to deliver their own assigned blows. FB-111s, F-4 Phantoms, and U.S. Navy Seventh Fleet attack aircraft were finishing up their day-long preemptive tactical strikes just as the radar-bombing, night-fighting Bufs started thundering down the Tam Dao mountain range ("Thud Ridge"). EB-66 "Destroyers," Navy & Marine EA-3B "Skywarriors" and EA-6B "Prowlers," and ECM-configured F-4s had already laid down a chaff corridor for the bombers and were now standing by to assist the B-52 electronic warfare officers with additional deception and jamming.

Yet more F-4 Phantoms (probably the most versatile American warplane of the Vietnam War) had joined up with the Stratofortresses in a protective MiG CAP escort, while below the Buf formations, F-105 and A-7 Hunter/Killer teams were going after individual SAM sites with antimissile missiles. Search and rescue HC-130 "Hercules" aircraft and HH-53 "Super Jolly Green Giant" helicopters stood by for the unavoidable, while orbiting overhead and to the side; waiting to fly bomb damage assessment sorties and provide on-going and follow-up reconnaissance, were "Olympic Torch" U-2R high-flying spy planes (similar to the U-2 Francis Gary Powers piloted when he was shot down over the Soviet Union in 1960), RC-135M "Combat Apple" recon aircraft (yet another version of the KC-135/Boeing 707 airliner), EC-121T "Super Constellation" threat alert/recon birds, DC-130 "Buffalo Hunter" recon drone launchers, and several examples of the almost indispensable SR-71 Habu. Out in the Gulf of Tonkin, the USS *Long Beach*, a nuclear-powered Navy cruiser positioned to monitor the enemy air order of battle—call sign "Red Crown"—was issuing a constant stream of MiG and SAM warnings (and sometimes vectors away from same) to the entire complement of Allied aircraft.

The B-52s needed all this help. Since the spring of 1972, the game's ante had been rising steadily. While no Arc Light Bufs had sustained significant enemy damage during the war's first seven years, that had changed with the April attacks in the Hanoi/Haiphong area. During the course of those raids and throughout the big Easter Offensive, several B-52s suffered serious battle hits. After that initial enemy success, whenever the heavy bombers ventured into the far North, the SAMs went after them with a vengeance. It therefore became only a matter of time before the inevitable happened.

On November 22, 1972, Olive Two was shot down after attacking a target near Vinh, North Vietnam. This was the first Stratofortress ever destroyed by hostile fire. The aircrew was barely able to nurse their mortally wounded bomber across the Mekong River before having to bail out near Nakhon Phanom, Thailand. Ostrozny, Foley, Rech, Estes, Stephens, and Sellers were all rescued.

That November was not a good time for the B-52 force. The increasingly unfavorable battle conditions had caused SAC to become so nervous about the threats to its nuclear bombers that the command began losing its nerve. More and more frequently, already-airborne B-52 waves were being recalled, not coincidentally after Omaha/Andersen had discovered that SAMs were very thick around the evening's target—this even though scores of fighters and other support aircraft were at that moment engaging the enemy in the heavies' behalf. Understandably enough, the fighter force leadership got seriously angry. As one of their generals put it, it was "very frustrating when B-52s cut and run with just a SAM indication." After a couple of weeks of this, SAC realized it was showing yellow and finally accepted the necessity for "press on" missions. On the whole, November of 1972 will go down as one of the more unseemly moments in the proud history of the U.S. Eighth Air Force.

Now, a month later, it was the night of December 18/19, and atonement was at hand. The opening round of Operation Linebacker Two was about to begin, with Snow One leading in a gaggle of twenty-one U-Tapao Ds. Their job was to hit the military airfields surrounding Hanoi (MiG suppression) while the balance of the first wave followed up with more airfield attacks and/or bored directly in on the other Hanoi area targets. To saturate enemy defenses and maximize mutual ECM support, all of the first-wave three-ship elements had further compressed the distances between themselves to a scant one minute—cells were barreling in almost literally on top of one another.

Brown cell was directly on the heels of Snow cell as the six D models swooped over Hao Lac airfield on the southwesterly side of Hanoi. While their 648 iron bombs rained down on the airfield, at least one MiG rose up to intercept. The MiG pilot took up the customary "six" attack position and began a stern assault on Brown cell, but unluckily for him, he had swung into the gunsights of the number-three tail gunner. Sergeant Turner let loose with a well-aimed burst from his Quad Fifties, and the MiG-21 went down in flames, the first ever shootdown scored by a B-52.

By that time, the first wave's attack was in full swing. Within minutes, the American UHF communication radios were saturated with battle-frenzied chatter. Everyone seemed to be talking at once—Red Crown threat warnings, bomber pilots yelling out SAM sightings, maneuvering calls from "who-knew?" and the unavoidable extraneous babbling that always happens during a desperate air fight. No one would have believed it possible for any single type of transmission to cut through the chaos, until it actually happened. It was the ghastliest sound imaginable—the shattering AHH-WAAH! AHH-WAAH! AHH-WAAH! from several emergency locator beacons—wailings so loud and insistent that they nearly blocked out everything else on the air. Buf crewmen were down.

Lilac Three was the first B-52 to be hit, struck by a SAM during the final stages of its bomb run against Kinh No. Badly damaged, the D model staggered away from the fight and somehow managed to limp back to U-Tapao on its own. Charcoal One, a G attacking the Yen Vien railyards, was not as fortunate. Just moments before bomb release, two SAMs hit the ship from behind, and less than a minute later the bomber began disintegrating. Rissi, Thomas, and Ferguson were killed. Johnson, Certain, and Simpson were captured, the first B-52 crewmen to become prisoners of war.

The second wave, a combined group of thirty Ds and Gs from Andersen, struck around midnight. Peach Two, a G model, dropped its bombs and had just entered SAC's required postrelease right-hand turn (and directly into the correctly forecasted hundred-knot headwind) when a SAM slammed into its left wing. Although the #1 and #2 engines were knocked out, the wing was on fire, and the forward compartment gunner had been wounded, the ship stayed airborne. The crew coaxed their stricken bomber over the border into friendly Thailand, where they promptly departed the doomed aircraft. Ashley, Vickers, Myers, Stegelin, Tramel, and Connor ejected, while Deputy Airborne Mission Commander Conner had to manually bail out through the hole left by the nav's downward ejection seat. All seven were picked up.

Rose One, a U-Tapao D model, led the third wave. Fifty-one Ds and Gs attacked at about five in the morning local, with the Hanoi Radio Tower one of their prime targets. As it turned out, this particular objective was within lethal range of up to eleven separate SAM launch sites. The wave leader was about to discover the bad guys running those sites had been closely observing bomber tactics and checking their watches and were prepared to ambush him when the predicted moment arrived and he appeared on their radar scopes. Bracketed by several antiaircraft missiles, its defensive electronic countermeasures overwhelmed, Rose One was hammered twice. One of the SAMs blew a hole in the fuselage big enough for the navigator-bombardiers to look out at the external bomb racks. Moments later, the cockpit burst into flames. Wilson, Brown, Alexander, and Barrows got out alive and were captured. Cooper and Poole were listed as missing.[4] A little later, another wave-three D model, Rainbow One, was hit by a SAM while on its bomb run against the Hanoi rail yards, but it was able to get safely back to U-Tapao.

By the time the sun rose over Hanoi on the morning of December 19th, the third and final wave had withdrawn and was returning to U-Tapao and Andersen. Out of the 129 B-52s launched, Eighth Air Force reported to Omaha that 94 percent of them had successfully released weapons against their assigned targets. Perhaps that was so, though nobody could say with any confidence how much damage had actually been done by those bombs. What could be said with certainty, however, was that the force had been met by an unexpectedly strong combination of antiaircraft artillery fire, MiG interceptors, and, most important, at least 164 surface-to-air missiles, yielding the enemy three Stratoforts shot down and two seriously damaged.

Publicly, Omaha put on a brave face; the official loss projections previously communicated to President Richard Nixon and National Security Adviser Henry Kissinger had been tabbed at 3 percent, a number purposely skewed to the high side to ensure SAC would look good by bringing in a better actual figure. And, indeed, by virtue of that earlier bit of rear end covering, the first day's actual losses were slightly lower than predicted. Although official eyebrows were raised, the Department of Defense civilian leadership chose to view the results as within understood parameters.

Privately, however, the SAC chieftains were aghast. No one with scrambled eggs on their service cap brims had thought for a moment so many B-52s would be damaged and/or lost. What's more, there was nothing that could immediately be done about it—because of the very long lead times in planning and executing the Linebacker missions, it had been necessary to get the Day Two launches under way even before all the Day One aircraft were fully recovered.

On Day Two, the bombers swung away from the airfields and concentrated more on North Vietnam's industrial infrastructure. Ninety-three Bufs went in, using almost precisely the same routes, altitudes, and tactics as Day One. The targets once again included the Hanoi Radio Station, the Yen Vien rail yards, and the Kinh No vehicle repair depot and fabrication plant, along with two new objectives—the Bac Giang war materiel transshipping point and the Thai

Nguyen thermal power plant, the latter located thirty miles north of Hanoi. The vast majority of bombers successfully struck their targets, though a few of the Gs were still having problems with their bomb release system and couldn't kick the weapons out. While North Vietnam launched approximately 180 SAMs, only two B-52s were damaged and none lost.[5]

The Strategic Air Command was lucky on Day Two, much more so than it either deserved or realized. Breathing a sigh of relief that the Day One losses hadn't been repeated and without benefit of any kind of orderly analysis as to what really had happened during the first two days, SAC commanders (temporarily lulled into a false sense of security) gave the go-ahead for the Third Day. Once again, the same approach headings, bombing altitudes, timing between cells and waves, and overall tactics from the previous two days would be used. Although almost all of the 2,000 frontline B-52 staff, flying officers, and gunners were deeply upset—indeed angry—over this decision to continue the attacks exactly as before, the official order had nevertheless been given, and in SAC that was that. Everybody swallowed hard and "popped to."

Everybody, that is, except Brig. Gen. Glenn Sullivan, the commander at U-Tapao. Not nearly as sanguine as the multistarred generals he reported to, he could not bring himself to support the status quo. With the full backing of his senior staff, he vigorously, and openly, dissented from SAC's Third Day plan. His 17th Air Division wanted new attack tactics, he said, and they wanted them right now. But it was like trying to head off an avalanche; Sullivan's direct communications with CINCSAC were ignored, his pleas swallowed up in the chaos of battle. The leadership at both Omaha and Andersen (through both action and inaction) made it clear the raids would continue as originally briefed. At least on the surface, SAC's top brass remained confident its force would be able to deliver yet another major blow to the enemy, with only minimal bomber attrition.

Instead, December 20/21, 1972, would become a Night of Judgment, collection time for all past due sins, a moment when all the shadowy entities—the B-52's resident gremlins, Murphy and his immutable laws, and the ever-present, always-capricious Gods of War—presented their promissory notes and demanded payment in full.

CHAPTER SIXTEEN

The Third Day

Over Laos: The Bleak Morning Hours

While the calendar had given over December 20th to the 21st in an eye blink, the weary and deeply apprehensive Third Day, third-wave aircrews were beginning to think the many dark hours bridging that Wednesday and Thursday would last into eternity. In an odd way, for some, the transit had become even more complex—their northbound passage was happening too slowly and too rapidly, both at the same time, an ambiguity that threatened the sanctity of Einsteinian time/space laws: "I hope we never get there, but let's hurry up and get it over with!"

As on the previous two nights, the lumbering parade was clawing its way up the Lao mountain chains, its preliminary objective an already well-traveled, arbitrary crossing in the sky the Americans had labeled the initial point. That dot on the map had been created by the simple expedient of uniting two previously unrelated lines of latitude and longitude—values with no special meaning on their own but when brought together at this particular moment, place, and circumstance had for the past three days come to represent the jumping-off spot for one of history's great air battles.

For the Dog model navigators out of U-Tapao, making their third trip in less than seventy-two hours along the same murky pathway, the navigation charts displaying that seemingly benign man-made symbol, IP, had already become tattered from heavy use. B-52 navigators did not favor the sterile, black-and-white strip maps handed out by SAC's bomb/nav shops, particularly while operating in "Indian country," and as a result often carried their own personal color charts, bearing the very latest on those cultural and topographic features deemed the most suitable for obtaining accurate mapping-radar fixes.[1] The wear and tear on such charts was especially noticeable along the attack route course lines, upon which numerous dead-reckoning circles and fix triangles had been penciled in, erased, then penciled in again on the subsequent mission, and where half a hundred ETA and heading calculations using plotter and dividers had left the paper porous from little punch holes.

The wave-three guys had been monitoring the command radios and knew things had gone grimly for the first two waves. Altogether, a total of ninety-nine bombers were tasked on Day Three. The first wavers (twenty-one Ds and twelve Gs) had several hours earlier worked over targets "Downtown"—the Hanoi rail repair facility, the Yen Vien rail yard, and the Ai Mo warehouse. As on the previous nights, the furious 100-knot winds from out of the northwest had scattered hither and yon the chaff corridors so earnestly sown by the F-4s and other ECM aircraft, meaning that once again the heavies were going down Thud Ridge virtually naked.[2]

It had already been demonstrated that B-52 electronic defensive capability, especially when up against the Spoon Rest/Fan Song network, was weakened considerably when the bombers had to go in without copious chaff masking and radar jamming from supplementary aircraft. The Buf crews had also learned over the course of the first two nights that their situation would further worsen if they didn't maintain strict cell integrity—should even one bomber became physically separated from the others, both it and the remaining two planes in the cell became extremely vulnerable to a radar "burn through" and antiaircraft missile lock on.

On the ground, the North Vietnamese SAM missile battalions, having at last figured out how to blast the hated B-52s out of the sky, had waited on the night's earlier first wave as a ravenous Doberman anticipates red meat. Their big chance arrived almost at once, when the three unclothed B-52Gs of Quilt cell came roaring in on the Yen Vien complex. Quilt Three was immediately in trouble; its EW had not only been saddled with an under-ECM-equipped G, but also what little spook stuff he did have wasn't working properly. Almost defenseless, Three was promptly nailed by a SAM while in the required posttarget combat break to the right—the tail wind that'd been so welcome while racing down the bomb run had once again turned deadly when a Stratofortress was nearly stopped in its tracks by a now-extraordinary headwind. The mangled G started sliding out of the sky, and when its downward vertical velocity exceeded 500 knots, the pilot ordered a bailout. Geloneck, Arcuri, Martini, and Madden became prisoners of war (POWs). Bombardier Spencer and EW Paul were killed in action.

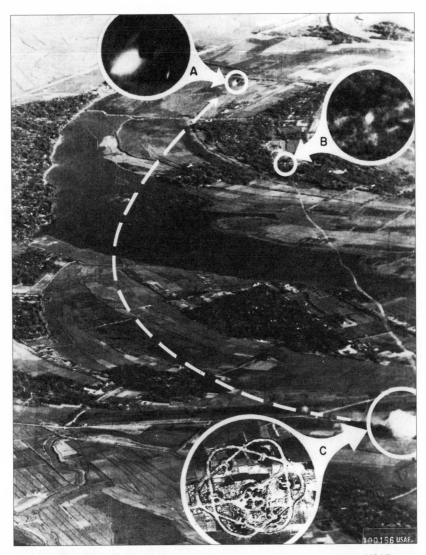

Fig. 28. Two North Vietnamese SA-2 Guidelines have been launched against a USAF recon aircraft early in the war. The dotted flight path of the still-coming missile shown in insert A traces back to its launch site (insert C). The missile in insert B (showing bottoms-up rear exhaust) has malfunctioned and will within a few seconds impact and explode in a populated area near Hanoi. *(U.S. Naval Institute Photo Archive)*

Four cells behind Quilt came Brass, another bunch of Gs headed for Yen Vien. During the harried postrelease combat break to the right, the Brass ships became separated from one another. The enemy seized on the cell's abrupt loss of ground speed, its prominent radar cross section while in the steep turn, and the collapse of mutual ECM support. A couple of well-aimed SAMs slammed into Brass Two, knocking out four engines. The aircraft managed to glide far enough to get into Thailand, with the crew bailing out over Nam Phong Marine Base. Ellinger, Casazza, Archie, Clement, Barroqueiro, and Schryer were all rescued.

Three cells behind Brass came Orange, a set of Ds engaged in yet another pounding of Yen Vien. While Orange One and Two were in the posttarget turn (and, again, with their ECM blanked out), Orange Three was left exposed. The enemy simultaneously launched up to twenty SAMs against the cell, and two of them struck Orange Three just before the Black Holers released their bombs. The heavy aircraft fluttered out of control, exploded mightily on the way to the ground, and, with what was left, crashed spectacularly just north of Hanoi. Somehow Granger and Klomann got out and were captured. Stuart, Perry, Lerner, and McLaughlin were listed as missing in action, but almost certainly had been killed in the midair explosion.

At roughly this point in the attack, a curious incident occurred. A D model electronic warfare officer named Smith, one of the very few Buf crewmen to have accrued over five hundred Arc Light combat missions, decided to take matters into his own hands when his airplane came under heavy attack. Configuring his ECM equipment just so, he hacked into the North Vietnamese antiaircraft communication radio network, whipped out his "lucky whistle," and let fly with a blast over the Guard frequency. The EW followed that startling piece of business with an angry shout: "Time out!" Perhaps the unorthodox countermeasures did confuse the North Vietnamese; there was an obedient pause in the SAM launches, and the crew successfully completed their bomb run. One thing could be said with certainty; electronic warfare officer stock shot up to all-time highs.

While Smith's cell got through OK, the enemy's blood was up. They were shooting down B-52s almost at will. The NVA couldn't wait for the second wave to attack; the entire Hanoi antiaircraft defensive network was now operating at fever pitch.

It was an entirely different story in the American camp. When word got back to SAC HDQS (via encrypted high-frequency [HF] radio reports from the airborne battle commanders) on how badly the first-wave short-tails had gotten creamed, the leadership came unglued. Of the twenty-seven wave-two bombers scheduled to attack, twelve were B-52Gs. While six of those Gs had been given some updated ECM equipment, making them a little less vulnerable, the other six were, electronically speaking, poor as church mice. With the hot Hanoi kitchen burning up his G model gooses, the commander in chief of

SAC himself decided to pull the plug. The six unmodified Gs were recalled.[3] The remaining fifteen Ds and six Gs in the second wave unloaded on their rail yard and power plant targets (escaping without losses) and boogied out of North Vietnam.

After the NVA was certain all the second-wave bombers had withdrawn, they did whatever they could to get fresh supplies of missiles quickly trucked in from storage warehouses and their SAM launchers reloaded. While that was going on, missile battalion commanders directed their tired radar and launch teams to stand easy for a short period. Have a smoke, get a bite to eat, catch forty. Do whatever was necessary to make yourself razor-sharp ready for what they knew for certain was the approaching American third wave.

At this point in the narrative, it might be helpful to step back from the battle's "big picture" and have a look at it from the viewpoint of one of those incoming third-wave Dog model crews. To that end, let's once again draft into service our hypothetical Blue Three gang from previous chapters. They'd have been grizzled old heads by this time, with perhaps two or three hundred Arc Light missions under their belts—and if they were coming out of U-Tapao, probably veterans of the first two nights as well. It's likely their squadron commander would have made them at least a cell leader—for the sake of this discussion, let's place them this night inside an equally hypothetical "Marble One" and position their three-ship element directly behind Straw cell, a D unit that actually participated in the December 20th wave-three attack. Like Straw cell, Marble cell would be attacking the Gia Lam rail yard in downtown Hanoi.

As we join our intrepid sixsome, they had just turned IP inbound. The pilots switched off their few remaining interior white lights, bathing the cockpit in night red. Down in the Black Hole, Marble One's magellan stood by while the navigation counters clicked over to his start-precision-turn latitude and longitude. When that instant arrived, he stepped on his floor mike switch.

"Pilot, nav. We are at the IP. Turn right heading one-four-five degrees. Accelerate to 470 knots true."

"Roger." The pilot turned to the heading while he nudged his eight throttles forward. Marble Two and Three silently followed suit, directly in trail.

As per what was now standard Linebacker procedure, the wave compressed itself even further, with Marble cell now only one minute behind Straw cell, and Straw precisely one minute behind the cell in front of them, and so on. Within Marble cell, the three airplanes closed to only fifteen seconds apart.

Command radios sizzled and hissed; many of the transmissions were coming in garbled and not a few walked over one another, effectively reducing their substance to so much gibberish. Up ahead, emergency locator beacons had been once again going off on an all too-regular basis—on Day One that wailing had terrified the bomber crews; now they were almost numb to it. As on the two previous missions, the night sky bristled with aircraft—B-52 bombers ahead and behind, low-flying SAM hunter/killers swooping and climbing, and comforting ECM aircraft hovering to the sides. Scores of agile American fighters were darting in and out of the Stratofortress formations, hungrily looking for MiGs.

Such proximity among friendlies, in the dark of night and heat of battle, did not come without considerable risk. During the Linebacker Two campaign, several F-4 Phantoms got too close and were nearly shot down by B-52 gunners. In fairness to the jocks, it was hard for them to stay with the bombers—their airplanes were unable to maintain the same high altitudes as the heavies for any length of time (afterburners were MiG-21 heat-seeking missile magnets), and it was extremely difficult for the F-4s to maintain proper position when the Bufs were evading SAMs or otherwise maneuvering. Easy it was, then, for a Phantom to inadvertently pass into a B-52 tail shooter's fire control radar coverage.

For his part, the Buf gunner was severely limited in his nighttime ability to differentiate between an F-4 and a MiG-21. To say nothing of the fact that he, like every other man on his crew, was scared witless—it was hard to see anything out in the blackness, and the Buf was sashaying all over the sky, its tail whipping around and slamming him from one side of his rear canopy to the other. Plus, angry missiles with lethal warheads were regularly zipping by his windshield; other B-52 gunners were blazing away at their own bogies, with hundreds of fiery rounds arcing out across the dark sky; and fast jets of unknown origin were screaming past him in a menacing manner—the world as a whole having seemingly disintegrated into absolute chaos. If modern day, thrill-seeking video-game-console players think their latest action download seems a bit too tame, they might sometime want to try Virtual Reality B-52 Linebacker Gunner on for size.

Once their ship was straight and level out of the IP inbound turn, the Marble One pilots leaned forward in their seats to visually assess what lay ahead. The Hanoi area night weather forecast was unfolding as advertised—thick overcast conditions between three and ten thousand feet, then pretty much VFR on top from there, plus a full moon—about the same as it had been on the first two nights. It would be relatively clear all the way in, which for a big ugly fat radar-bomber trying to stay invisible wasn't all that good.

The jet stream tailwind was also about the same as the first nights. A speed of 470 knots of true airspeed at 35,000 feet (very roughly equal to 540 miles an hour), aided by a 100-knot-plus tailwind, yielded a ground speed approaching 700 mph, about 10 miles per minute, or very nearly equivalent to the speed of sound at sea level. With all that push, Marble One's bomb run would not last much more than ten minutes.

There was a great deal to do in that short time, and the bulk of the work fell on the Black Hole navigator-bombardiers. They got right to it, with the nav reeling off the checklist challenges to the RN.

"Bomb doors circuit breakers set?"

"MADREC in Auto?"

"Bomb release mode selector switch set as briefed?"

"External racks loaded light switch on?"

Next came the installation of the critical ballistic and offset aiming data into the bombing and navigation analog computer.

Nav: "Bombing altitude?"

The RN read it back, adding "Set to OAP Two." He would be dropping the bombs with his electronic crosshairs centered on the second offset aiming point.

Nav: "ATF and Trail?"

The RN recited the weapon's actual time of fall in seconds and the horizontal distance in feet the bombs would travel.

Nav: "Offset One?"

The numeric data on the first aiming point, those values the offset aiming system was going to "fool" the bombing computer and by extension the airplane itself, were carefully enunciated.

Nav: "Offset Two?"

The vital second set of values, the drop numbers, were methodically repeated back by the RN, then cross-checked yet one more time by the nav. The team's concentration on these tasks was utter; everything except the rote and discipline of the bomb run sequence had to be pushed from their conscious thoughts. Many Black Hole gangs became so fixated, they sometimes were only vaguely aware of SAM warnings and threat advisories issued by their EWs, ignoring the airplane's twisting and turning even when hanging nearly upside down in their ejection seat harnesses.

"Pilot," the EW said laconically. "I'm picking up a lot of Spoon Rest radar search activity, but there's nothing pointed at us yet. And the LSL has been crossed." They had actually passed the Lethal SAM Line earlier, but while that event had been a big deal and worthy of special mention on the first trip, tonight it rated only an "oh, by the way."

Hiss-hiss, the AC acknowledged.

The bombardier-navigators continued running down their checklists.

Nav: "Bomb release interval control switch set in Train."

RN: "Rog, BRIC counters and interval set as briefed. BRIC lights are on."

When the bombs started to release, amber lights on a panel to the radar navigator's left would begin blinking, indicating the release was in progress.

The two men plowed through still more items.

"Vertical camera on."

"ETA to bomb release time, on time."

"Release circuits connected."

"Master bomb control switch on."

"Arming switches set."

The RN peered intently at the BNS radar's ten-inch screen as he switched it from the navigational 360-degree sweep-scan into sector-scan, the pie-shaped bombing mode that focused the magnetron's energy into a specific direction and magnified the returns. He grasped the tracking handle with his right hand and manipulated the electronic crosshairs to where he wanted them, adjusting antenna tilt, video gain, and receiver gain as needed.

"Nav, radar. Confirm I have acquired and am tracking OAP One, Mountain Peak."

The radar navigator was on a very distinctive, isolated paint in the Tam Dao range, located a few score miles west of Hanoi. The return had been picked for its excellent radar reflective qualities from dozens of candidate images provided by SR-71 overflys. Normally, the OAP would have had a jazzy nickname,[4] but Linebacker had brought an entire new level of seriousness to the Andersen and U-T target planners.

The nav leaned across his narrow table, to where his nose was nearly touching the glass on his smaller, five-inch repeater. "Roger, radar. I confirm your crosshairs are on Mountain Peak."

"Update your position counters," the radar nav directed. This will be their last navigation fix before release, and maybe for some time thereafter, depending on how things went.

The RN quickly changed gears.

"Pilot, radar. Bomb Run Checklist complete. I have positive ID on OAP One. Center the PDI."

Hiss-hiss.

Marble One was seven minutes from release, expecting OAP Two acquisition in another one minute.

"SAM UPLINK! ONE RING!"

Marble One's electronic warfare officer had detected the dreaded SA-2 Fan Song tracking and missile guidance radar, the "ring" call an indication of the relative strength of the signal. "Go in this direction," the enemy uplink electrons were saying to at least one *just-launched* antiaircraft missile, "to destroy a Yang Khi Fatted Calf." The beam-riding Guideline had responded on a downlink, "Yes, Comrade, I understand. Death to enemies of the people!" The American EW, listening very closely to this conversation—audio feedback and interpretation were the very essence of his work—instantly cranked his ALT 22 and ALT 32 pulse jammers up to maximum.

Red Crown: "SAM launch! SAM launch! Northwest of Hanoi!"

"TWO RINGS!" The EW's voice carried a new urgency.

Instinctively, and after checking that his crosshairs were still synchronized on OAP One, the RN dropped his head to the optical bombsight between his knees for a quick look-see. After spinning the contraption into focus, he rotated the optics out toward the night horizon, observing along the way scores of ominous light streaks visible through the 10,000-foot cloud deck. A whole lot of stuff was happening underneath the scud, and all of it was bad.

He reset the instrument to its maximum 6X magnification and twisted the viewer to a point beneath the ship, his heart skipping a beat when two large telephone poles with fire spurting out their bottoms came blasting out of the gloom. A moment later, they tipped their spear points at Marble cell. The missiles, trailing silver, doughnut-like exhausts, did not move to either side relative to the cloudy background and their noses grew larger and larger as they rocketed skyward.

The RN barked into his mike, "Two SAMs with our name on them!"

"I see them!" the copilot yelled. "Pilot, BREAK LEFT!"

At that moment, the crew was more thankful than ever the "no-evasion" order prior to bomb release had been rescinded. The pilot cranked the beast into an I-don't-believe-it 80-degree bank, practically standing the thing on its left wing. The maneuver had its intended effect—the SAMs immediately lost their electronic-beam concentration.

The EW keyed his mike, sounding very relieved. "Missiles veering away."

But just a handful of seconds later, he was back on ship's intercom. "MULTIPLE SAMS!"

With four and one-half minutes on the To Go meter, the night sky around

Marble cell lit up with dozens of streaking, deadly Roman candles. B-52 ship-to-ship radios erupted.

"UPLINK! SIX O'CLOCK!"

"SAM! SAM! TWO RINGS!"

"VISUAL SAM! MANEUVER!"

"BEHIND YOU, LOOK OUT!"

"MANEUVER! MANEUVER! CLOSING FAST!"

Down in the Black Hole, the bombardier-navigators could only hold on for the carny ride, blocking their ears to the uncontrolled shrieking on the radios and cinching themselves even tighter into their ejection seats. Although the "fun" was in full swing outside, they simply could not permit themselves to be distracted by it. They had to concentrate on the bomb run.

And that was getting tougher and tougher. Besides everything else, the Buf's maneuvering gyrations were raising hell with the radar stabilization unit. Heavy spoking, called "wagon wheel tracks," appeared on the RN's screen, blanking out the aiming point. When the AC really bent the thing to one side, the entire BNS caged itself in self-defense for several seconds at a time. The bombardier's hands were a blur on the tuning controls and tracking handle; he would have to use every trick in his bag.

Abruptly, as suddenly as they had appeared, the SAMs vanished. Taking advantage of the momentary lull, the Marble One pilots leveled the ship and recentered the PDI.

"Pilot, this is tail gunner. We're OK." Guns knew without being asked that the AC would want a quick, down-and-dirty report on the ship's condition. "A couple real close calls, one just missed the Number 7 and Number 8 engine pod. Marble Two and Three are still with us."

Hiss-hiss.

"Crew, this is radar." Things were happening fast; the To Go meter was relentlessly ticking down. "I'm switching to OAP Two, the Paul Doumer Bridge." He was late making the shift; the SAM attack and 100-knot tailwind had really thrown his timing off. "Nav, confirm I am on the second OAP."

The nav leaned forward. "Roger, I have you on the bridge, about a thousand meters northwest of the mark."

"Correcting." The RN had seen his placement and was already dragging the crosshairs over to the exact aiming point. The Doumer Bridge (also known as the Long Bien Bridge), a massive, steel structure built by the French during their colonial days, was the primary artery crossing the mile-wide Red River in the central district of Hanoi. The radar nav was looking to center the hairs on the span's easternmost concrete and brick pylon.

"Nav," the RN said, after he was satisfied he had the bridge pylon zeroed in, "confirm I am on OAP Two, Doumer Bridge."

The nav quickly confirmed same.

"Stand by," the RN said a moment later, "for target confirmation."

This would be the final verification, the last of hundreds of cross-checks he and the other American bombardiers would be making all night long to ensure the B-52 force struck what it was supposed to, that the attack would not fall victim to enemy propaganda and the international antiwar press by inadvertently bombing what could later be reported as "hospitals, schools, or orphanages." Just as important, insofar as the crews were concerned anyway, was the need to avoid hitting certain nearby buildings such as the Hanoi Hilton, one of several locations housing American prisoners of war. At any rate, there was no room for mistakes, especially with a delegation of highly visible American antiwar activists, the most conspicuous of which was folksinger Joan Baez, actually in Hanoi at that very moment. Marble One's bombardier disengaged the offset aiming system and allowed his crosshairs to settle on the target itself.

"Radar nav, this is nav. I confirm you are directly on the Hanoi Gia Lam railroad yards and repair shops."

"Roger," the RN said, really hurrying things up—they were flat-out rocketing down Thud Ridge, "target is verified and cross-checks are complete. Returning to OAP Two, the Doumer Bridge, for final aiming. Break-break. Pilot, radar. We are at sixty seconds To Go. I'm going to hold the bomb bay doors until ten seconds TG, damned if I'll give their radar any more to paint until we have to." The RN had said that last defiantly, fully aware he was throwing the book out on yet one more sacred piece of SAC dogma.

"Agreed," the AC said, his tone positive and reassuring. "PDI is centered and we are straight and level."

The RN wrapped his right hand tightly around the tracking handle and directed all his thoughts at keeping the crosshairs on the Paul Doumer bridge pylon. Just as with the Norden optical bombsight, the radar crosshairs might start drifting, especially if the BNS Doppler feed was bad. When that happened, the RN would drag the hairs back to the aiming point, thereby "killing" the wind's effect. Meanwhile, those minute changes would be instantly fed into the bombing computer and the appropriate corrections displayed on the TG meter and PDI. The pilot turned as needed; the time To Go was automatically lengthened or shortened. This synchronizing process would continue all the way through to release.

"Thirty seconds TG," the nav said. "Now if they'll just hold off shooting at us for another minute or two!"

Indeed, Marble cell was enjoying a brief respite, mostly at the expense of Straw cell directly in front of them, who seemingly had drawn the attention of nearly every SAM battery in North Vietnam.

Straw Two was about to get the worst of it. The fifth bomber to come in over Gia Lam, the D model took four very near misses during the bomb run, yet somehow the crew had managed to drop on the target. Their luck ran out, however, in the postrelease turn to the right. A SAM slammed into a wing, taking out two engines and wounding the pilot and navigator, though the ship stayed in the air. But not for long; the men were just able to get the Buf back across the Lao border before forced to leave it. Johnson, Farmer, Russo, Fairbanks, and Barclift were picked up by fast-responding Jolly Greens, but the RN, Gould, was never found.

At ten seconds To Go, the Marble One radar nav toggled the bomb bay door switch, and the massive panels groaned open. The screeching cockpit and slipstream noises took on an even more tense quality, as if the ship had sucked in its breath and was holding it.

The Marble One nav counted the seconds down off the TG meter. "Five, four, three, two, one . . ."

"Bombs away," the RN said almost conversationally, as the BNS automatically initiated the drop sequence. Ten seconds later he engaged the spring-loaded emergency armed release switch, dumping any weapons that might still be left in or on the ship.[5]

"Break to the right!" the nav yelled.

Anticipating the required posttarget turn, the Marble One pilot had already kicked his right rudder hard while simultaneously throwing the yoke over about as far as it would go.

"UPLINK! THREE AND A HALF RINGS!"

Nobody on board had ever heard that call before. The EW, his voice in an octave range the crew had never heard before either, could barely choke out a follow-up transmission.

"Hard lock! A SAM has us wired!" He tried to say more, but it came out strangled.

"Talk to me, E-dub! We can't see it!" the pilot said frantically.

"I got every jammer at max!" the EW yelled out to no one in particular. "I'm pumping chaff!" To *hell* with the 'only use chaff against MiGs' order.[6]

"I see it!" the tail gunner exclaimed, "coming in low and fast, rear portside . . . Jesus Christ, MANEUVER! MANEU—"

Too late.

For just a moment, the navigator-bombardiers down in the Black Hole thought the universe itself had come to a sudden and spectacular end, and in very nearly the same fashion it began thirteen billion years earlier—with a brilliant flash and a big bang. Or more precisely, a big KAWAANG! The accompanying white light penetrated the bomber's skin like X rays, passing through the crew cabin as if the fuselage did not exist. The RN and nav were instantly stunned into helplessness, swallowed up by a foul, whirling, deafening incomprehensibility. They had no explanation for the sudden whoosh of clouded, condensated air, or why the lower compartment had suddenly filled with flying debris, nor could they fathom how come it was suddenly so cold in the cabin, and where was that heavy odor of burnt gunpowder coming from?

"EXPLOSIVE DECOMPRESSION!" the aircraft commander bellowed. "CREW GO TO EMERGENCY PRESSURE BREATH!"

The missile had detonated forty meters short of the Buf's left buttock, loosing thousands of deadly shards in every direction. Although the aircraft had escaped a direct hit—what surely would have been fatal—the ship had nevertheless been badly damaged. The worst of it struck the left wing and that same side of the fuselage—fragments had penetrated the 47 Section, the now-empty bomb bay, and the Black Hole, near the amplifier/tube racks behind the radar navigator's ejection seat. Most of the navigation systems and bombing radar were knocked out, plus the RN had been peppered by small pieces of shredded metal. The bombardier was writhing in his seat from the sharp, stinging pains on his left side, so discombobulated he thought for an instant he'd just awakened from a coma and several demented flight surgeons were sticking him with a hundred dull needles.

If that wasn't enough, the RN's oxygen mask had come loose from the force of impact and he could feel the air rushing from his lungs, like two balloons collapsing inside him. Still stunned by the shock of the explosion and unable to grasp why he couldn't catch his breath, panic set in and he began thrashing about in his seat harness. The alarmed nav did his best to calm the other man via sign language—the noise was indescribable—shaking his own attached oh-two mask in an exaggerated manner with one hand and directing the beam from his Sanyo flashlight directly on it with the other. The lower compartment had been virtually blacked out, with only a little ambient red and white lighting coming from the few instruments and dials still functioning. At last, the RN got the idea. With a shaky nod of understanding, he raised his trembling hands to his mask and, after fumbling with the bayonet clip for a few moments, finally got it reattached to his helmet.

Only seconds after the radar nav had gulped in several delicious lungfuls of pure oxygen and was beginning to settle down, he became aware of an acute discomfort in his bowels—while the air pressure inside his body still hovered at that found near 8,000 feet mean sea level (preimpact cabin psi), the North Vietnamese Army had now equalized the crew compartment's atmosphere with the ship's current altitude of 30,000 plus feet. The laws of physics prevailed; both he and the nav began passing large amounts of gas, and probably other material as well.

The rest of the crew were in the same boat. Everybody knew it was critical that they get the bomber down into thicker air, and fast. Fortunately, both pilots were uninjured and handling the crisis well; the copilot shined his flashlight on the gauges while the AC wrestled with the rudder, yoke, and throttles of the rapidly descending bomber. Despite great difficulty in handling the crippled beast, the pilot was able to maintain control.

By this time, the decompression vapor had largely dissipated in the crew cabin. The RN was quickly rallying from his oxygen deprivation, and both he and the nav were training their Sanyos on the Black Hole's critical gauges, especially the altimeter, N-1 compass, and airspeed indicator. As per doctrine, the navigator periodically called out altitude and airspeed to the pilots during the emergency descent. The AC and copilot had kept their situational awareness throughout, immediately taking up and holding a southwesterly course—toward Thailand.

When the airplane reached 10,000 feet, where the outside air was at last breathable, the pilot hauled back on the yoke and added what power he could muster to maintain altitude and a reasonably healthy airspeed. Within moments, the altimeter hands stopped their free fall and the slipstream noises returned to nearly normal. Each of the six men took a deep and grateful breath. Maybe a couple. Without being asked for it, the nav radioed up a refined compass heading to where he hoped they were going.

"Crew, this is the pilot. We've lost engines three and four, and the electrical and hydraulic systems are screwed up good, but the thing seems to be holding together for now. How's everybody doing?"

The nav piped up. "Radar's been hit."

The RN came right back, playing the matter down. "I'm OK. Feels like I took a load of birdshot on my left side—stings like hell. I'm gonna need a new green bag, but all the parts are still here and working."

"OK," the pilot responded, trying not to sound as worried as he was, "but let me know if things get any worse. Nav, I'm counting on you to keep an eye on him."

"Don't I always," the nav chortled, the first attempt any of the fellows had made at humor all day. The RN responded in kind—right hand upraised, middle finger extended.

"Hey, gunner," the pilot said, moving things along, "how we looking from where you sit?"

"Sir," the gunner instantly responded, "the three and four pod is dinged good and still trailing smoke, but there's no fire that I can see. You are venting quite a bit of JP-4 out that wing; some of the panels are ripped up. All the other lifting and control surfaces look OK. It feels like its flying halfway decent from here." D tail gunners could sense when a Buf was out of rig or otherwise not performing correctly—the tip of the whip was a mighty sensitive observation post.

Marble One's "aft compartment commander" hadn't forgotten about external threats either. "Near as I can tell, pilot, all the SAM activity is to the rear, and there's no sign of any bogeys trailing us." A wounded B-52 would be easy prey for a marauding MiG.

"E-Dub here, roger that. My scopes show us clear of any threats."

"And pilot," the copilot chimed in, "even though we're losing fuel out the left wing, we should be OK for U-T." He had done his job properly when they turned IP inbound by switching the engines to the fullest tanks and opening all the cross-feed valves.

"Roger," the aircraft commander said, deciding against either an immediate bailout or emergency landing somewhere in northern Thailand. "Crew, we're on our way to U-Tapao. Strap yourselves in tight and stay real alert in case everything all-of-a-sudden goes to hell in a handbasket. Radar, keep monitoring heading, airspeed, and altitude, yell if anything looks funny; nav, get your butt up here in the IP seat and bring along a flashlight. I got no lights and can't see diddley-squat on the panels, and I need the copilot to talk to U-T approach and help me fly this beast."[7]

Things were going to turn out all right for Marble One; although their ship had suffered substantial battle damage, it was a tough Dog model and could handle the problems. Its old-fashioned, noninterdependent operating systems did not take each other out when one of them was hit, as was happening all too frequently in the Gs. The Marble fellows would arrive safely back at their base on the Gulf of Siam less than an hour later—shaken and a little giddy, but extremely proud they had accomplished their mission and brought themselves and their shot-up B-52 back home in one piece.

Meanwhile, the battle over Hanoi continued to rage. A flock of third-wave Gs was storming the Kinh No vehicle repair complex, with Olive cell in the lead. The crews had by now figured out that being the lead airplane was the most dangerous attack position; the NVA were increasingly ready, willing, and able to zero in on the first bomber that appeared on their radar scopes. And that's exactly what happened in this case—when Olive One went into the standard posttarget combat break to the right, it was promptly nailed, going down hard and fast. Nagahiro and Beens ejected and became prisoners. Walters, Johnson, Lynn, and Bebus were killed outright—Heggen died a week later in an NVA hospital from his wounds; he'd been sitting in the IP seat as a deputy airborne commander and was forced to manually bail out through the nav's hatch hole.

Tan cell arrived over Kinh No eight minutes later. The number three B-52G had lost its bombing radar and became separated from the other two aircraft while attempting a Bonus Deal procedure directed by Tan Two's forward-cabin gunner. Isolated from the others, Three was hit from below just before reaching the bomb release line. The airplane immediately went into a dive. Moments later, another missile slammed into it. Tan Three disintegrated so rapidly that only Gunner Lollar survived the shoot down and his subsequent imprisonment. Craddock, Lockhart, Kirby, Darr, and Perry were gone.

Even with that, the NVA wasn't quite finished with America's "invincible" Strategic Air Command. The last element that attacked that night, the three Ds of Brick cell, demonstrated with exclamation-point clarity the pure insanity of the required PTT (posttarget turn). While Brick Two was dutifully cranking it around, a SAM ripped into its right wing and fuselage. The veteran bomber shook the hit off and made it home, but that was the final straw for Buf aircrews; they wanted nothing more to do with Omaha's postrelease tactics.

Although Brick cell brought an end to Day Three combat, the aftershocks were only just beginning. Out of ninety-nine bombers, four Gs and two Ds had been shot down, with one additional D seriously damaged, a 7 percent attrition rate. Even SAC's original (padded) 3 percent loss projection paled in comparison, a hue that no doubt matched Omaha's complexion. If Strategic Air Command's brass had been horrified after the Day One losses, they were near paralytic after December 20/21.

The only positive to come out of the catastrophe was to bring everybody from the lowest brown bar to CINCSAC into complete agreement: The attack tactics had to be modified. By any measure that was excellent news, but the same planning and logistical obstacles the leaders had been facing since Day One were still in place—with the long lead times involved in every phase of the complicated operation, how in the world could a new, on-the-fly direction be implemented without creating an even bigger disaster? The sheer size and scope of Linebacker had given it an almost unstoppable, unchangeable momentum—even before the new tactics-change decisions could be finalized and communicated down through the chain of command, it was already bus time for the Day Four crews.

SAC gulped hard. On the one hand, it would be madness to send the force up in the same manner as the first three days; but on the other, Omaha could not NOT launch some kind of attack on the evening of the 21st—under the circumstances, such an act would have been completely unacceptable to the White House. The presidential proviso in the original orders to "be prepared to extend operations past three days" had just been invoked; the enemy wasn't close to giving up, and President Richard Nixon wanted Operation Linebacker Two continued "indefinitely."

Desperately short of options, the Strategic Air Command did the only thing it felt it could: hold back all the long-range Andersen bombers from the Day Four mission into North Vietnam. This did two important things—it bought more time for essential planning and analysis (again, Guam was nearly six hours flying time from Hanoi, with corresponding longer lead times) and, even more critically, it temporarily removed the shooting-gallery Gs from the battle. (They would never again be used directly over Hanoi.) Only two squadrons of the more survivable, closer-based U-Tapao Ds were to go into Route Pack Six on Day Four, fewer than one third of the bombers sent on each of the preceding three days.

SAC does not appear to have been entirely candid with Washington about its revised strategy, most particularly as to the location of the targets the B-52 force as a whole would be attacking beginning on Day Four. The official Air Force history of the Linebacker Two campaign, written in the late 1970s, states that at this point "Andersen committed 30 aircraft [per day] to support of the war in *South Vietnam* [italics added], reverting to the standard separate three-ship cyclic operations." The reasons given in that official monograph for resuming regular Arc Light missions were: 1) to support the ground war in the south, and 2) to provide experience for new Linebacker crews coming in from the States. Maybe that was the case, but one cannot suppress a deep suspicion this questionable use of the bomber force in the midst of a great battle was actually an attempt to obfuscate SAC's unwillingness to continue 100-plane raids on North Vietnam.

As it happened, that aspect of the game plan proved not so terribly difficult to sell (get away with?). At such a critical moment, nobody in Washington could have imagined the resumption of routine Arc Light missions was remotely in the cards—it was so played down in the reports that the switch to the south didn't register until days later—and an observer standing at the end of the Thai and Guamanian runways would still have seen about the same number of Day Four bombers taking off as had launched on Days One through Three (though with no idea where those B-52s were actually headed).

Of course, the Buf aircrews would not have been tuned in to these palace intrigues. And even if they had, there would have been neither time or value in discussing them, nor would it have affected anything in their routines if they had. No matter if it was from U-T or The Rock, North Vietnam Linebacker or South Vietnam Arc Light, a crewdog's daily allotment of twenty-four hours during December of 1972 was going to be consumed in exactly the same manner—flying, briefing to fly, or getting a few hours shut-eye so he was ready to fly. If there *were* a few moments left to squander on any personal reflections, a man might squeeze in a prayer or two asking that he not screw up or get killed.

By now, the clock, which could not have cared less about any of this, was demanding another launch. U-Tapao's Fourth Day (night of December 21/22) began in the same manner and with the same routines as its previous three missions, though with twelve fewer bombers, mostly because of crew and aircraft availability. Thirty big black uglies lined up on Runway 36 and, with their tall tails pointed at the Gulf of Siam, took off one right after the other and headed north.

Fortunately for the men aboard (and for that matter, all the Buf crewmen in the theater), the U-T commanders had refused to back away from SAC's internal knife fight. Gen. Glenn Sullivan and his colonels, despite having been continually rebuffed by higher authority over the past three days, had never stopped pleading their case. Now, in the aftermath of the Third Day debacle and Omaha/Andersen's tactic's epiphany, they had finally achieved the break-through they'd so desperately sought. Although most of the approved changes (e.g., approach angles, bombing altitudes, timing between cells and waves) could not be streamed in until Day Five, some fast staff work did yield one very well-received last-minute Day Four modification—the PTT was elimi-nated, and instead most bombers continued straight ahead for a "feet-wet exit" over the Gulf of Tonkin.

The thirty Ds of Day Four had been assigned three Hanoi area targets—six to Quang Te airfield, twelve to the Ven Dien supply depot, and twelve to the Bac Mai airfield/storage area. About seventy-five ECM, fighter, and tactical strike aircraft flew in support of the attack, which began a little after 3:30 am local on the 22nd and ended about fifteen minutes later. Although the Americans had gained a lot of battle savviness and were using only first-line Dog models, it was still a tough fight.

Those bombers striking Quang Te and Ven Dien hit their targets and escaped unscathed, despite encountering many SAMs. Not so the Bufs sent against Bac Mai. Once again a malfunctioning aircraft became SAM prey while attempting a Bonus Deal. Immediately after departing the IP, the wave leader, Scarlet One, lost its bombing radar. During the cell's attempted realignment, whereby Scarlet Two took over One, Three moved up to Two, and One swung around to the rear and assumed the Three position, the trio became separated. At the same time, Three's gunner started firing at a bogey he believed was a MiG (it might have been an F-4) while his pilot began taking evasive action. Meanwhile, the ship's frantic EW, who was dealing with both radar-directed flak and multiple SAM threat radars, had a critical jammer overload and fail. With Scarlet Three's ECM now thoroughly compromised and the airplane isolated because of the cell change and MiG avoidance maneuvers, the North Vietnamese Fan Song homing beam "burned through." The first two SAMs streaked by Scarlet Three and just missed, but a second pair following moments later found their mark. Bennett, Alley, and Copack were killed; Giroux, Camerota,[8] and LeBlanc became POWs.

Three minutes later, Blue cell attacked that same Bac Mai complex. Blue One's bomb run had been proceeding normally when the airplane was suddenly and overwhelmingly bracketed by a six-SAM salvo. Thirty seconds from bombs away, with the ship hit hard and burning fiercely, the AC hit the red ABANDON light. That quick decision by the pilot saved the entire crew, because the airplane blew up only a minute or two after the last man had departed. Yuill, Drummond, Bernasconi, Mayall, Conlee, and Morgan were captured. Although several of the men had been wounded, they all survived the war.

With eleven B-52s having now been shot down in four days, SAC went into another tizzy. Even though the attack tactics were undergoing a complete revamp and bombs were still being laid on the assigned targets with a decent accuracy percentage, the cost was simply coming in too high. While the ivory tower geniuses at Andersen and Omaha understood it was out of the question to completely stand down the daily strikes and get properly reorganized— Nixon would have them guillotined—it was also clear they could not continue sending up even the D model bombers on an essentially "same-o, same-o" basis. Again, what to do? Once more, the options were limited, at least in the short term. (One must constantly keep in mind only handfuls of hours were available if any changes were to materialize on the subsequent mission.)

It was at this juncture that Omaha came fully to its senses and transferred the daily mission planning to the Eighth Air Force staff on Andersen, where it should have been all along. Tactical battle plans could now be drawn up and implemented by the commanders on the spot, rather than emerging from a poorly informed, sterile environment half a world away. There was more good news—feedback from crews, flexibility in attack plans, and immediate reactions to fluid battle conditions were to now be an integral part of the planning process.

Still, for Day Five, none of that stuff was ready to go and time had once more run out. The crews were filing into the briefing theater and Eighth on Andersen had to make one more can't-wait-another-minute decision. And so it did: All the Day Five attacks were to be shifted away from the crack Hanoi SAM batteries.

U-T was ordered to send up another thirty B-52Ds, their objectives the less heavily defended, though still lucrative, targets at Haiphong—primarily its railroad support structure and petroleum products storage facilities—located on the Gulf of Tonkin coast about fifty miles east of Hanoi. Happily for the crews, some of the coming tactics, improvements that had already been approved and in the works could be incorporated into this mission. One of those wrinkles even showed some imagination. Instead of lining up to the northwest in Laos and making a bomb run across the entire breadth of North Vietnam, the Bufs would come in from the south across the ocean, dip to the left a tad to drop their weapons, and then immediately scoot back to the right and out over the Tonkin Gulf. Not only did this route keep the bombers out of enemy territory for almost the entire mission, but it also afforded an ocean rescue in the event a bailout became necessary. Having a fast-response Jolly Green hovering over one's life raft was infinitely preferred to looking up from a muddy rice paddy at a straw-hatted farmer brandishing a pitchfork.

The target shift and new tactics thoroughly faked the NVA out. During the early morning (though still dark) hours of December 23rd, Snow cell led Gold, Yellow, Ebony, Ruby, Amber, Walnut, Rust, Red, and Ivory in for the attack. They split into three groups some distance out, then at sixty miles from the harbor city, abruptly fanned out in a series of feints, staggering the time and distance between each cell. Sixty-five F-105s, A-7s, F-4s, EB-66s, and EA-6Bs were right alongside, hunting for SAM launchers, sowing chaff (which didn't blow away from high winds for a change), and jamming the enemy radars. Only forty-three SAMs came up after the attackers, thanks to the surprise element and excellent suppression work from the support aircraft. Walnut and Red cells did get "hosed down" by several SAM batteries when they ripped through the petroleum storage area, but they and everybody else got through the raid OK; in fact, for the first time since the operation began, not one Buf received battle damage.

On Day Six (Saturday/Sunday, December 23/24), thirty Bufs went up again. Guam was now back in the Linebacker mix, sending twelve Ds out to go along with eighteen Ds from U-T. Also, the 43rd Strategic Wing at Andersen had been ordered to send two dozen of its D crews to Thailand via C-141 Starlifter to relieve U-Ts tremendous daily sortie burden and replace their combat losses. Those crews remaining on The Rock were by now well rested and ready to get back into the Linebacker fight, especially now that there was a growing feeling SAC was getting its act together. Targets for that night were three SAM sites and the Lang Dang rail yards on the north side of Haiphong. Again entry and exit was from the Gulf of Tonkin. And again, the objectives were successfully struck, with no losses or aircraft damaged.

On Day Seven, and for the fourth day in a row, thirty D models (these all from U-T) were launched, but this time, in a calculated move to keep the NVA off balance, the bombers returned to their original approaches from the northwest out of Laos. And on this mission, the raiders also went back to Hanoi, bombing the Thai Nguyen and Kep railroad yards. Yet more of the new combat tactics were successfully introduced, with no aircraft lost, though one Buf was struck by flak, the only occasion during Linebacker that enemy Triple A scored a hit. Also, Black and Ruby cells were engaged by MiGs; one bogey got careless behind Ruby Three and Airman First Class Moore shot him down, the second and final confirmed MiG killing by a Buf gunner.[9]

By the time the last of the Day Seven bombers landed, the obligatory Christmas pause had gotten under way. Since the beginning of the war, the Americans had allowed this Christian holiday to interfere with its prosecution. The civilian leadership in Washington could not be deterred from its belief the Western "peace on earth goodwill to all men" message might somehow manifest itself on Buddhist Asians. The enemy, after taking a few minutes each year to laugh at the stupidity of their foe, had unfailingly used the bombing halts to replenish their strength and get ready for another round of fighting. Sure enough, in December 1972, Nixon ordered a thirty-six-hour Christmas truce, and sure enough, Hanoi took its usual advantage.

This time, however, there was a big difference. The Americans were furious, their Strategic Air Command bloodied and humbled. From the Pentagon to U-Tapao, the lights burned brightly. The U.S. Air Force was determined to turn the tables, to use the day and a half pause to its advantage. Bombers were ordered repaired and fitted out like never before, very large numbers of aircrewmen were sent into crew rest, bomb dump and weapon jammer troops worked day and night filling clip-in assemblies, and Eighth Air Force staff tacticians, target planners, and the bomb/nav shops shifted into overdrive. Like Popeye after eating a can of spinach, SAC was twirling its huge mailed arm above its head, preparing to deliver a mighty blow.

CHAPTER SEVENTEEN

Getting Smart ... and Finishing Them Off

The Eighth Day, December 26, 1972

The groundlings had done their part. The 43rd Combat Support Group (Andersen), 303rd Consolidated Aircraft Maintenance Wing (Andersen), and 340th Consolidated Aircraft Maintenance Wing (CAMW) (U-Tapao) had the aircraft and weapons at or as near optimum as humanly possible. The commanders of the 43rd Strategic Wing (Andersen), 72nd SW (Andersen), and the 307th SW (U-T) had their aircrews mentally prepared as never before. The Eighth Air Force staff, which up to this point had been cut out of nearly all the action by Omaha, had risen to the occasion by producing an outstanding and well-balanced attack plan.

Combat crew morale, emerging from its Day Three low, had shot up across the board. The flyer's fresh positive thinking became infectious; when the time came for the just-off-the-bus aircrews to take ownership of the bombers, the machines had nearly to be wrested away from their maintainers and weapon jammer troops. The renewed confidence the coming mission was bringing percolated all the way to the top; the entire Strategic Air Command found itself reenergized.

North Vietnam was to be attacked by 120 B-52s. U-Tapao would send up everything it could muster, planned at forty-two D models. Andersen committed to seventy-eight bombers—forty-five Gs and thirty-three Ds. Seventh Air Force (TAC)—and the U.S. Navy stood ready with a huge supporting contingent of 113 aircraft. The combined strength of the strike force would be rivaled only by the gigantic Day One attack, except that this time the Americans had gotten maybe a hundred times smarter about how to wield their hammers.

Seven waves of B-52s were to bomb ten targets—one in the city of Thai Nguy-

26 DEC 1972

LEGEND

- ┄┄┄┄ CHINESE BUFFER ZONE
- ───── APPROXIMATE SAM COVERAGE
- ▲ TARGETS
- ──→ BOMBER ROUTE IN
- ········ BOMBER ROUTE OUT
- COLOR CALL SIGN OF CELL

TARGETS

1	THAI NGUYEN	18
2	KINH NO COMPLEX	9
3	DUC NOI RAILROAD	9
4	HANOI RAILROAD	9
5	HANOI PETROLEUM STORAGE	9
6	GIAP NHI RAILROAD	18
7	SAM VN 549	3
8	VAN DIEN VEHICLE	15
9	HAIPHONG RAILROAD	15
10	HAIPHONG TRANSFORMER	15
		120

113 SUPPORT AIRCRAFT

EB-66, EA-3A & EA-6B (NAVY), EA-6A (MARINE) ECM
F-4 CHAFF
F-4 CHAFF ESCORT
F-4 (AF & NAVY) MIG CAP
F-4, B-52 ESCORT
F-105 & A-7 (NAVY) IRON HAND
F-4 HUNTER/KILLER

B-52 CELLS/TARGET TIMES

'D' GUAM		'G' GUAM		'D' U-TAPAO	
SNOW	2230	OPAL	2230	BLACK	2230
SLATE	2232	LAVENDER	2232	RUBY	2232
CREAM	2236	WINE	2235	RAINBOW	2235
LILAC	2238	SABLE	2238	INDIGO	2237
PINTO	2242	LEMON	2241	BROWN	2240
COBALT	2245			ASH	2244
		PAINT	2230		
RUST	2230	BRICK	2233	PINK	2230
MAROON	2232	GRAPE	2236	WHITE	2232
AMBER	2235	PURPLE	2239	IVORY	2235
SILVER	2238	COPPER	2242	YELLOW	2238
RED	2241			EBONY	2242
		MAPLE	2230	SMOKE	2245
		HAZEL	2233		
		AQUA	2236	GOLD	2245
		BRONZE	2239		
		VIOLET	2242	WALNUT	2245

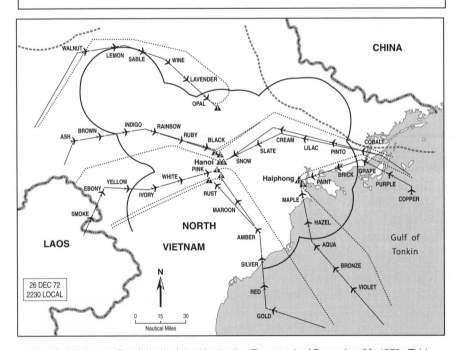

Fig. 29. Mission profile of the decisive Linebacker Two attack of December 26, 1972. *(Table and map based on illustrations from USAF Monograph, Linebacker II: A View from The Rock, 1985; courtesy Air University Press, Maxwell AFB, AL)*

en (forty miles north of Hanoi), two in Haiphong, and seven in Hanoi. It would be a simultaneous attack: All bombs, repeat, all eight thousand bombs, were to be released during a single fifteen-minute time frame. Cells would come in at different altitudes and axes of attack, with variable time spacing between each of them. High and low elements would crisscross each other's track, making it absolutely critical that lead navigators hit their exact time on target (TOT). If that timing was even a quarter-minute off, a high cell might inadvertently drop its load on a low one, to say nothing of the increased possibility of midair collisions. ECM defensive tactics had been significantly enhanced, a very large dividend accrued from the accumulated combat experiences, new recon info, and greater knowledge of enemy frequencies and techniques. Only D models would penetrate Hanoi airspace; the Gs could get plenty accomplished by working over less SAM-intense locations. There would be no more big postrelease combat turns; the bombers were to simply scatter away in every direction as fast as they could.

Although the attack plan in all its parts was quite complex, the basic objectives were fundamental: overwhelm the enemy's defenses, obliterate the assigned targets, and destroy North Vietnam's will to continue the war.

Snow cell kicked it off, leading wave one from out of the northeast in an attack against the Hanoi Gia Lam rail yards and the petroleum products storage area at Gia Thuong. Wave two, with Opal in front, blew down from northern Laos and struck the Thai Nguyen rail yards. Rust brought wave three in from across the Gulf of Tonkin and hit SAM sites and the Van Dien vehicle depot in Hanoi. Pink and the balance of wave four came up from the southwest and pounded the Giap Nhi railroad complex on Hanoi's south side. Wave five, with Black out front, came in from the northwest to blast the Kinh No complex and the rail yards at Duc Noi. Waves six and seven, led by Paint and Maple coming in from two different directions, made a "double-barreled attack" on Haiphong's railroad facilities and electric transformer station.

To be sure, and despite all the meticulous planning and huge array of American firepower, there were glitches. An air emergency at Kadena held up a group of KC-135 tankers for fifteen minutes before they could take off for their Point Golf refueling appointment with Guam's wave-three bombers. Fortunately, thanks to terrific navigation and timing triangle hocus-pocus by Rust One's Black Holers (along with some serious postrefueling throttle bending), the third wave was able to effect a rendezvous, get its gas, and make up the lost time. (Had they not, it would have been necessary to scrub the entire, no-longer-simultaneous attack.) Then there were all the things going on behind the scenes that never seem to make it into the popular imagination, like the trials of the aircraft maintenance troops at U-Tapao, who had been stretched so thin that they and their aircraft were nearly used up. In spite of herculean efforts by the 340th CAMW, only thirty-eight U-T Dog models made it off the runway (out of the planned forty-two). Six of the scheduled machines flat out died on the tarmac, though the two spares did get airborne. And the air fighting itself was back alley. The Hanoi night sky "looked like the world's biggest Fourth of July celebration." While the crews did a good job evading the scores of SAMs they encountered, not everybody got through.

Ebony and Ash cells were two of the four U-T elements that had to go in with two ships rather than three, because of the net-four launch aborts. Ebony Two had lost an engine before turning IP inbound against Giap Nhi and was already at risk. Additionally, as part of only a two-ship element, they were looking at even more trouble because of the incomplete cell's degraded ECM jamming. Shortly before bombs away, Ebony Two was isolated by an enemy Fan Song radar and struck hard by a missile. The pilot was killed instantly, but somehow the copilot and radar navigator held everything together until "bombs away." Immediately thereafter, however, another SAM struck.

With unmistakable finality, Ebony Two flipped over on its back and began to break apart. The copilot gave the bail-out order and the crew started punching out. Moments later, the B-52 turned supernova, and the North Vietnamese sky lit up for a hundred miles in every direction. Thousands of gallons of burning JP-4 hung as if suspended in the sky, while shattered remnants of the great ship slowly fluttered to earth like dead leaves. Morris was already gone from the first SAM and Wimbrow was likely killed as a result of the second. The huge explosion blew Gunner Cook out of the airplane, he who had still been in the aircraft because communication was cut off from the forward compartment and the ABANDON signal hadn't flashed in the tail. Cook survived and became a POW (as did Hudson, LaBeau, and Vavroch), but after repatriation, he lost both legs to unhealable wounds.

Ash One, another U-Tapao D model, found itself in a similar two-ship cell configuration and, essentially, the same thing happened.[1] Ash cell couldn't summon enough jamming to ward off a Fan Song uplink near Kinh No and the lead ship took a missile. Though severely damaged, with seven and eight on fire, the airplane nevertheless managed to stay airborne. Less than an hour later, the crew would make a valiant attempt to land their crippled airplane at U-Tapao. Cream One and Two also received damage, but made it safely back to The Rock.

Except for this "attrition," the mission was an unqualified success. To put it in plain English: On Day Eight, the Americans kicked the bejesus out of the North Vietnamese. Determined to keep the pressure on, and realizing they were playing a winning hand, SAC made Day Nine a repeat of Eight.

Because of the vast distances involved and correspondingly long recovery cycles, Guam could only get thirty bombers ready in time for Day Nine. U-T was able to scrounge up another thirty, which raised the raid total to sixty Bufs (twenty-one Gs and thirty-nine Ds). As it happened, this halving of the force did not have as much of a negative effect as might be presumed: Eighth Air Force was already running out of targets. Most notably, it was judged that no more attacks on Haiphong were required; the city's infrastructure and harbor had been completely neutralized. Therefore, on the ninth day, the bombers were able to concentrate their efforts on several particularly annoying Hanoi SAM sites (hopefully the Ds could silence the last of the big threats to the heavies), along with the Van Dien supply depot and the Lang Dang, Duc Noi, and Trung Quang rail yards.

This was destined to be the final day of "SAM's coming in salvos." The NVA had decided they would shoot their wad in one last-ditch attempt to stave off the Stratofortresses. If an unrestrained, coordinated antiaircraft missile onslaught had occurred earlier in the battle similar to the one that took place on Day Nine, B-52s would have dropped like flies. But by this later date, the Americans understood how to play the game, and only two Bufs didn't make it through.

Ash Two had dropped its bombs on a SAM site and was departing the target area when it got nailed by one of a boatload of missiles fired in a huge, simultaneous spread. Although the D model was severely damaged and the pilot wounded, the AC coaxed the crippled aircraft into Laos, where he and his crew bailed out. Despite the rescue choppers having to penetrate fairly deep into that potentially hostile airspace, they were able to extract Mize, Gruters, North, Robinson, Anderson, and Whalen.

Four minutes later, Cobalt One was only seconds away from releasing on its Trung Quang target when it took a nearly direct hit between the forward wheel well and right wing root, killing navigator Fryer outright and probably EW Johnson, though he might have been lost during or just after ejection. Lewis, Cusimano, Condon, and Gough did get out of the thing, but were captured. Six minutes later, Black Three, yet another D model, received shrapnel damage over Duc Noi. The boys stabilized the ship and managed to make it back to U-Tapao without any more excitement than what they'd already gotten that night.

And so ended Day Nine; despite the losses, it was the second night in a row the Bufs had thoroughly ripped up Hanoi. Although the Americans did not know it at the time, the enemy's air defenses had been virtually wiped out.

Day Ten arrived and sixty more B-52s struck the same railroads and SAM sites on a direct follow-up from the previous evening. Only a few surface-to-air missiles came up in greeting, the first real indication to the aircrews that the fat lady was warming up in the wings. No B-52s were lost or damaged. Everyone took great pleasure in hearing the last of the responses to the airborne commander's postrelease roll call:

"Orange cell, out with three."

"Quilt, out with three."

"Violet, out with three."

Came Day Eleven, December 29,[2] and once again sixty B-52s attacked Hanoi, blasting the smithereens out of the Phuc Yen and Trai Ca SAM storage facilities (housing large numbers of missile components in their shipping crates, ready for assembly) and what was left of the Lang Dang railroad yards. Unbeknownst to the crews, the North Vietnamese leaders had already signaled U.S. president Richard Nixon they were ready to return to the peace table. Before the last B-52 landed from Day Eleven, a presidential order had gone out to Eighth to discontinue bombing above the 20th Parallel and stand down from Operation Linebacker Two.

Still, it wasn't quite over. Arc Light immediately resumed its regular sortie cycle, just to make sure the North Vietnamese diplomats arriving back in Paris to meet with National Security Adviser Henry Kissinger didn't forget why they were there. On January 3, 1973, during a B-52 attack on a truck park near the coastal city of Vinh, North Vietnam (located below 20 degrees north latitude), Ruby Two was hit just after bomb release. The U-Tapao D model turned easterly and made an immediate feet-wet exit into the Gulf of Tonkin. With the ship rapidly folding on them, Wickline, Milcarek, Klingbeil, McTernan, Fergason, and Killgore bailed out. Although beat up pretty good, they were all pulled out of the water. As it happened, shortly before Linebacker Two began, Ostrozny had been shot down in Olive Two while also attacking Vinh. Oz and Wickline became the bookends to the "eleven-day war."

Over the next few months, U.S. air forces kept the pressure on by way of sporadic raiding, which mostly served as reminders to North Vietnam that they were required to continue implementing and honoring the January 27th Paris peace agreements. By August 1973, that process was complete. The U.S. Army had by then withdrawn the last of its troops from South Vietnam, and only a few Marines were still in-country, left behind to guard the American embassy in Saigon. The U.S. Navy had already detached its carriers from the Gulf of Tonkin and redeployed the fleet. The U.S. Air Force fully departed all of South Vietnam and Thailand; SAC's B-52s, KC-135s, aircrews, and ground support units had returned to North America (save a small garrison that remained on Guam). The Strategic Air Command began a gradual process of putting the "dirty little conventional war" behind it and restoring the force's full attention to the old adversaries—Red China and the Soviet Union. The Cold War was back on the front burner.

And the B-52 Arc Light/Linebacker era passed into history.

CHAPTER EIGHTEEN

The Twenty-First-Century Buf/BUFF

Following the end of the Southeast Asian war in 1973, the aging "Big Belly" D model bombers were integrated back into the rest of the nuclear deterrent Stratofortress fleet, though they continued to retain their secondary tasking role as American's primary "iron bomb" weapons platform. By 1983, however, the "D" airframes were finally worn out and the last of them had to be withdrawn from service.[1] At that point, the B-52G model was designated the Air Force's primary heavy bombardment response to nonnuclear "conventional war" threats.

Throughout the balance of the 1970s and 1980s, fundamental Strategic Air Command nuclear defense doctrine, the bomber fleet, and the ground Alert program continued to function in essentially the same manner as it had since SAC's inception. After the dissolution of the Soviet Union and an end to the Cold War, however, the nation's "ready in fifteen minutes" deterrent posture was no longer deemed necessary. Therefore, on September 27, 1991, by presidential decree, the nation's rapid-response ground alert forces permanently stood down. For the first time in thirty-four years, no American nuclear bomber was poised to launch on a moment's notice.

Despite this tremendous relaxation in the nation's defense posture, no one doubted the world remained a dangerous place. Furthermore, and though future conflicts were much less likely to be exchanges between global superpowers, the nuclear threat wasn't likely to entirely vanish either. There were still a lot of atomic and hydrogen bombs lying around, and in some cases those weapons weren't safeguarded as carefully as the United States would have preferred. What's more, many old national antagonisms were resurfacing, with limited regional wars rapidly becoming more common. And then there was the emerging, frightening new threat to America's security: worldwide terrorism.

Also by that time, the dynamic technological breakthroughs of the previous several decades (microchips, miniaturized electronic components, high-speed computers, and communication satellites) had begun to fully manifest themselves in the B-52. The remaining Stratofortresses (about 160 Gs and 100 Hs) underwent major modifications to accommodate all the latest in digital flight systems/instrumentation, automated navigational systems, and state-of-the-art weaponry.

Specifically, the crude video game/toy technology of the 1970s had by 1990 morphed into complex cockpit digital/graphic monitors (so-called "glass displays") that transformed much of the modern pilot's instrumentation into colorful TV/computer-like screens. For the first time since Albert F. Hegenberger's work in the 1920s, the pilot's steam gauges were no longer "kings" of the instrument panel. Additionally, the advent of the satellite-fed Global Positioning System (GPS) had led to a complete Black Hole makeover,[2] resulting in a navigational advance every bit as significant as the World War II magnetron and H2S mapping radar. Instead of laboriously extracting lines of positions from natural heavenly bodies to fix the plane's position, navigators could now obtain that same information with a twist of their fingers.

Perhaps most important, weapons delivery systems were dramatically enhanced across the board. Short-range attack missiles (SRAMs) could now be delivered from the internal bomb bay. Plus, heavy stores adaptor beams (replacing the old Hound Dog mounting racks used in Vietnam) were installed under the wings, arming the B-52 with external air-launched cruise missiles (ALCMs).

By the early 1990s, the B-52's maritime defense role had also been substantially expanded, from a "collateral responsibility to a major mission." Patrolling B-52s, armed with Harpoon ship-killing missiles, now had the ability "to neutralize or destroy enemy naval forces and to protect friendly naval forces and shipping . . . [O]perations may consist of counter air operations, aerial minelaying, reconnaissance and interdiction of enemy naval surface and sub-surface forces, port facilities, and shipping."

As a result of these dramatic changes in geopolitics, technology, capability, and mission objectives, and with the half-century-old concepts of "strategic" and "tactical" air warfare now blurred beyond recognition, the Pentagon initiated a major defense reorganization. On June 1, 1992, the Strategic Air Command was dissolved. On that same day, SAC's assets, along with Tactical Air Command's fighters, the nation's ICBM force, and certain recon/support units were integrated into a single new entity called Air Combat Command

(ACC), headquartered at Langley AFB, Virginia. The remaining B-52s, along with the "modern heavies," the B-1B Lancer (a total of 100 built) and the stealthy (but very expensive) B-2 Spirit (21 built), were folded into the newly reconstituted 8th and 12th Air Forces.

Today it is the H model Buf/BUFF one reads about, the "B-52 bomber" that is being sent out to launch underwing and bomb-bayed cruise missiles and "smart" bombs on pin-point terrorist targets. At the beginning of 2009, ninety-two B-52Hs were still in the nation's operational bomber inventory. That number, however, is certain to dwindle as airframe deterioration, parts unavailability, system cannibalizations, and the inevitable "attrition" incidents continue to take their toll. As this is written, Congress has apparently agreed to allow the Air Force to begin retiring an additional seventeen aircraft, which, if implemented, would leave some seventy-five operational H models going forward. Whatever final number shakes out, the bombers will continue to be located at two bases—Minot AFB, North Dakota (5th Bomb Wing) and Barksdale AFB, Louisiana (2nd BW). Those Hs remaining are scheduled to stay on active duty at least until 2018 and possibly as long as 2040, though that latter date is increasingly being questioned as the realities of the fleet's condition become more and more apparent. For old-time B-52 aircrewmen, the very idea of the BUFF lasting until 2040 is a staggering thought. If such a thing occurred, the Stratofortress' operational life span would exceed eighty-five years, something no other warbird anywhere on the planet has come close to achieving. (The B-17 lasted just eight to ten years as a front-line combat aircraft.)

That kind of longevity seems all the more remarkable when one reflects on how comparatively little the machine's outward appearance has changed in fifty years. Because the plane's basic airframe design is so tremendously flexible, the Air Force has throughout the many decades been able to regularly incorporate into it the very latest in navigation, flight control, and weapon systems—modifications that can continue as even more advanced technologies present themselves. Also, because of almost uncanny 1950s' engineering prescience, the bomber's unlimited (with aerial refueling) range, large payload capacity, and extended loitering capability has made it a nearly ideal weapons platform in the ongoing war against terror.

Nearly twenty years would pass before the BUFF again found itself back in a "hot" war. This time it came in Southwest Asia, where long-brewing trouble in Iraq finally boiled over. In mid-January 1991, Operation Desert Storm was launched in retaliation for Saddam Hussein's earlier invasion of Kuwait.

Although the B-52G models (by then the Stratofortress fleet's sole conventional weapons carrier) were nearing the end of their life,[3] they nevertheless became an essential component of the U.S. counterattack against occupying Iraqi forces.

The Gs enjoyed a very high level of success during Desert Storm, in large part because of the post-Vietnam heavy stores adaptor modification mentioned earlier, which in addition to newly arming the B-52 with external cruise missiles also increased the Gs' conventional bomb tonnage carrying capacity to nearly double what it had been during Linebacker. The airplane could now carry fifty-one Mark 117 750-pound conventional bombs (twenty-seven bomb-bayed internals and twenty-four wing-mounted externals), giving it a per-plane punching power nearly comparable to that of the old "Big Belly" D. Not surprisingly, and as was the case with the Viet Cong and NVA, the Iraqi enemy came to regard the B-52 as the most feared of all the allied weapons arrayed against it.

The Gs played an especially important role during the opening hours of Desert Storm, one so sensitive to overall national security that the details were withheld from the general public for a year. Seven B-52Gs secretly launched from the 2nd Bomb Wing at Barksdale AFB, Louisiana, to attack targets in Iraq, halfway around the world. The bombers were armed with conventionally warheaded versions (each equivalent to a 2,000-pound bomb) of the new AGM-86B air-to-ground nuclear-tipped cruise missile, a Top Secret weapon system that had only recently been added to the SAC deterrent arsenal. The surprise attack by these just-off-the-shelf CALCMs (conventional air-launched cruise missiles) was devastating, both in terms of targets destroyed and the sudden strike's shock value—within a ten-minute time span thirty-three of the thirty-five launched cruise missiles obliterated their assigned targets.[4] (The mission did have its problems, which didn't affect the attack's strategic outcome, and which we will not dwell on here.) To the seven aircrews onboard (including extra pilots and Black Holers), it was a job well done, though the squadron still faced a staggering fifteen-hour deadhead back to North America, bringing their total sortie length to thirty-five hours. The successful landings at Barksdale also carried with them something of a personal distinction for the exhausted men, one at least carefully noted by former and current bomber types—to that date, it was the longest duration combat mission in history.

Four B-52 bases were used during what is today sometimes referred to as the "first Gulf War." The foundation air facility, in a sense the equivalent of Andersen AFB, Guam, during the Vietnam War, was on the island of Diego

Garcia in the Indian Ocean. Other remote launch bases included RAF Fairford in the United Kingdom and Moron, Spain. The most forward-operating station, and arguably the one of greatest value (for the same proximity reasons Vietnam's U-Tapao was so important), was at Jeddah, Saudi Arabia. Between seventy-four and eighty-six B-52Gs (accounts vary) were engaged in Operation Desert Storm.[5]

Later in the 1990s, the B-52 was once more called into action. Long-simmering political turmoil in the Balkans (a sore spot for centuries) was rapidly turning into armed conflict and genocide. While Operation Allied Force was not nearly the military engagement that Desert Storm was, at least six B-52Hs and two B-2s did see some action, though it is fair to argue the mere threat of those two weapon platforms was probably just as important as their actual use. Described by one historian as the "very peculiar air war over Serbia," the conflict was fortunately short-lived and, in the end, a reasonably successful political conclusion was achieved.

From a purely military standpoint, the Yugoslavian trouble did produce one remarkable event—the successful introduction of "smart bombs." More properly called JDAMs (joint direct-attack munitions), a smart bomb is essentially a combination of the old and new—a relatively inexpensive GPS/inertial guidance navigation kit is strapped to an individual dumb iron bomb and the combined assembly is dropped and then "flown" directly down to an exact set of preselected target coordinates (fifteen-nautical-mile range). Thanks to this remarkable example of Yankee ingenuity, bombs no longer had to be dropped in an often wasteful series of "strings," but could instead be individually released against separate targets, theoretically increasing the actual destructive effectiveness of a B-52 bombload of adapted Mark 117s as much as fifty-fold.

Such a remarkable dividend (only slightly exaggerated) comes from precision. Since the very first ballistically aimed gravity bombs were dropped a century ago, it has been an accepted military axiom that, because of the inherent and unavoidable trigonometric difficulties, most of the weapons would miss their target. Even by Vietnam, a roughly 500-foot circular error on an entire radar-aimed string was still considered OK. But now, with the "smart bomb" JDAM modification, a singly released 750-pounder could almost guarantee a thirty-foot circular error (CE) 100 percent of the time, in any weather. During Desert Storm in 1991, the great bulk of American air-dropped ordnance had been delivered the old-fashioned "dumb" way; by the 1999 Kosovo operation, 90 percent of it was coming from these new precision weapons.

Two years later came the 9/11 tragedy. Very shortly thereafter, a furious United States launched massive air raids (about ten B-52Hs were included in the heavy bomber component) against its perpetrators—Al Qaeda terrorists and the Taliban located in Afghanistan. Altogether during the course of Operation Enduring Freedom, American attack aircraft, in very close coordination with U.S. Special Forces that were targeting the enemy from the ground (just a couple of hundred brave men altogether, some from horseback—evoking images of nineteenth-century cavalry charges along the nearby Khyber Pass), delivered six thousand JDAMs and six thousand laser-guided bombs, accounting for about two-thirds of all dropped bomb tonnage. These combined air/ground strike teams proved remarkably successful with their real-time attacks against such highly "perishable" and/or moving guerrilla targets—what was, in fact, the old Arc Light Bugle Note concept carried through to the nth degree. By the end of March 2002, the Al Qaeda terror network in Afghanistan had itself been "terrorized," its organization destroyed, and the Taliban government driven from power (though as this is written, current events suggest the final stages of the Afghan campaign have yet to play out).

In the spring of 2003, Operation Iraqi Freedom, or the "second Gulf War," was initiated. For the B-52Hs, the action began on March 21, when BUFFs from RAF Fairford and Diego Garcia joined seven hundred other attack aircraft todeliver the "shock and awe" assault against Saddam Hussein's regime. Over the next several weeks, "Stratoforts ranged across the entire country, attacking command and control centers, communications facilities, and defenseemplacements." The B-52s were particular effective in "preparing the battlefield ahead of rapidly advancing Coalition ground forces."

During Iraqi Freedom, the big bombers fully matured into their new twenty-first-century role. Working in complete concert with joint and unified allied commands, the BUFFs were available on a 24/7 basis, ready to throw anything and everything they had at the bad guys, including for the first time in combat, the new CBU-105 wind-corrected munitions dispensers (WCMDs), or "smart-guided" cluster bombs.[6] By the time open hostilities in Iraq ended in late April 2003, the approximately twenty-eight B-52Hs engaged had once again demonstrated to the world—if it indeed still needed any convincing—that America's Big Ugly Fat Fellow still had, and would continue to have into the foreseeable future, one heck of a punch.

This is what the B-52H Stratofortress long-range multirole bomber brings to the party today:

- Continues to be USAF's principal nuclear strike vehicle, conventional weapons platform, and "power projector."
- Current total weapons payload capacity of 70,000 pounds.
- Nuclear weapons capability that includes advanced cruise missiles(ACMs), air-launched cruise missiles (ALCMs), and gravity bombs.
- Conventional weapons capability that includes antiship Harpoon mis siles, selected Navy mines, air-to-ground Raptor missiles, convention al ALCMs, joint stand-off weapons (JSOWs), JDAMs, WCMDs, and gravity bombs.
- The very latest in ECM, including multiband threat recognition and multiple threat jammers, multiple threat radar warning systems, digital warning receivers that can simultaneously identify up to sixteen radar signals, jammers with multiple-band 360-degree coverage, false target generators, noise jammers, tail warning sets, and infrared flare and chaff dispensers.
- The latest in low-altitude, electro-optical forward image viewing, plus recent upgrades in radar altimeters, heading and reference systems, inertial navigation systems, and a bomb/nav computer network (to help handle the new precision weapons) called the Offensive Avionics System (OAS).
- Worldwide reach, unlimited operational range (with air refueling).
- All-weather, day/night navigation and strike capability.

No doubt more "brush-fire" conflicts of the Desert Storm, Allied Force, Enduring Freedom, and Iraqi Freedom variety will be coming our way in the decades to come. USAF Air Combat Command (ACC), "the primary provider of combat air forces to America's combatant commands," has a large and imposing roster of fast-response attack aircraft ready to meet that threat, including (but not limited to) the B-52H, the B-1B Lancer bomber, the B-2 Spirit stealth bomber, the backbone F-15 Eagle and F-16 Fighting Falcon tactical/strike fighters, the F-22 Raptor advanced stealth fighter (replacing the F-117, retired in 2008), and the in-development, extremely versatile F-35 Lightning II Joint Strike Fighter. Operating under the new joint service operational philosophy (all theater Army, Navy, and Air Force units reporting to a single unified command), these aircraft will be a major factor in keeping the United States the world's dominant air power.

And to further ensure that edge will not be lost, ACC has ginned up something entirely new, a revolutionary class of weapon platforms that might very well become the leading attack element in all future conflicts. We are talking here about the amazing breakthrough of all-weather, remote-controlled, unmanned aerial vehicles (UAVs), pilotless aircraft that have the astonishing ability to conduct crucial reconnaissance and bomb enemy targets while under the remote control of an operator many miles away.

Although various types of drones and remote-flown aircraft have been used for decades (particularly target drones), a true UAV capability, as we understand it today, did not become available until the 1990s. The most important of these first-generation UAVs (they are now coming in all sizes and shapes—from hand-launched models to regular airplane dimensions) was the RQ-1/MQ-1 Predator, "a long-endurance, medium-altitude unmanned aircraft system for surveillance and reconnaissance missions." Powered by a simple four-cylinder 115 HP engine, the robot craft cruises at 84 mph, has a range of 400 nautical miles, and a ceiling of 25,000 feet. Although modest in size and performance, the tireless Predator has, since its 1995 debut in Bosnia, been continuously gathering critically important and almost certainly otherwise unattainable intelligence from trouble spots all over the globe.

Following the success of the Predator, more advanced UAVs were quickly brought on-line. The next generation Global Hawk UAV-3 offered even more sophistication with regard to remote reconnaissance, and it was followed by the cutting-edge MQ-9 Reaper, which was introduced to "hot fieldwork" in 2005 (with a final decision on its full rollout scheduled for 2009). The Reaper moved the UAV up from not just a great surveillance vehicle but also a lethal attack weapon, the Air Force's first hunter-killer UAV. It's "more powerful than the Predator [which has been subsequently armed with warheads as well] and is designed to go after time-sensitive targets with persistence and precision, and destroy or disable those targets with 500-pound bombs and Hellfire missiles."

We can be assured that as these words are written, there are in the works yet more projects aimed at improving even the Reaper. It is frankly astonishing how much flight/combat technology has advanced in just a few decades, and, what's more, continues to gain headway at a seemingly ever-increasing pace—is it not a distinct possibility that in the not-so-distant future many, if not most, attack aircraft will be flown robotically?[7]

Yet, before we are completely swept away by these extraordinary Buck

Rogers–type weapons, perhaps an old-fashioned bomber crewdog might offer up a caveat or two. To be perfectly blunt, it would be a mistake to swallow whole this tempting "war on the cheap" bait dangling in front of us and completely abandon the concept of manned airborne weapon systems. There are real dangers in allowing our air defense forces to become overreliant on pure technology, a caution that particularly applies to future, fully automated (no-pilot), stealth-type fighter/bombers and the current drone-styled unmanned aerial vehicles. While in the eyes of the lay public, video game war making and attack robots are almost irresistibly dazzling, those same features can potentially render a weapon system too remote from the battlefield, subjecting the vehicle to unknown, unrecognized hazards and perhaps even making their "no-risk" employment dangerously overattractive.

Certainly no argument can be made against the to-date success of robotic craft in meeting their primary mission requirements of reconnaissance and clandestine hunter-killer actions. They have performed beyond all expectations and at a refreshingly modest cost. Yet it must be pointed out that most of these automated systems have not yet been completely proven out under sustained heavy operations while taking direct enemy fire, which is to say they have not yet been thoroughly battle tested. Individuals who have been in combat can say with the certainty of personal experience that the more complex and automatic a weapon system is, the more likely it is to break down (and remain unrepairable) in the fiery chaos of a prolonged and desperate fight. One has only to refer back a few pages to the fate of the then "more modern, electronically interlocking systems" Linebacker B-52Gs for a classic example.

To say all this another way, there is real peril in 1) putting too much faith in ultrasophisticated weapon technology that cannot absorb even the slightest battle damage without it proving fatal to the equipment (think of the modern automobile electronic ignition module and how even the tiniest foreign object—a BB pellet would do it—can completely disable the entire vehicle), and 2) not taking into account a largely undiscussed, but quite serious disadvantage of remote robotic combat—the absence of sometimes critical on-the-spot human judgment and ingenuity. While there can be no question these futuristic weapons systems can and must be aggressively developed and deployed, it should never be forgotten that this is all fertile ground for one or more catastrophic violations of Murphy's Law, and thumbing one's nose at that ancient leprechaun and gremlin chieftain is not something to take lightly.

Alas, such ponderings are no longer within the actionable provinces of Vietnam-era B-52 aircrewmen. They who were schooled in the now obsolete

ASQ-48 and -38 bombing and navigation systems are themselvesbecoming obsolete, unfamiliar (sometimes even unnerved) by the modern war technologies and aircrew philosophies embraced by their warrior children and grandchildren. Products of an analog rather than a digital age, these dinosaurs and their Vietnam/Cold War B-52s are to the young people of today relics from an ancient past. The time cannot be very far off when their out-of-date story slides permanently into the mist (save a few obscure history books) and that will be the last heard of "Peace Is Our Profession," Mole Holes, Coco exercises, tall tail Bufs, ear-splitting J-57 water takeoffs, sextant observations, "the counters," pilot's deflection indicators, radar synchronous deliveries, offset aiming points, ATF, TRAIL, and "dumb bombs."

And pretty darn soon, the last will be heard of "navigators" and "bombardiers" as well. In 2004 the Air Force announced those positions (along with the "electronic warfare officer") would be phased out over the next half decade. In their place, to fill the nonpilot officer aircrew slots, will come the combat systems operator (CSO). The long-range plan involves a joint-service venture, calling for all Air Force and U.S. Navy CSO training to be jointly and variously conducted at Randolph AFB, Texas, and Pensacola Naval Air Station (NAS), Florida, with Pensacola eventually becoming the sole facility. The men and women selected for CSO will learn three basic subspecialties: basic (or panel) navigator, EWO, and weapons systems operator/officer (WSO).[8] According to official USAF release-ese, "the goal is to develop a young officer with superior airmanship and some knowledge of weapons employment and electronic warfare tactics." New CSO graduates "will fly missions in bomber, strike fighter, airlift, tanker, and electronic warfare aircraft." In other words, because of the tremendous advances in technology and automation, it has become possible to combine navigator, bombardier, electronic warfare officer, and weapons systems officer training into a single program.

Even most of the dinosaurs would have to agree such a change makes sense—just as the coming of all-metal, multiengine monoplane bombers in the 1930s called for formally trained nonpilot aircrew, so likewise does the era of automated satellite navigation, digital electronic flight systems, programmable smart bombs, cruise missiles, and unmanned aerial vehicles require fewer but more technologically sophisticated aircrewpersons. What's more, the Pentagon insists the new program will improve nonpilot aircrew career prospects, something sorely needed in an Air Force with a long tradition of "pilot" promotional bias. Perhaps it will work out that way—in 2007 the USAF announced a certain number of qualified CSOs (minimum of Federal

Aviation Administration [FAA] private pilot certification required) would be trained to operate UAVs, relieving the expensive requirement of having the vehicles flown only by rated service pilots and opening up new possibilities in the size of a robot aircraft fleet and its overall combat capability.

And so there it is—in the space of less than one human lifetime (1940–2004), the rated military professions of navigator, bombardier, and electronic warfare officer were born, grew up during a world war, came into their majority and middle age during several regional wars and a global Cold War, and then died quietly and nearly unnoticed. To paraphrase the almost self-mocking epitaph inscribed on more than one frontier Boot Hill tombstone: "They lived a short, but hard life."

AFTERWORD

While contemporary academicians, scholars, and historians continue to formally debate, discuss, teach, and write about the long-term effect of the Vietnam War and the B-52's role in it—as well they should—even casual mention of the subject to the Stratofortress Combat Crews themselves generates a much more visceral reaction. This is especially the case with the Linebacker Two veterans. For them, that last big deciding battle was the defining moment of not only the war but their own lives as well. Whatever personal remembrances and perceptions of that time they still carry with them today are instead far more likely to be focused through the prism of a single one-star general officer.

Furious over Omaha's deeply flawed Linebacker Two attack plan, Brig. Gen. Glenn Sullivan, commander of the 17th Air Division at U-Tapao, made a risky personal decision to contact CINCSAC directly and raise hell over the manner in which the battle was being waged. By slashing across the chain of command and openly waving the red flag, Sullivan accomplished three things: 1) desperately needed changes in air combat tactics, which probably saved the operation from disaster, 2) the undying gratitude of the B-52 crews, and 3) the ruination of his own career. Top generals have long memories regarding other senior officers who bypass channels and make them look bad, and SAC's were no exception. Passed over for promotion, Sullivan was retired a couple of years later, departing this life in obscurity on January 29, 1998.

That invisibleness is likely to remain, thanks to self-serving historical monographs that ignored his contributions, official position papers that distorted the battle's events, another star or two that were not to be, and the lost fame that was his rightful due. And yet, in a way, one that perhaps would be difficult for nonaircrew to understand, those thirty-five years of establishment snubs are no longer of any real consequence. Only one thing ever was, and still remains, important—what he left behind in the hearts of the men who served under him. For there can be not a doubt that when the Maker's

Balance Sheets are finally reconciled and the B-52 Linebacker aircrews are summoned for their Last Great Mission together, it will be Glenn Sullivan flying Wave Lead.

The general would probably be the first to agree that SAC's primary personality trait, its deeply embedded doctrinaire philosophy, was both its strength and its Achilles heel. That dominant characteristic can be traced all the way back to the creation, when Curtis LeMay decided that groupthink and collective decision making, as opposed to individual initiative, would be the foundation on which he built his Strategic Air Command. And, frankly, the concept worked quite nicely in a Cold War nuclear deterrence environment—when one is dealing with atomic weapons, there can be no room for improvisation or mistakes. Strict organizational rules, careful attention to detail in all activities, precise flight training syllabuses, absolutely no deviation from established air or ground alert procedures, human reliability, fail safe, positive control—those were the pillars that held up the House of SAC.

But while that formalized, inflexible approach served Strategic Air Command and the nation well in a "Peace Is Our Profession" Cold War environment, it caused many problems in the conventional Vietnam conflict. Men engaged in hot combat must be light on their feet and not wedded to any specific methodology, ready on a moment's notice to react to changing battlefield conditions—promptly chucking that which doesn't work and replacing it with that which does. And there was the real quandary when it came to Southeast Asia, and especially Operation Linebacker Two. The very qualities most prized in a conventional fight were so completely counterintuitive to long-established SAC culture that it nearly resulted in a catastrophe over Hanoi.

And now, on behalf of all who have patiently journeyed with us through these many pages, we must ask the terrible question: How could the SAC leadership, they who had done such a remarkably good job running their aspect of the war for seven and one-half years, have so completely botched the planning for the climactic Linebacker Two battle?

Surely the generals were intelligent, dedicated men. Surely they had the best interest of the country at heart. Most top SAC leaders were heavily decorated World War II veterans, courageous bomber and fighter pilots all. Both CINCSAC and the Eighth Air Force commander were aces several times over. Such men were not amateurs at war, nor did they spook easily. Why, then, with all that battle-hardened experience, did Omaha rush into the planning with such apparent carelessness? Why were the nearly fatal planning flaws not perceived at the outset? Why wasn't quick and decisive action taken to correct those problems once they had been so clearly manifested after Day One, possibly averting the Day Three disaster? Why did the leadership shun both initial combat crew input to the attack plan and subsequent feedback during Days One through Three? Most stunningly, how could they have so completely disregarded the desperate pleas coming from their farthest forward-field general?

Reader, here is the task. Take a few moments to consider all that has been presented in this book regarding Strategic Air Command doctrine and culture, and then put yourself in the place of the top Linebacker commanders, along with all the institutional and personal baggage each man carried on December 18, 1972. Upon such reflection, and after discounting the wisdom of hindsight, can one still be so very surprised that when SAC first found itself sucked into a poorly understood, unwanted conventional Southeast Asian war, it would preserve its operational integrity by transferring long-established (nuclear) procedures into the new iron-bomb Arc Light program? And that, when the Linebacker Two operation abruptly and unexpectedly dropped into its lap after seven-plus years of doing everything a certain way under the Arc Light tent, Omaha would resist spur-of-the-moment ideas and revert to those same long-practiced, widely accepted tactics? And that, while attempting to direct the campaign from ten thousand miles away, a career fighter pilot who probably shouldn't have been CINC-SAC in the first place would hamstring the line commanders further by not admitting to himself that he'd lost control? And that, now worried even sicker about keeping everything right with the White House, said same supreme commander would continue to hold the entire operation under tight in-house control at Omaha? And that, because of the resulting built-in communication delays, inattention to fast-breaking battlefield intelligence, conflicting personal agendas up and down the chain of command, an inbred fear within SAC of opposing any higher ranking officer, and the overall confusion of war, subordinate colonels and generals would become unwitting coconspirators in the breakdown?

To veteran Arc Light and Linebacker aircrewmen, no, none of it comes as a surprise. Deeply unfortunate and disappointing? To be sure. But not a surprise.

In the final analysis, however, and despite all the mistakes, dissembling, and, yes, probably needless waste of men and bombers, the job still got done. The contemporary 1973 verdict on the Christmas bombings has held up on appeal. Historians continue to agree that Linebacker Two achieved its limited but nevertheless crucial geopolitical goals: the honorable extrication of the nation from the war.

As for those questionable Linebacker attack tactics, it is probably safe to say that in the great scheme of things, they are destined to remain historical footnotes—important to the participants, certainly, but irrelevant to the final result. What will be remembered is that North Vietnam returned to the Paris Peace talks in early January 1973, and they did it for three basic reasons: 1) Their defensive capability had collapsed, 2) a large portion of North Vietnam's national infrastructure had already been destroyed, and 3) continued B-52 bombing against the country's defenseless cities meant complete annihilation.

The only thing that could have stopped Linebacker Two from succeeding was the Soviet-supplied SA-2 Guideline surface-to-air missile. Surprisingly, pre-Linebacker threat concerns had been almost entirely focused on MiGs and B-52 midair collisions; Omaha completely underestimated the SAM threat. While the enemy fighters and flak had constantly to be monitored, it was the SAMs that did the damage. And, oddly enough, they ultimately decided the battle, though in a way no one could possibly have predicted.

By relying almost solely on limited quantities of imported antiaircraft missiles for its defense, the NVA had made the crucial mistake of gathering all its eggs in one basket. They then, in the heat of battle, compounded the error by succumbing to zeal. The unrelenting attacks by the B-52s and other U.S. strike aircraft so enraged the North Vietnamese army that the enemy was provoked into expending missiles wholesale, sometimes in salvos of six or eight against a single target. As a result, in their unrestrained enthusiasm to shoot the bombers down, the North Vietnamese ran themselves out of irreplaceable ammunition. There was an even stranger twist; a chilling argument can be made that SAC's poor tactics—that is, B-52 bombers turned missile bait—actually worked to the Americans' advantage. Think of the fight-movie characters Rocky Balboa and Apollo Creed. Rocky made Creed throw so many punches that, even though many of them landed, Rocky was strong enough to wear Creed out from the effort and thus achieve the final knockout.

In the parlance of another sport, American football, this is called "winning ugly." When studying military history, one finds that such outcomes are more often the case than not; rare it is that great victories come through heroic feats of arms or brilliant generalship. Far likelier, the matter comes down to who had the best luck, which side made the fewest mistakes, who had the most weapons and greatest logistical capability, and which of the belligerents was strong enough to wrestle the other fellow to the ground. As the football coaches declare after having emerged victorious from one of their own slug-fests, no matter how unbecoming the game might have been to spectators, "it still counts as a win."

It should also be mentioned (one hesitates to say in passing) that relative to previous large air battles waged over dense urban areas, especially the World War II carpet-bombing bloodbaths that took hundreds of thousands of civilian lives, Linebacker-inflicted ground casualties were comparatively light, fewer than two thousand Vietnamese. This result can be attributed to both the United States' authentic desire to avoid human "collateral damage" and the dedicated professionalism of American combat airmen.

A few days following the sixty-ship attack on the evening of December 29/30, 1972, what in all probability was the world's last massed, heavy bomber raid, North Vietnam returned to the conference table. After a few more weeks of diplomatic wrangling, the Paris Peace Accords were signed on January 27, 1973. Between February 12 and April 1, 591 American prisoners of war were released under "Operation Homecoming." In the fall of that year, completely war-exhausted as a nation and with its POWs now back on American soil, the United States took itself permanently out of the Southeast Asian conflict.

The terms of the Paris treaty and its aftermath left the South Vietnamese to mostly fend for themselves. The "decent interval," as former U.S. national security adviser and secretary of state Henry Kissinger characterized that period between the Yankee departure from Southeast Asia and when it became certain the United States would never again intervene militarily in South Vietnam's behalf, lasted about two years. By April 1975 the end had come. Broadcasting images forever engraved on the American psyche, television sets across the nation depicted the final horror—helicopters evacuating hordes of loyalist refugees from atop downtown Saigon buildings. The people's desperation to leave was matched only by the bitterness of all the U.S. soldiers who had sacrificed so much to prevent such an event from ever happening.

In Hanoi there was great joy. From the North Vietnamese viewpoint, the long war of liberation had at last been won. After centuries of struggle, the country was reunified and rid of foreign influences—free of China, free of

Japan, free of France, free of America. Following a years-long interregnum of bitter internal strife and continuing border conflicts (especially with Cambodia and China), Vietnam rejoined the family of nations. Diplomatic relations were restored between the two onetime enemies and, wonder of wonders, a former American POW, Douglas "Pete" Peterson, was appointed the first U.S. ambassador to the Socialist Republic of Vietnam.

Operation Linebacker Two was costly to the relatively small, tightly knit Stratofortress community. Over the course of eleven days and 729 sorties, six B-52s suffered minor hits, three were seriously damaged, and fifteen were shot down (all by SAMs). Ninety-two Buf crew members had been in the bombers lost. Of that number, twenty-six were rescued, thirty-three were captured, and thirty-three were killed. (Although several men may still technically be missing in action, all that had been in that classification are now believed dead.) Also, two additional B-52s were shot down just before and after the battle, with all twelve men aboard rescued.

That wasn't the only American blood spilled—the Air Force's tactical fighters, ECM platforms, and support birds, along with U.S. Marine and Naval Aviation, paid a price as well. Those losses included two Navy A-6A carrier strike aircraft, one Marine A-6A strike aircraft, one Navy A-7C carrier strike aircraft, one Navy A-7E carrier strike aircraft, one Marine F-4J carrier fighter, one Navy RA-5C recon aircraft, two Air Force F111A fighter-bombers, two Air Force F-4E fighter/chaff sowers, one Air Force EB-66 ECM/chaff sower, and one HH-53 Jolly Green Giant rescue helicopter. Two of these aircraft were lost to SAMs, three to MiGs, three to flak, one to small arms (Jolly Green), one to engine failure (EB-66), and three others to unknown causes. From among the crewmen that flew those machines, two were rescued, eight were captured, and eleven were killed in action—with perhaps two more unrecorded casualties, unknown to all but their mates and families.

During the Linebacker Two operation, 15,000 tons of bombs were dropped from B-52 Stratofortresses on thirty-four targets that included military airfields, electric power plants and transmission facilities, petroleum refineries, war materiel storage warehouses, assembly plants, railroad stations and transshipment yards, surface-to-air missile storage and launch sites, and the enemy's communication, command, and control network. The NVA launched about one thousand SAMs against the heavy bombers, of which only a relatively small number actually hit their prey.

As for those Buf crewdogs who survived what they refer to among themselves as either "the eleven-day war" or "the Christmas bombing," most were still alive at the dawn of the new millennium. A few continued to work; the majority had retired to the golf course or fishing boat. For many, the Linebacker operation had receded so far into the past that it almost seemed like it had happened to someone else, as if the memories were no longer their own but, instead, of a film they'd once seen or a book long ago read. They knew that wasn't so, of course, but the disconnect was there, and it had continued to grow over the years, the details of that December slowly dissolving away.

Yet there were days when all of it came rushing back with ice-water clarity—when the morning newspapers describing the latest foreign outrage would be angrily thrown against the breakfast dishes. Suddenly, the gray eagles found themselves aroused young warriors again, and it was only the night before they were over Hanoi. For just an instant, not a few wondered if the Air Force might take them back, that maybe there was still something useful they could do. That perhaps they might be allowed to strike just one more blow against those who would destroy all that B-52 combat crewmen had dedicated their lives to preserve. One of their own's personal story illustrates this anguish better than anything else.

It began on the night of December 26, 1972. He was the copilot on Ash One when it was struck by a SAM while attacking Hanoi's Kinh No rail yard. With the aircraft commander and gunner wounded and the B-52D severely crippled, the crew headed for U-Tapao. During final approach, the pilot encountered flight control problems and when the copilot lowered the gear, the ship stopped responding to yoke and rudder. The pilot attempted a go-around but the aircraft stalled and crashed off the end of the runway. Gunner Grippin escaped when the tail broke off on impact, but Turner, Joyner, Marshall, and Tabler perished, with only the copilot surviving in the forward compartment. Grievously wounded, he was pulled from the burning wreckage by a gallant Buf pilot who had only just landed himself. Expected to die and with last rites administered, the copilot somehow survived.

On a sunny morning nearly three decades later, former B-52 copilot, Defense Intelligence Agency analyst, and retired Lt. Col. Robert J. Hymel was on duty at his desk in the Pentagon. While preparing to move to a new work station, he was killed when a hostile aircraft crashed into the building. Mindful of the irony in his death, his wife, Pat, said she was grateful God had given them another twenty-nine years together. Bob Hymel's last action came on Tuesday, September 11, 2001.

And the beat goes on . . . .

ACKNOWLEDGMENTS

The bulk of the source material for this effort came from my own SAC/Arc Light experiences and personal library of aviation books, military files (orders, maps, charts, logs, etc.), government textbooks, flight manuals, family letters, odd keepsakes/ephemera, forty-year-old scrapbooks, and photo albums. As extensive as that data was, however, it did not provide everything required to round out the bigger picture. This was especially the case with regard to the chapters on early navigation and bombing, the final stages of the Vietnam War, Operation Linebacker Two, and the post-Vietnam B-52 role. A full accounting of those additional references used, plus the key components of my private records, can be found in the bibliography.

Although I did participate in several of the battles discussed in the text, I personally did not haul Linebacker mail. By that time, December of 1972, I was back in the world and living the soft life. As a consequence, it was essential to interview (mostly via e-mail) individual combat crew members who had flown in the "eleven-day war." A few of those men rate special mention. Craig Mizner and his 7th Bomb Wing "Crew E-57 Dog Patch" history were a gold mine of Linebacker lore—plus his navigator, Bill Beavers, read portions of the manuscript and passed along many helpful and specific nav-bomb insights. I am also very grateful to Kincheloe's Crew E-16 radar navigator Wilton Strickland, who flew six out of the eleven Linebacker Two missions and provided a tremendous amount of information on the inbound routes, IPs, offset aiming points, and targets along the Red River valley and in Hanoi and Haiphong. Wilton also steered me to an excellent article written by the late David Zook, an electronic warfare officer who flew four LB2 missions (see bibliography for link). Others who made valuable Linebacker contributions included Dennis Carrier (navigator), Scott Freeman (electronic weapons officer), Phil Newsom (nav), Denny Whalen (radar navigator), and Ray Sullivan (Brig. Gen. Glenn Sullivan's son) and his Teleproduction Group Web site. (See bibliography.)

I also realized I needed a much better grasp of electronic warfare officer wizardry. Arc Light veteran and UNT classmate John Clemen reviewed portions of the manuscript and shared many particulars about ECM/black box procedures and nomenclature. "Raven" Phil Rowe, who has written prolifically on the web about electronic warfare and his B-52 experiences, cleared up a lot of stuff I had been wondering about for forty years. Bill Senkel, an old 306th Bomb Wing colleague, Arc Light veteran, and Korean War–era "Old Crow" carefully read and commented on the entire manuscript in his always-thorough and reliable manner.

Many thanks are due the 306th Bomb Wing Alumni Association for its large measure of cooperation and encouragement. Special mentions go to the aforementioned Bill Senkel; long-time B-52D aircraft commanders and Arc Light veterans Tim Daugherty, George "Tony" Sayre, and Charlie Hale; and radar navigator Joe Demes. Joe, whose nav/bomb career began with World War II B-26s (fifty-eight missions over France and Germany) and extended well into the B-52D/Vietnam era, led the manuscript reading rounds and made sure I received timely feedback.

I am also deeply grateful to a number of our World War II and Korean War brethren for their many articles through the years in the Air Force Navigators Observers Association (AFNOA) newsletters. Particular nods go to Bruce Callander, Ken Ablett, and John Howland for their incisive and valuable written work on navigation and bombing. (See bibliography.) Ken Ablett also reviewed portions of the manuscript and offered many constructive comments and corrections. Bombardier Russell Woinowsk, another AFNOA member who flew heavy bomber combat missions during both World War II and Korea, had some very interesting Norden and Sperry perspectives, having himself been among the nation's first formally trained instructor bombardiers (graduated with the first three classes of 125 men). Trained in 1940 at Lowry's Instructor Bombardier School, Russell personally helped establish the new bombardier schools going up at Barksdale, Ellington, Midland, and Big Springs.

The Internet is a wonderful resource (when cautiously used), supplying a great deal of technical data and locating what would otherwise be difficult to access primary source information. Those sites providing specific contributions are listed in the bibliography.

A deep-seated need by former B-52 combat crewmen to tell their individual stories has in recent years resulted in a growing number of self-published books (listed separately in the bibliography, along with individual thumbnail summaries and ordering information). These efforts helped enormously to jog my memory and fill in the blanks. Wilton Strickland's *In the BUFF* and AC/pilot James Hooppaw's *Where the Buf Fellows Roamed* were especially useful. All of them would be of interest to anyone wishing to learn more about B-52 "inside stuff."

Special thanks are due Rick Russell and the Naval Institute Press for believing in the raw manuscript and to Elizabeth Bauman, George Keating, Judy Heise, Susan Corrado, Gary Kessler, Chris Robinson, and the rest of the hard-working NIP team for their help in shaping it into a finished book.

There is one published source I am compelled to especially single out. Marshall L. Michel's book, *The Eleven Days of Christmas* (see bibliography), stands out above all others as the most important and accurate analysis ever done of the Linebacker Two campaign. For the first time, Michel tells the complete story—warts and all—and from both the American and North Vietnamese points of view. He traveled to Hanoi and personally interviewed NVA commanders and SAM missile battery crews who actually participated in the battle, recording priceless perspectives that have significantly increased our understanding of what happened. I am extremely indebted to Michel, not only for writing such a well-documented book but also for the inspiration his work provided. (I started thinking about *Flying from the Black Hole* immediately after putting *Eleven Days* down.)

Specifically (but not exclusively), Michel should be given credit for bringing into the full light of day the following about Operation Linebacker Two:

- Providing the most exhaustive chronology of events yet published leading up to and during the battle.

- Exposing the conflicts of interest and subsequent communications /leadership breakdowns within SAC's chain of command.

- Debunking self-serving official U.S. Air Force monographs and pointing out the unsavory disconnect between the Air Force's candid, in-house after-action LB2 battle reports and its subsequent "CYA" public position.

- An in-depth analysis of the controversial late-1970s magazine articles written and/or inspired by Dana Drenkowski, a former F-4 and B-52 pilot, regarding the Air Force's lapses during the battle. Michel concludes the charges by Drenkowski, who was publicly vilified by the Air Force at that time, were largely correct.

- Thoroughly airing the ugly realities of the poor attack tactics used during the first three days.

- Laying to rest the long-standing, untrue rumors regarding wholesale B-52 crew mutinies during Linebacker (a handful of men did refuse to fly—Michel believes fewer than five, a smaller number percentage-wise than that seen during 8th Air Force's World War II assault against Nazi Germany).

- Perspectives on the battle from the North Vietnamese army's viewpoint —exclusive interviews with key enemy soldiers that provide both a fuller understanding of the Linebacker battle and a fascinating insight as to the tenaciousness of the enemy and why they prevailed in the end.

- Helping to resurrect the official reputation of Brig. Gen. Glenn Sullivan.

- Pointing out a striking, watershed moment—the December 29, 1972, raid may have been the last great massed bomber attack in history.

Himself a former F-4 Phantom pilot who flew combat missions during Linebacker Two (how very ironic it took a fighter jock to properly tell the story!), Michel's book is the gold standard on the subject, a must-read for anyone interested in the most decisive air battle of the Vietnam War.

Lastly, it is important to say aloud that whatever weaknesses and outright blunders *Flying from the Black Hole* might still contain are my responsibility alone.

NOTES

CHAPTER 2. A BOOMING SOUND

1. "What good is it?" harrumphed a Parisian to the American diplomat standing next to him, as the two observed an earlier unmanned Montgolfier ascension. "What good," retorted Dr. Benjamin Franklin, "is a new-born baby?"
2. Henceforth, our discussions will be confined to American-manufactured aircraft, unless otherwise noted.
3. U.S. Army Air Corps 2nd Lt. Orvis Nelson went from Kelly Field Keystones in 1933, to the transitional biwing Curtiss Condors when he flew the mail for the Army in February/March 1934, to the Martin B-10Bs at Hamilton Field, California, in 1935. It was like going from a covered wagon to a Ford Model T to a Maserati.
4. A few comments about "standard" aircraft performance numbers: Published specifications and officially supplied flight data should always be handled with care; better it is to think of the information as the machine's "in-a-perfect-world" capability rather than an expected everyday result. Performance always varies between test factory aircraft functioning in ideal environments and the values generated from an entire fleet of airplanes operating over an extended period of time under daily flying and maintenance conditions. Also, unfiltered "official" statistics nearly always originate with the plane maker and/or the military end user, either of whom may have certain axes to grind with the data's publication. Lastly, what is almost never made clear to lay readers is that any aircraft's performance involves tradeoffs in payload, speed, and range.

   For example, most aviation reference books list maximum cruise speed of the B-17G at 300 to 315 mph. Those numbers would bring wry smiles to former Fort crew; it was a rare event for any war-time B-17 to crank out the miles that fast. Why this seeming contradiction? Here's a quick illustration that sheds some light: If a lightly loaded B-17G is cruising in the thinner air at 25,000 or 30,000 feet, and the throttles are wide open, and nobody cares about gas consumption, the airplane might crank out the promised 300 mph. But if that same Fort is loaded to the gills with gas and bombs and forced to plug along in lower, denser air, and the engines need to run on lean mixtures and at reduced power settings because the airplane is headed deep into Germany and it's going to be close as to whether there's enough juice to get back to England, the crew might have trouble coaxing out 150 mph. A reasonable cruise speed for a "normally" operating World War II B-17 was in the neighborhood of 160 to 180 mph.

CHAPTER 3. THE BIG UGLY FELLER

1. The Boeing engineers present at the Van Cleve included Vaughn Blumenthal, Art Carlsen, Maynard Pennell, George Schairer, Ed Wells, and "Bob" Withington. Among

the uniforms that sent them there were Curtis LeMay, "Pete" Warden, and K. B. Wolfe. Later, others joined the team—U.S. Air Force test pilots Tex Johnson and Guy Townsend, along with Richard Loesch and Art Curran; USAF's John Elrod, representing the bombardier/navigators; and engineers John Alexander, "Bev" Hodges, "Larry" Lee, George Martin, Jack Nelson, and T. A. Wilson, along with executive Wellwood Beall, all of Boeing. Many others also made important contributions to the multiyear development program; these were the men either there at the beginning or key to the final result.

2. Interestingly, twenty-seven of the B models became sneaky recon birds instead of operational bombers.

3. The Hound Dog, with one missile mounted under each wing, was operational SAC armament for many years. It could carry a nuclear warhead, was capable of Mach 2+, and had roughly a 500-mile range. The navigator was responsible for programming it in flight; a rather onerous, extra duty most navs did not care for, though the pilots didn't mind the Hound Dogs—their turbojet engines could be used as extra thrust in an emergency. The AGM-28's technology was relatively primitive, and it was difficult while airborne to maintain a good current position inside the missile's "brain," an absolute requirement if one of those just-launched little pointy white things was to have any chance of hitting its target. SAC believed in the Hound Dog, however, and the entire B-52 fleet was quickly modified to accept it. The next-generation, technologically superior Skybolt was canceled by the Kennedy administration, even though it appeared to be working as advertised in the test program. (Whether it was actually needed is, of course, another matter—the Soviet Union did fold without it.) Apparently, however, much of the Skybolt research and development (R&D) did not go to waste, as we see manifested today in the nation's outstanding cruise missile capability.

4. These extra crew positions represent a typical B-52D. Some bombers also had an instructor EW position, which like the bunk station wasn't officially legal for a man to occupy during takeoffs and landings—not to say such things didn't happen once in a while. Other models had slightly different extra-crew seating arrangements, particularly the Gs and Hs.

5. The B-47 had a three-man crew. The RO was alone in a small lower compartment near the nose; the pilot and copilot sat in fighter pilot–like tandem fashion under a clear canopy atop the fuselage. The copilot was able to reverse his rear seat so he could also function as the tail gunner.

6. Most Vietnam-era B-52 crewmen consider the three-letter "Buf/BUF" acronym the purer form. Recent usage, however, has favored the capitalized "BUFF," which is perhaps OK in that it preserves the expression as the bold four-letter word it ought to be.

CHAPTER 4. LEMAY

1. It was "atomic bombs" and "atomic war" before the 1953 development of thermonuclear weapons, after which it became "hydrogen bombs." Subsequently, such phrases as "nuclear bomb" and "nuclear war" were used more and more frequently.

2. Astonishingly, records indicate that on January 1, 1947, the United States had only nine atomic bombs in its inventory (later in the year, President Harry Truman privately told one of his old World War I "Battery B" mates that the nation didn't have much of a club to use against the Russians, because he "only had fourteen atomic bombs"), an

indication of just how difficult and expensive it was (and hopefully still is) to manufacture weapons-grade uranium and/or plutonium.

3. The SAC "spot promotion" system was bitterly resented by Air Force officers in other commands, especially the fighter pilots, whose role in the new age of SAC bomber hegemony was already becoming seriously diminished.

4. The last KC-97 was built on the same day the first KC-135 jet tanker came off the line. The KC-97s were just too slow for the B-52 (the tank had to go into a shallow dive to keep the Stratofortress above stall speed) and the Air Force replaced them with 135s as quickly as possible.

5. "Bombs Away" LeMay, as he was sometimes referred to, was the inspiration for the foaming-at-the-mouth general played by the actor George C. Scott in the movie Dr. Strangelove.

CHAPTER 5. EARLY NAVIGATORS AND BOMB AIMERS

1. "Knot" isn't an abbreviation for "nautical" mile (the two words are phonetic coincidences). And to say "knots per hour" is incorrect; the word knot already incorporates velocity. Still, the two terms are connected. Because one minute of latitude equals one nautical mile (handy when using dividers to measure miles on a chart), it became a natural convention for sailors, and later flyers, to cause "one knot" to become equal to "one nautical mile per hour."

2. Latitude is the angular distance north or south of the equator, as measured from 0 degrees at the equator through 90 degrees at the poles. Latitude lines are always parallel to the equator and each other; sixty nautical miles separate each degree of latitude.

3. Longitude represents the east or west angular component on the globe, as measured from 0 through 180 degrees beginning at the Prime Meridian located at Greenwich, England. The International Dateline is precisely opposite Greenwich on the other side of the Earth, 180 degrees away (except where it has been arbitrarily redrawn for political/cultural reasons). Longitude lines converge at both poles; they are not parallel, with the distance between each degree decreasing as latitude increases. Incidentally, most scholars believe the concepts of "latitude" and "longitude" were systemized by the AD second-century Greek/Roman geographer and mapmaker Claudius Ptolemy.

4. The two are essentially the same instrument. A sextant has a maximum angle of 60 degrees between its reflecting mirrors. (Its observable arc describes one-sixth of a circle, or 60 degrees.) An octant (describing one-eighth of a circle) has 45 degrees between mirrors. Octants were used initially in airplanes, but preferences had switched almost exclusively to sextants (greater viewing and operating flexibility) by World War II. Also, because of motion and other three-dimensional issues, aircraft sextants use an enclosed "bubble" to establish an artificial (celestial) horizon. Marine sextants measure altitude above the visible horizon and do not require a bubble.

5. "Fix" is navigator speak for a known position, as opposed to a "DR," a dead-reckoning or presumed position. Each has its own distinct symbol on a working chart: Fix = a triangle with a dot inside it, rendered $\triangle$; DR = a circle with a dot inside it, rendered $\odot$.

6. Dead reckoning or, more precisely, "deduced navigation" can be defined as a pencil and plot method of determining an airplane's current position by advancing a previous-known position using only heading, estimated wind/drift, airspeed, and time elapsed.

7. The landing near Clifden was marred by John Alcock's unwitting descent into what looked like a level meadow but was, in fact, a spongy bog. The aircraft got dinged, but nobody

was hurt. Both men subsequently received a hero's welcome in England. Interestingly, in those very early days of aerial ocean travel, it was believed the navigator, with his seemingly magical pathfinding skills, was more important to the enterprise's success than the pilot.

8. The early development history of aircraft charts, logs, engine meters, flight instrumentation, and formal navigation techniques was much messier (and may never be altogether sorted out) than this brief summary implies. It is difficult today to give specific credit to any one individual or country—during and just after World War I, all the North American and European countries, Imperial Germany especially, made important procedural and technical contributions to the new sciences of flight control and air navigation, sometimes simultaneously.

9. Other significant milestones arising from and/or inspired by Albert F. Hegenberger's team included: The first Army Instrument Flying Course occurred at Kelly Field in 1930. The first dedicated sectional aeronautical chart appeared in 1930. The first DGs (directional gyros) were in use by 1932. Army air navigation procedures were being officially described and separated as dead reckoning, pilotage, celestial, and radio by 1933. The first of the modern-type DR circular slide rules appeared about 1934. The first official Army Air Corps "Celestial Air Navigation" text, written by Lt. Thomas Thurlow, was issued at March Field, California, in 1934.

10. It is stunning how small the U.S. Army Air Corps was at that perilous time. According to Maj. Gen. Norris Harbold (see bibliography), on July 1, 1936, "[among all Army pilots] there were 61 DR navigators, and 30 celestial navigators. . . . There were but 1,789 officers and flying cadets in the [entire] Air Corps on this same date."

11. It is not widely known that the Sperry Company also manufactured gyro-stabilized World War II bombsights. Early on, there were severe shortages of the Norden, and as a consequence, many bomber squadrons were equipped with the more readily available Sperry S-1s. Both sights had their proponents, though the edge had to go to the Norden. The Sperry weighed 75 pounds, versus 35 pounds for the Norden, no small matter from a handling standpoint. Even more important, official military tests conducted from 1940 to 1942 reported that the Norden was superior in ease of operation, accuracy, and maintenance. By late 1944, nearly all the Sperry sights had been replaced by Nordens. By then, the roughly cylindrically shaped, always specially guarded Norden had acquired the inevitable nicknames: in Europe, it was known as "The Football"; in the Pacific, it was "The Blue Ox."

12. Most notably up to that point was an air raid early warning radar designed by Robert Watson-Watt, first employed during the 1940 Battle of Britain.

13. Because of their all-weather, day/night capability, those aircraft equipped with the new H2S systems were usually used as leaders and pathfinders. The bombers had not been designed with a radar operator position, and, as a consequence, the radar equipment and extra crewman had to be jammed into the forward fuselage next to the radio operator. The earliest sets were big, black boxes with huge circular antennas encased in leather that protruded out the device's upper corners. From even a short distance away, the apparatus tended to look like a giant mouse. As a result, and much to the dismay of those first radar operator/bombardiers, they got stuck with being named the "Mickey Men." Two additional comments: 1) The onboard "Mickey" radar sets had no connection with the Oboe/Gee H Cat and Mouse remote transmitter stations, and 2) While the Germans did not have an H2S-type capability, they did have the rough equivalent of Oboe, which they called Knickebein.

14. This discussion simplifies what was an uneven, drawn-out transformation from an all-

pilot bomber crew (excluding enlisted positions) to the formal mix of pilot and non pilot rated officer airmen that was present in the Army Air Force at the time of Pearl Harbor. Also, a word about "observers." This position has long been a nebulous specialty, confusing even to those familiar with military aviation. Basically, the job was kind of a catchall, a crewman who accommodated certain nonpiloting airborne duties that often changed and were difficult to otherwise quantify. It was during World War I (1917) that the man who rode with the pilot first received the official designation of "aerial observer." He had many jobs in those open cockpit days—gunner, navigator, reconnaissance specialist, in-flight repair technician, keeper of the thermos bottle, and so forth. The "observer" title continued to describe nearly all nonpilot officer aircrewmen well into the 1930s and, in some cases, even beyond.

15. Sixty plus years later, the nation's collective memory of the U.S. Army posts that trained nearly 100,000 World War II navigators and bombardiers (both optical and radar) has dimmed to the point of nearly winking out. So as not to allow the irreparable to happen, here are the name/locations of those now nearly forgotten training facilities, as compiled from material published in the Air Force Navigators Observers Association (AFNOA) newsletters. Situated in the milder-weather American south and west, they included Barksdale, LA; Big Springs, TX; Boca Raton, FL; Brooks, TX; Carlsbad, NM; Childress, TX; Coral Gables, FL; Deming, NM; Ellington, TX; Higley, AZ; Hobbs, NM; Hondo, TX; Kelly, TX; Kirtland, NM; Lowry, CO; Mather, CA; Midland, TX; Roswell, NM; Selman, LA; San Angelo, TX; San Marcos, TX; Turner, GA; and Victorville, CA.

16. Some newly graduated World War II navigators and bombardiers were first made "flight officers," then commissioned second lieutenants approximately six months later.

CHAPTER 6. TRAINING THE COLD WAR MAGELLAN

1. Before the Air Force moved the EWO school to Mather, most B-52 "spooks" were trained at Keesler AFB near Biloxi, MS. Also, in a carryover from World War II practices, some of the very early B-52 EWOs were enlisted, noncommissioned officers (sergeants).

2. A common answer "Zoomies" gave when asked what they thought of their "free education" at Colorado Springs went something like this: "I wouldn't do it again for a million dollars." Pause. "But I wouldn't trade it for a million either."

3. ROTC distinguished military graduates (DMGs) were also awarded regular commissions.

4. With Mather the Air Force's only nonpilot flying officer aircrew training facility, that added up to A LOT of second lieutenants in one location. On any given day, over a thousand brown bars (plus many first lieutenants in the advanced schools) could be found scurrying about the base, or in classrooms, or on the flight line. It was quite a revolving door—Mather UNT classes started and graduated every two weeks, with about thirty-five to fifty men in each class. Designated numerically, Class 65-10, for example, graduated its members during the tenth week of 1965.

5. The failure by too many students to properly accomplish too few of these instructions brought an end to UNT parasailing—the large number of broken legs, sprained ankles, and other injuries put a serious crimp in the graduation rate. This was before modern parachutists had devised ways of greatly slowing the rate of descent.

6. Named in 1965 after Lt. Edwin Bleckley, the first aerial observer to receive the Medal of Honor. Bleckley was decorated posthumously in 1918 for his heroic action while

dropping critical supplies to World War I's famed "Lost Battalion."

7. The Mather school inherited an infamous phrase carried over from the days when Texas bases trained most Air Force navigators. On those not infrequent occasions when a celestial student became "temporarily disoriented," he would sometimes resort to a quick look out the window before plotting (or more correctly "backing in") his position. Instructors always referred to this as a Dubhe, Deneb, and Dallas three-star fix.

CHAPTER 7. STRATOFORTRESS BOMBARDIER TRAINING

1. The many types of observer, navigator, bombardier, radar operator, and electronic warfare officer wings issued by the Army and the Air Force beginning in 1917 had by the Vietnam War–era been standardized into a single badge. Navigator-Observer silver wings were identical to the pilot's badge except for a different shield design, which portrayed the USAF Coat of Arms; "its heraldic symbolization depicts Air Force power, in the indivisible mediums of air and space, over all earthbound objects." Once a navigator/observer had achieved seven years of experience and two thousand hours flying time, he became a senior navigator/observer and was authorized to affix a star above his wings. After fifteen years of flying duty and three thousand hours logged time, he wore a silver wreath around his star and was called a master navigator/observer. In the B-52, the navigator, radar navigator, and electronic warfare officer wore the same wings and were all subject to the same senior and master badge criteria.

2. The American version of H2S was designated H2X, which evolved into the APS-15 bombing radar. Because of the postwar proliferation of American-made equipment, the earlier acronyms soon fell into disuse. By the B-36 era, few U.S. personnel were able to connect the dots back to radar bombardment's British origins.

3. Another important bomb aiming transition occurred in the Peacemakers. The Norden-type optical bombsights were finally relegated to backup emergency use only. Although the device was retained in the B-36 (indeed, an optical bombsight would persist all the way into the B-52F), the checklists now gave it just minor peripheral duties, such as poststrike bomb damage assessment. The seemingly insignificant, routinely distributed tech orders directing this change had, in fact, heralded a major turning point—only radar could provide what the future Atomic Age required: all-weather, day or night bombardment.

4. In yet another example of the high fluidity in Air Force nonpilot aircrew positions, this course had a name change in the early 1960s as well, having been previously designated RBN, or radar bombing navigation training.

5. It was at NBT that the boys first learned the Black Hole in-flight trouble-shooting mantra: "RESET, RECYCLE, REPLACE," meaning that when something malfunctioned, first try resetting the related circuit breakers; if that didn't work, try recycling the appropriate switches; and if that still didn't do it, try replacing certain vacuum tubes and/or amplifiers. It was amazing how often this relatively simple exercise cleared up what had initially appeared to be a serious problem.

6. Two men were permanently paired with one another during the entire NBT course, the fellows alternating between the RN and nav positions on their simulator rides and training flights. At the risk of repeating material discussed in previous chapters, in the B-52, the left-seater was predominately the crew bombardier, and he was called the radar navigator. He was also the Black Hole's boss. The man in the right seat was

predominately the crew navigator, and though also trained as a bombardier, was always referred to as the navigator. As a practical matter, both men did both jobs, the one continually covering for the other. After several years seasoning, and if willing and qualified, the B-52 navigator could be upgraded to radar nav and assigned his own nav on a new crew.

7. The first, and most important, article of the Code of Conduct read: "I am an American fighting man. I serve in the forces which guard my country and our way of life. I am prepared to give my life in their defense."

CHAPTER 8. WELCOME TO THE BIG LEAGUES

1. There was one exception to Castle's unique role. During certain periods, the 4017th CCTS could not provide enough properly trained SAC crews in a timely fashion, and the 6th Bombardment Wing at Walker AFB near Roswell, NM, picked up the slack. The Roswell training was essentially identical to Castle's.

2. A rough ride was fairly typical during low-level flight. The B-52 had been built as a high-altitude bomber; after the Soviets developed the deadly SA-2 Guideline antiaircraft missile, SAC's nuclear tactics shifted to tree-top attacks. The crews suffered the physical consequences.

CHAPTER 9. GETTING SAC'EMCISED

1. The Fs were actually the first B-52s to enter the war (in 1965), but they were soon replaced. And it was only at the very end, in 1972, that the Gs were brought in to bolster the Linebacker operations. A sprinkling of Cs showed up in the early years, but they were so similar to the Ds that nobody really noticed. Aside from these exceptions, B-52 operations in Southeast Asia was an all-D model show.

2. There was an even worse scenario. An individual B-52 crew member (especially a pilot)might serve a couple of TDY tours with SAC, then get a one-year PCS into Tactical Air Command flying fighters, transport, or recon in Vietnam, AND THEN get transferred back to SAC and a fresh cycle of unlimited B-52 TDY duty. And, while we are on the subject, there was another nasty clinker on the coal grate. Faced with a deck stacked so heavily against them, many SAC junior officers who had planned on making the Air Force a career reluctantly resigned their commissions (often some of the best men) to escape the madness. This also happened in the other armed services, no doubt contributing to the American military's decade-long decline following the Vietnam War.

3. Named after the U.S. senators who secured the funds to have them built. LeMay also had a hand in getting this done; before the building of these desperately needed quarters, many military families lived in near squalor.

4. If a young officer had been given the navigator chair in a crew that was essentially intact except for his slot, the crew might be ready for certification in just a few weeks. If he was part of a newly formed crew, however, it might take two or three months.

5. Why the obsession with time on a nuclear strike? KC-135 tankers, essential to reaching the target, had to be rendezvoused with at exact, predetermined en route points and times. Also, many strategic Soviet targets were scheduled for multiple strikes, all of which required coordination. Imagine trying to find a radar aiming point on a target that had been already obliterated by a missile a few minutes earlier. That naturally raises

another question: Why, then, schedule the bomber strike at all? Answer: Maybe the prior missile, or even another bomber, couldn't make it to the target. Follow-up "make sure" strikes against critical installations were an integral part of the SIOP nuclear war plan. Also, sometimes a target would require more than one nuke to knock it completely out.

6. B-29 bombardier Ferebee told of an interesting sequence on the Hiroshima mission when the 9,000-pound "Little Boy" left the Enola Gay. Although the crew had been briefed on the weapon's effects, none of the men, except maybe the pilot, Paul Tibbets, really understood what the "device" was capable of. While in their breakaway turn, Ferebee took a notion to watch it go off through the Norden optics. After a few seconds of bending over the sight, he suddenly remembered the stern warnings about the flash and threw his head back. Moments later, a terrific beam of blinding light, like a laser, blasted up through the optic's lenses and against the greenhouse ceiling. Ferebee said if he'd kept his head down, the flash would have taken out an eye. And that was from a "puny" twenty-kiloton bomb, what today would be considered almost a field tactical nuke.

7. Although the B-52 carried the same navigational radio aids (VOR, DME, TACAN, etc.) as other military and civilian aircraft, that equipment was rarely used. The reason is clear when one realizes that in the event of a nuclear war, all the world's navigation radio aids would be put out of commission—either opposing forces would close down their own stations (so they couldn't be homed in on) or the tremendous electromagnetic waves radiating out from thermonuclear blasts would neutralize them. As a result, SAC determined early on that its crews would conduct all their navigation without benefit of any outside radio aid.

8. A nautical mile is equivalent to 6,080 feet; an "English" or statute mile is 5,280 feet. Aviators must exercise great care not to mix them up.

9. In a tradition carried over from radar-equipped World War II B-17s, B-24s, and B-29s, followed by postwar heavies like the B-50 and B-36, the B-52 crew pecking order was: AC/pilot, RN, copilot, nav, EWO, and gunner. An individual's military rank had no bearing on this hierarchy.

CHAPTER 10. TURNING ON THE ARC LIGHT

1. A popular back-of-the-jacket message seen and heard throughout Southeast Asia was a seriously irreverent play on the 23rd Psalm: "Yea, though I walk through the valley of the shadow of death, I will fear no evil; for I am the meanest mother———— in the valley."

2. B-52 crews looked at radar bomb scoring teams differently after experiencing Sky Spot releases. Where before the RBS guys were viewed as a threat, that is, someone who could give them a "bad bomb" (one or two during an Operational Readiness Inspection [ORI] could be lethal to a LeMay-type SAC career), Vietnam Sky Spot/MSQ/Bugle Note controllers were regarded as the "good guys."

3. Housing on Andersen for TDY cadre wings like McCoy's 306th was adequate until Linebacker Two, when extreme overcrowding made it necessary to house enlisted personnel in hundreds of twelve-person "Canvas Courts" (aka tents) and at a place dubbed "Tin City." Tin City was something else—obsolete, metal housing sheds were "refurbished" just enough to cram in thousands of extra maintainers and munitions handlers. Living conditions were harsh: twelve-hour minimum work shifts, marginal chow, no respite from coral dust and stultifying tropical heat, constant flight line noise, zero personal

space, overtaxed latrines, the list goes on. B-52 Combat Crewmen were cramped (entire six-man crews were squeezed into quarters designed for two) but much better off, with a solid roof over their heads and, even more important, air-conditioning.

4. Caricatures of the popular Peanuts strip were a favorite. One can imagine the racy situations the talented but slightly perverted Andersen cartoonists got Charlie Brown and Lucy into. The idea caught on at Kadena and U-Tapao as well, after Arc Light set up shop at those bases. Air Division staff turned a blind eye to this harmless, yet somehow important, diversion, something that would have been unimaginable back home in LeMay's Strategic Air Command. The author's personal favorite? Two hungry vultures are hunkered down on a bare tree branch, desperately searching for carrion. One turns to the other and says: "Patience my ass, I'm going to kill something."

5. This chapter describes a normal Arc Light Andersen preflight, performed entirely by the flying crew themselves. During the hectic 1972 Linebacker operations, and because of the very long missions (fifteen to sixteen hours), most of the preflights were conducted by B-52 aircrews not flying that day. Also, it should be noted the Linebacker bomb loads varied considerably from the basic Arc Light mixes described in these pages.

6. "MAlfunction DEtection and REcording" was critical to the monitoring of the BNS and autopilot systems.

7. Among the unsung heroes behind the B-52 are its maintenance men, particularly the ground crew chiefs. Until Vietnam reared its ugly head, SAC crew chiefs usually served long apprenticeships before they were given a Stratofortress. In those earlier days, bomber crew chiefs were somewhat akin to the graying, grizzled sergeants one saw in World War II battle movies, wise old Ward Bonds who knew as much or more about "their" airplane than anyone else and never let anybody forget it. But after a few years of the man-eating operations in Southeast Asia, circumstances became much different. By the time the 1972 Linebacker engagements rolled around, bomber crews were more likely to encounter a squeaky-voiced, first-hitch airman first class who couldn't yet legally buy a drink or even get into the NCO club. Yet . . . somehow . . . those young American boys had to, and did, grow up overnight. SAC may have been stretched precariously thin in one of its most critical positions, but those Linebacker flight line youngsters, most of whom by Day Three bore the look of men who'd spent the last twenty years at the bottom of a coal mine, wound up performing their duties in so gallant a manner it would have brought tears to even the toughest John Wayne fictional character.

8. Among the other experts were "Uncle Ned," who handled maintenance issues; "Uncle Tom," coordinator for ground movement and location of aircraft; and "Cousin Fred," supervisor of taxi and towing operations.

9. Late in World War II, after Guam had been recaptured from Japan, the Army Air Force established then–North Field on the northern tip of the island, at Pati Point. Building the runways proved to be a daunting task; the underlying coral was like granite. Rather than wrestle the terrain to the mat, civil engineers accommodated to the topography, and the result was a pronounced dip in the middle of Runways 06 Left and 06 Right (and their reciprocals, 24L and 24R). Most Arc Light launches were to the northeast on 06R, the longest available strip of concrete. In 1947 the field became North Guam Air Force Base. Two years later it was renamed in honor of Army Air Force Brig. Gen. James Andersen, air chief of staff on Guam before he went down in the Pacific during the war against Japan.

CHAPTER 11. FIRST COMBAT MISSION

1. The trawlers off Andersen were to play a significant role during Linebacker Two. Very specific reports on takeoff times and the number of B-52s in each wave were sent to the Soviet embassy in Hanoi, which relayed that information to the Soviets' North Vietnamese allies.

2. The use of the much more comfortable headset during "noncritical phases of flight" was an Arc Light gray area. Everybody used them in Southeast Asia, and the brass looked the other way; whereas during Stateside nuclear practice sorties, even during the Vietnam War, the custom was not tolerated. On a North American flight immediately following an Arc Light tour, the author had an Outstanding Rating on his semiannual Effectiveness Report reduced an entire grade because he forgot where he was and slipped the headset on and his chute off during a high-altitude celestial leg. Unfortunately, the squadron commander was not only a stickler for regs, he was ABOARD the aircraft. Again, one did not mess with LeMay's Strategic Air Command.

3. Actually, there was a very small window/porthole aft of the radar navigator's left side instrument panel, behind his left shoulder. Clearly a design afterthought, it was as useless as it was nearly invisible.

4. Not to be confused with the infamous World War II Bataan ("Death March") Peninsula, located near Manila several hundred miles to the south.

5. One of the many early legends surrounding the World War II Norden bombsight claimed the device could "put a bomb in a pickle barrel from 20,000 feet." The long used insider phrase "pickle out the bombs" and the official name "pickle switch" (which also was about the size of a big pickle) probably were derived from that "capability."

6. The route back was more direct—straight across the Philippines. Without bombs onboard, overfly permission was granted to returning B-52s.

7. When flying at high altitudes, the Earth's horizon can appear lower than its "normal" horizontal position—the higher the aircraft, the lower the horizon appears—a phenomenon known as "dip."

8. The weather-dynamic troposphere extends up to roughly 30,000 feet, where the stratosphere begins and where the B-52 generally operates, hence the name Stratofortress. From an atmospheric standpoint, above 50,000 feet (the operational ceiling of the Buf) is essentially Space.

9. This exchange might also have included a reference to the infamous Vietnam "Falcon Code." The code was devised especially for use over the command radios in order to both abbreviate and mask certain choice comments that otherwise couldn't be made. In this case, the veteran might have said: "Nice going, kid. I'll give you a One-Oh-Nine." A "109" translated as "Beautiful, just f—ing beautiful!" Other examples among the thirty-to-forty most popular phrases included: "Beats the s— out of me" (103); "This place sucks" (107); "F— you very much" (108); and "Pardon me, sir, but I believe you have me confused with somebody who gives a s— "(269). One quickly gets the idea.

CHAPTER 12. THE SOUTHEAST ASIAN WAR GAMES

1. On January 23, 1968, the USS *Pueblo*, a Navy intel ship operating close to the Korean peninsula, was seized by the North Koreans. The spectacular incident sparked an

international crisis, resulting in a reinforced American military presence throughout the western Pacific.

2. The still-fresh memory of U.S. bombings of the Japanese homelands during World War II, the B-52's association with nuclear weapons (think Hiroshima and Nagasaki), and the almost as radioactive "reversion issue" (the return of Okinawa to Japan), made continued Buf operations at Kadena too politically hot.

3. The only other all-weather, day/night platform was the FB-111 supersonic swingwing medium bomber that came along late in the war. Designed as an interim weapon system between the B-52 and the next generation, it had limited operational utility (B-58 Hustler redux)—only seventy-six were built. The few that were left when the B-1B Lancer arrived were mothballed.

4. Allied troops from South Korea, Australia, New Zealand, Thailand, and the Philippines fought alongside the U.S. and South Vietnamese armies during the Vietnam War.

5. Subelements of the plan were called Breakfast, Lunch, Snack, Dinner, Dessert, and Supper. Somebody with operational naming power was enjoying himself.

6. Considering all the hush-hush and obfuscation surrounding these attacks, it's not surprising that confusing and conflicting accounts continue to appear in reference books and on the Internet, particularly as to when the Cambodian raids first started (air incursion in March 1969, ground incursion in May 1970); where the weapons were dropped from and on what during any given mission (B-52s could "throw" their bombs several miles, meaning they didn't necessarily have to penetrate Cambodian airspace to hit targets on that side); the extent of an "incursion" (both sides of the border could receive bombs on a single strike); and what the bomber crews knew and recorded on their charts and logs. As to that latter point, special SAC staffers filling out the official paperwork were directed to "back in" preselected "cover" targets and courses that were located inside nearby Vietnam, deleting the actual targets and aircraft positions in Cambodia. There was hell to pay in 1973 when those "bombing data falsifications" were revealed to an angry U.S. Congress.

7. Not surprisingly, the secrecy lid blew off just a couple of months later when the *New York Times* broke the story, though Prince Norodom Sihanouk of Cambodia did not subsequently lodge a protest and the article pretty much stayed below the public radar. For the next year, when reporters suspected there had been a Cambodian bombing, American officials responded by saying that if it did happen, it was "accidental."

8. On May 14, 1969, elements of the ARVN and American 101st Airborne Division assaulted Hill 937, Ap Bia Mountain, one mile from the Lao border. After six days of fierce fighting, with severe losses on both sides (hence the name "Hamburger Hill"), the Allies took the mountain. Then, as had been done at Khe Sanh and other similar actions, the remote prize was very quietly abandoned by the United States a few days later. On top of all this, the horrible My Lai Massacre story was breaking at the same time. Such "victories" only seemed to emphasize even more the apparent purposelessness of the war.

9. It only became Linebacker "I" after Linebacker "II" was authorized later in the year, in the same manner The World War only became World War I after the second one had started. There has been speculation the term "Linebacker" was chosen because the name might appeal to (and gain favor with) football fan Richard Nixon.

CHAPTER 13. BACK TO SAC

1. The Soviets launched the world's first artificial satellite just three days later, on October 4, 1957. With Sputnik, the concept of intercontinental missile warfare had become a reality.

2. This reaction time was arrived at by calculating the average number of minutes it would take an ICBM to strike a continental U.S. target once it had been detected by the Ballistic Missile Early Warning System (BMEWS).

3. The United States maintained at least twelve B-52s on continuous Chrome Dome airborne alert for several years, that exact number a very closely held secret at the time.

4. There was one exception. In October 1969, in a fit of pique (his so-called "madman strategy"), Richard Nixon tried to rattle the cages of the Soviets (who were supplying 85 percent of the NVA's war-making materiel), China, and North Vietnam by initiating Operation Giant Lance. It was intended to suggest the president might do anything (maybe even nuke Hanoi?) to end the Vietnam War. For several weeks, B-52s once again hauled nuclear weapons on airborne alert, basically using the old Chrome Dome routes and procedures. In November the administration made a determination its objectives had been met and terminated the program. However, nothing at all had changed on either the diplomatic or political front—it's entirely possible the Soviets, like the U.S. public, failed to even notice the alert. To the best of the author's knowledge, American bombers have not been authorized to carry nuclear weapons aloft since the end of the Giant Lance operation.

5. With only a very few exceptions, the SAC/Arc Light/Linebacker Combat Crews remained uncontaminated by the rampant drug use that by 1971 had gravely crippled U.S. ground forces in Asia.

6. A never-ending cycle of seeing her husband off to Arc Light, an even heavier than usual Alert schedule after he rotated back home to the States, and then watching him once again return to Arc Light would have brought even a saint to her knees. Divorce rates in the B-52D community soared in the late 1960s and early 1970s, but it seems more a wonder so many wives stayed the course.

7. Readers will note that the author mentions these items again and again. SAC was equally relentless about reminding the men of their duties and responsibilities around nuclear weapons and to ensure they continually guarded against COMPLACENCY of any sort. Combat crewmen had to wholly understand the Positive Control nature of the entire war plan, which included certain "fail-safe" procedures essential to avoiding mishandling the weapons and/or jeopardizing the integrity of the overall mission. Furthermore, no one man was ever allowed near a nuclear bomb or a B-52 loaded with nuclear weapons, the minimum in proximity being "two-men (qualified), no-lone." Such matters were regularly tested using surprise Alert quizzes, with 100 percent test scores mandatory.

8. Curtis LeMay, who is still remembered by many only for his excesses, was strongly opposed to any kind of an electronic "Captain Midnight Secret Decoder Machine" to handle the authentication, launch, and strike methodology, for precisely the reasons so gleefully exploited at his expense in movies like *Fail-Safe* and *Dr. Strangelove*.

9. The Command Post had a similar system of checks and balances, whereby it could only act after receiving a properly authenticated message from the president (via CINC-SAC in Omaha), or after 1961, from the orbiting "Looking Glass" aicraft, a specially modified KC-135 Stratotanker that served as SAC's Airborne Command Post. Looking

Glass aircraft were always manned by a general officer, operated around the clock, and served as SAC's backup headquarters should the land-based command and control network be knocked out. The Airborne Command Post stayed in business all the way to the end of the Cold War, standing down only when SAC did in the early 1990s.

CHAPTER 14. WON'T SOMEBODY PLEASE TURN OUT THE ARC LIGHT?

1. The final missions against Vietnamese targets came in January 1973, on the heels of Operation Linebacker Two. Although the peace terms announced in Paris and signed on January 27th had ended the "Vietnam War," unfortunately for the peoples of Indochina, Southeast Asian in-fighting raged on for several more years. Immediately following the Paris Peace Accords, which also guaranteed the neutrality of Cambodia and Laos, the U.S. military pledged its support to the Lao and Cambodian governments against Pathet Lao and Khmer Rouge insurgents. B-52 crews continued to drop iron bombs in both those countries until August 1973, when the U.S. concluded enough was enough and ended American air combat in Southeast Asia once and for ever.

2. There was also something else in the mix, a subtle but no less debilitating psychological issue completely overlooked by nearly everyone (including most Vietnam War historians) and one only vaguely perceived by the worn-down Arc Light crews themselves. Nobody knew at the start it would take seven years before Hanoi figured out how to bring down a B-52.

3. The semiofficial military newspaper that first appeared during the Civil War. It was permanently resurrected by Gen. John Pershing during World War I.

4. This tune stayed on the O Club juke for a very long time. Here are the chorus lyrics, sung in Peggy Lee's classically haunting manner:

> Is that all there is?
> Is that all there is?
> If that's all there is my friends,
> then let's keep dancing.
> Let's break out the booze
> and have a ball,
> if that's all there is.

5. Rules of Thumb on decorations: Every Arc Light aircrewman who flew even a single combat mission was eligible to wear the Vietnam Service Medal and the Republic of Vietnam Campaign Medal. Twenty missions rated an Air Medal (AM), with an Oak Leaf Cluster (i.e., another Air Medal) coming with each additional twenty. Those men who had accumulated 150 combat missions could be recommended for (and usually received) a Distinguished Flying Cross (DFC). Also, for most, if not all of the war, those who had accumulated over 200 missions were given a special non-decoration award—a solid silver commemorative cigarette box. In early 1972, when the Bufs started flying into Route Pack Six and the Red River valley (thereby making their crewmen "River Rats"), extra mission credits were added to each sortie, which counted for AM and DFC merit awards. It should be noted that the very great majority of Arc Light medals were awarded for MERIT, as opposed to HEROISM. Heroic medals and decorations, much more commonplace during Linebacker Two, were handled separately from merit awards and with the much greater level of respect they deserved.

CHAPTER 15. DECEMBER 18/19, 1972—LINEBACKER TWO'S FIRST DAY

1. Andersen was assigned fifty-three D models and ninety-nine Gs; U-T had fifty-four Ds. SAC gave the two bases about three hundred B-52 aircrews.
2. Bonus Deals could also be conducted in G models, despite the clumsiness and other potential problems associated with having the tail gunner's eyeballs remotely located in the forward cabin.
3. The long flight from Guam on this first day of Linebacker Two had a silver lining, at least as far as the navigator-bombardiers were concerned. It gave them time to study their target's offset aiming points, simulated radar images, and SR-71 photos—the vital drop information that had been so cavalierly tossed through the hatches moments before takeoff. The U-Tapao crews didn't launch for many hours later, and their target folders had arrived in time for ample study before takeoff.
4. Gunner Poole and Navigator Cooper went down with the ship. Their remains were finally found, identified, and returned to their families in 2003. They were buried at Arlington National Cemetery.
5. One of the damaged bombers, Hazel Three, was the only Linebacker G model to have been struck by a SAM and not brought down.

CHAPTER 16. THE THIRD DAY

1. Those very detailed maps were called Special SEA Operational Navigation Charts (SOC), identical in look and scale (1:1,000,000) to the standard USAF ONC (Operational Navigation Chart). As a rule of thumb, an inch was equivalent to about sixteen statute miles.
2. These "chaff corridors" were a two-edged sword. While masking individual B-52s from targeting radars, they also highlighted to the enemy the bomber route of attack. A "chaff blanket" used later was more effective.
3. There continues to be much discussion about this recall in military and historical circles. The essential point revolves around whether it was a legitimate on-the-spot tactical maneuver or if, as one researcher put it, SAC turned from their targets in "fear of losses." Was the recall a prudent move or had the North Vietnamese army accomplished something not even the Luftwaffe could do at Schweinfurt, Regensburg, and Ploesti? The matter is complex, charged with emotion, and beyond the scope of this book.
4. Arc Light offset aiming points were typically given such whimsical monikers as "Ting Tong," "Adam's Peak," "Maiden's Breast," "Fly Trap," "Pussy Peak," "Mitten Mountain," and so forth. Also, it should be noted that the Buf BNS could load up and use as many as four offset aiming points, and most of the Linebacker bombardiers took advantage of that capability. For the sake of narrative clarity, we use only two here.
5. Many Linebacker Two releases had train times as short as three seconds.
6. There is evidence to suggest the initial "don't pump chaff at SAMs, only at MiGs" directives (also discussed in chapter 1) came about because there were not enough aluminum chaff bundles and/or ground crews to simultaneously and completely fill all of the B-52 dispensers during 100+ bomber raids.
7. The dialogue used on Marble One's bomb run is considerably more formal and less hurried (in the interest of clarity to the reader) than what actually would have been heard. Intercom exchanges between combat crew, who knew each other intimately, were usually much more cryptic, especially in the heat of an intense, high-stakes fight. Previously

mentioned B-52D radar navigator, Wilton Strickland, graciously shared several of his personal Linebacker Two bomb run sound tape recordings with the author. Here are a few actual, verbatim excerpts from those tapes:

Pilot/copilot: "OK, there's some more coming up, I think. And another, and another." "What's the bomb run heading?" "He's in a turn." "There's two at eleven o'clock."

Radar nav: "You have the coordinates for the final GPI there, nav?" "Do you have a visual on 'em, pilot?" "Range is eleven thou." "Still on the point!" "Let's get the hell outa here!"

Nav: "Are you turning?" "Just lost Doppler." "OK, radar, let's go down to the target." "You're on OAP 1." "EAR!"

EW: "Uplink! Maneuver!" "Frequency is 9400, radar."

Gunner: "There's two of 'em." "five o'clock, six o'clock! Coming right up!" "He just blew up!" "There must be five of 'em!"

8. EW Camerota successfully evaded for two weeks but it was just too difficult to pull off a Jolly Green rescue that deep into enemy territory. Nearly dead from exposure, he finally had no choice but to "submit to capture."

9. Some military historians have suggested that the two MiG-21 kills by tail gunners Turner and Moore are not substantiated by North Vietnamese combat records. The Buf crews involved strongly support their gunners' claims, and both victories continue to be officially credited by the U.S. Air Force. Three other MiG claims by Buf gunners were disallowed.

CHAPTER 17. GETTING SMART . . . AND FINISHING THEM OFF

1. That was the end of two-ship elements. From then on, whenever an airplane dropped out, the two remaining bombers would marry another cell, forming a new five-ship cell.

2. December 18 to 29 makes twelve days, less one day for the Christmas pause equals eleven days of battle.

CHAPTER 18. THE TWENTY-FIRST-CENTURY BUF/BUF

1. The long-term storage of the Es and Fs at the "Bone Yard," aka Davis-Montham AFB, Tucson, AZ, was completed in 1978 and had preceded the retirement of the more capable Vietnam War Ds.

2. GPS, the primary means of worldwide navigation today, uses a grid of twenty-four satellites (at least four visible from any point on Earth) to fix one's location by determining precisely how long it takes (using an atomic clock set to "Zulu" time) for the signals to travel between the satellites and an individual GPS receiver. The latitude and longitude readouts are accurate to within less than ten meters and still improving.

3. Coincident with the Desert Storm operation, the B-52Gs were being phased out of the USAF inventory under terms of the recently negotiated Strategic Arms Reduction Treaty (START). Fortunately, there were still enough Gs in the inventory to prevent this separate diplomatic action from becoming a hindrance to the relatively short-lived Desert Storm requirements. By the end of 1992, all the B-52Gs had been destroyed (a START requirement, as opposed to the usual storage), except for a few static museum displays.

4. Despite the general public impression left by Desert Storm's opening ALCM and Tomahawk cruise-missile attacks by B-52s and the battleship USS *Missouri*, plus dramatic television coverage of laser-guided aerial strikes by stealth-type fighter/bombers, the

greater portion of delivered ordnance was not of the cruise missile or "smart bomb" variety, but came instead from standard gravity weapons using long-proven carpet bombing techniques. The B-52Gs alone were credited with delivering 40 percent of all weapons dropped by coalition forces during the six-week conflict.

5. Although a few Desert Storm B-52s did sustain battle damage, none were lost in action, though one had a catastrophic electrical failure on its way back to Diego Garcia and went down in the Indian Ocean—three of the six crew were killed.

6. To briefly clarify a few technical points: JDAMS and laser-guided weapons are separate system concepts. JDAMs are guided by GPS to a targeted set of latitude/longitude coordinates. Laser/electro-optic guided systems essentially work by placing a laser "spot" on a target and causing the weapon to home in on it. In 2006 the Air Force revealed that the "Litening AT Targeting Pod" was now available for combat use by the B-52H fleet. According to official releases, "the Litening AT uses high-definition, electro-optical sensors and airborne lasers to aid the aircrew with target detection, identification, and weapons guidance precision." The new system gives the overall theater commanders "the capability to have a precision weapon platform airborne in the battle area for long periods of time, which will help in attacking targets that are time sensitive and fleeting."

7. Future Congresses will likely feel increasing pressure to fund even more UAV programs in exchange for building fewer attack aircraft and training fewer pilots, as the funding requirements for UAVs become smaller in comparison to the other. Also, legislators are bound to be more and more mindful of the political advantages in not sending human aircrew into high-risk situations. Incidentally, as of March 31, 2007, just 13,545 pilots and 4,371 CSO-type nonrated officer aircrew (combined new CSOs, new WSOs, old navigators, old bombardiers, and old EWOs—the transition is not yet complete) were on active duty in the United States Air Force, a fraction of the Vietnam War–era total.

8. The reader has no doubt noted the almost exclusive use of the masculine pronoun throughout this work. That is because through the Vietnam War and for some time thereafter, there were NO female B-52 aircrew. Today, of course, the cockpit is open to both genders. The author understands that as this is written, there are about twenty women serving in the B-52H. And, yes indeed, all the old-time Buf guys do wonder how the pee can deal works.

Abbreviations and Acronyms

ABC	airborne mission commander
AC	aircraft commander
ACC	Air Combat Command
ACM	advanced cruise missile
ADC	Air Defense Command
ADF	automatic direction finding
ADIZ	air defense identification zone
AFA	Air Force Academy
AFNOA	Air Force Navigators Observers Association
AGM	air-to-ground missile
ALCM	air-launched cruise missile
AM	Air Medal
ARA	airborne radar approach
ARVN	Army of the Republic of Vietnam
ATC	Air Training Command
ATF	actual time of fall
BDA	bomb damage assessment
BMEWS	Ballistic Missile Early Warning System
BNP	basic navigation procedures
BNS	bombing and navigation system
BOQ	bachelors office quarters
BRIC	bomb release interval control
BRL	bomb release line
BUF/BUFF	Big Ugly (Fat) "Fellow" (B-52)

BX	base exchange
CALCMS	conventional air-launched cruise missiles
CAMW	Consolidated Aircraft Maintenance Wing
CAP	Combat Air Patrol
CCTS	Combat Crew Training Squadron
CE	circular error
CFI	certificated flight instructor
CINCSAC	commander in chief Strategic Air Command
COSVN HQ	Central Office for South Vietnam–Headquarters (North Vietnamese army)
CP	command post
CSO	combat systems operator
DEFCON	Defense Readiness Condition
DFC	Distinguished Flying Cross
DG	directional gyros
DME	distance-measuring equipment
DMG	ROTC distinguished military graduate
DMZ	Demilitarized Zone
DR	dead reckoning
EAR	emergency armed release
ECM	electronic countermeasures
E&E	escape and evasion
EGT	exhaust gas temperature
EMERGCONS	Emergency Conditions
ETA	estimated time of arrival
EW	electronic warfare; electronic warfare officer
EWO	electronic warfare officer
EWOT	Electronic Warfare Officer Training
FAA	Federal Aviation Administration
FNG	"fluking" new guys

GCI	Ground Control Intercept
GPI	ground position indicator
GPS	Global Positioning System
HE	high explosive
HF	high frequency
HHCL	"H" Hour Control Line (nuclear)
ICBM	intercontinental ballistic missile
IFF	identification friend or foe
IFR	instrument flight rules
ILS	instrument-landing system
IN	instructor navigator
IP	instructor pilot; initial point
JADMS	joint direct-attack munitions
JSOW	joint stand-off weapon
LB2	Linebacker 2
LORAN	Long Range Navigation
LOS	line of sight
LSL	Lethal SAM Line
MAC	Military Airlift Command
MACV	U.S. Military Assistance Command–Vietnam
MADREC	malfunction, detection, and recording
MARS	Military Affiliated Radio System
MATS	Military Air Transport Service
MMS	Munitions Maintenance Service
nav	navigator-bombardier
NBT	Navigator Bombardier Training
NCO	noncommissioned officer
NVA	North Vietnamese army
OAP	offset aiming point
OAS	Offensive Avionics System

OCS	Officer Candidate School
OER	Officer Effectiveness Report
ONC	Operational Navigation Chart
OPS	base operations
ORI	Operational Readiness Inspection
OSI	Office of Special Investigations
OTS	Officer Training School
PCS	permanent change of station
PDI	pilot's deflection indicator
PLF	parachute landing fall
POW	prisoner of war
PTT	posttarget turn
radar	radio detection and ranging
radar nav	radar navigator/bombardier
R&D	research and development
RBN	radar bombing navigation training
RBS	radar bomb scoring
RDF	radio direction finding
RIO	radar intercept officer
RN	radar navigator (see radar nav)
RO	radar observer/navigator/bombardier
ROTC	Reserve Officer Training Corps
RSI	radar scope interpretation
RTU	Replacement Training Unit
SAC	Strategic Air Command
SAM	surface-to-air missile
SAR	search and rescue
SEA	Southeast Asia
SIOP	Single Integrated Operations Plan (nuclear)
SOC	Special SEA Operational Navigation Charts

SOS	Squadron Officers School
SRAMS	short-range attack missiles
START	Strategic Arms Reduction Treaty
TA	terrain avoidance
TAC	Tactical Air Command
tacair	tactical air
TDY	temporary duty
TG	time to go (bomb run)
TOT	time on target
UAV	unmanned aerial vehicle
UHF	ultrahigh frequency
UNT	Undergraduate Navigator Training
UPT	Undergraduate Pilot School
USAF	U.S. Air Force
USO	United Service Organization
VC	Viet Cong
VFR	visual flight rules
VHF	very high frequency
VOR	VHF omnidirectional range navigation
WCMD	wind-corrected munitions dispenser
WSO	weapon systems operator/officer

BIBLIOGRAPHY

BOOKS

Bonds, Ray, ed. *The Vietnam War: The Illustrated History of the Conflict in Southeast Asia.* New York: Crown Publishers, 1979.

Bowditch, Nathaniel. *American Practical Navigator: An Epitome of Navigation and Nautical Astronomy.* Washington, DC: United States Hydrographic Office/U.S. Government Printing Office, 1939.

Bowers, Peter M. *Boeing B-29 Superfortress.* North Branch, MN: Specialty Press/Warbird Tech Series, Volume 14, 1999.

Bowman, John S., ed. *The Vietnam War: Day by Day.* New York: Barnes & Noble Books/Brompton Books, 1989.

Boyne, Walter J. *Boeing B-52: A Documentary History.* London: Jane's Publishing Company Limited, 1981.

————. *The Influence of Air Power upon History.* Gretna, LA: Pelican Publishing Company, 2003.

Broughton, J. *Thud Ridge.* New York: Bantam Books, 1969.

Budiansky, Stephen. *Air Power: The Men, Machines, and Ideas That Revolutionized War, from Kitty Hawk to Iraq.* New York: Penguin Books, 2004.

Chant, Chris. *The World's Great Bombers.* New York: Barnes & Noble Books/Amber Books Ltd, 2000.

Compere, Tom, and William Vogel, eds. *The Air Force Blue Book: Volume I.* New York: Military Publishing Institute, 1959.

Dorr, Robert, and Lindsay Peacock. *Boeing's Cold War Warrior: B-52 Stratofortress.* London: Osprey Publishing, 1995.

Emde, Heiner. *Conquerors of the Air: The Evolution of Aircraft 1903–1945.* New York: Viking Press, 1968.

Eschmann, Karl J. *Linebacker: The Untold Story of the Air Raids over North Vietnam.* New York: Ivy Books/Ballantine, 1989.

Ginter, Steve, and Nick Williams. *Convair: T-29 Flying Classroom.* Simi Valley, CA: self-published.

Hallion, Richard P. *Storm over Iraq: Air Power and the Gulf War.* Washington, DC: Smithsonian Institution Press, 1992.

Harbold, Norris B. *The Log of Air Navigation.* San Antonio, TX: The Naylor Company, 1970.

Higham, Robin, ed. *Flying American Combat Aircraft.* Mechanicsburg, PA: Stackpole Books, 2005.

Jacobsen, M., and R. Wagner. *B-36 in Action.* Carrollton, TX: Squadron/Signal Publications, 1980.

Johnsen, Frederick A. *Boeing B-17 Flying Fortress.* North Branch, MN: Specialty Press/ Warbird Tech Series, Volume 7, 2001.

———. *Consolidated B-24 Liberator.* North Branch, MN: Specialty Press/Warbird Tech Series, Volume 1, 2001.

Michel, Marshall L. *Clashes: Air Combat over North Vietnam.* Annapolis, MD: Naval Institute Press, 1997.

———. *The Eleven Days of Christmas: America's Last Vietnam Battle.* San Francisco, CA: Encounter Books, 2002.

Taylor, John, and Kenneth Munson. *History of Aviation.* New York: Crown Publishers, 1972.

Tillman, Barrett. *LeMay.* New York: Palgrave MacMillan, 2007.

U.S. Office of Air Force History. *Linebacker II: A View from the Rock,* USAF Southeast Asia Monograph Series, Volume VI, Monograph 8. Washington, DC: Office of Air Force History, 1985.

U.S. War Department. *Guam: Operations of the 77th Division,* Armed Forces in Action Series. Washington, DC: Historical Division, War Department, 1946.

Wallace, Graham. *The Flight of Alcock & Brown: 14–15 June 1919.* London: Putnam, 1955.

MILITARY MANUALS/TEXTBOOKS

Air Navigation: AF Manual 51-40, Volume 1. Washington, DC: U.S. Department of the Air Force, 1968.

Air Science II: Air Force ROTC ConAC Manual 50-2. Mitchel AFB, New York: Headquarters U.S. Continental Air Command, 1949.

Air Weapons Aircrew Handout. APO San Francisco: HDQS 4252D Strategic Wing (SAC), "CURRENT INFO FILE SCAT HANDOUT," staple-bound SEA weapons update for B-52Ds, January 1970.

Instrument Flying Handbook. Washington, DC: U.S. Department of Transportation, Federal Aviation Administration, AC 61-27C, 1980.

Student Study Guides. Mather AFB: Undergraduate Navigator Training (UNT), 1966.
  Applicable SSGs:
  "Aircraft & Navigation Equipment" Workbook
  "Basic Navigation Procedures" Workbook
  "Day Celestial" Workbook
  "Earth's Surface" Workbook
  "Night Celestial" Workbook
  "Plotting Techniques" Workbook

Student Study Guides. Mather AFB: Navigator Bombardier Training (NBT), 1967.

Applicable SSGs:
"ASQ-48 Computers" Workbook
"ASQ-48 Radar" Workbook
"Basic Operations" Workbook
"Crew Duties, Mission Requirements" Workbook

T.O. 1B-52C-1 "Dash One." Tech Order/Flight Manual B-52C and B-52D. Published under authority of the Secretary of the Air Force, 1970.

T.O. 1B-52C-1-1-2. B-52C and D Radar Navigator's/Navigator's Manual, Secretary of the Air Force, 1970.

T.O. 1-1C-1-5. Air Refueling Procedures B-52B-F, Secretary of the Air Force, 1969.

T.O. 1B-52C-34-2-1. Aircrew Conventional Munitions Delivery Manual B-52C-H, Secretary of the Air Force, 1969.

T.O. 1B-52C-1CL-2. USAF In-Flight Crew Check Lists: NAV/RN Nuclear Bombing Procedures, 1970.

T.O. 1B-52C-1CL-2. USAF In-Flight Crew Check Lists: NAV/RN Conventional Bombing Procedures, 1970.

MISCELLANEOUS PRINT SOURCES

Ablett, Ken. *Air Navigation: The Way It Was.* Booklet reproduced by AFNOA with permission from Col. Ken Ablett, USAF Ret. and AFNOA Historian, 2006.

Air Force Navigators Observers Association Newsletter. AFNOA, 88878 SW 96th Street, Unit A, Ocala, FL 344481: Former observers, navigators, bombardiers, and electronic warfare officers alumni periodical newsletter.

Airport and Course Data. Manual prepared for United Air Lines by Boeing School of Aeronautics (seven-ring insertable binder for regular updates, similar to modern Jeppesen Airways Manuals—used by O. M. Nelson, Mainliner Captain, UAL), 1939.

Boyne, Walter. "LeMay." *Air Force Association Magazine* 81:3 (March 1998).

————. "Linebacker II." *Air Force Association Magazine* 80:11 (November 1997).

Bowers, Ray L. "Five Pathfinders: The Origins of Air Navigation." *Air University Review* (July–August 1971).

B-52 Stratofortress Association News. 498 Carthage Drive, Beavercreek, OH 45434: Former Combat Crew and other B-52 alumni periodical newsletter.

Callander, Bruce D. "The Short Heyday of the Bombardier." *Air Force Times* (9 April 1984; Reprinted in AFNOA newsletter).

"Combat Crew: Strategic Air Command." Offutt AFB, NE: SAC in-house monthly pamphlet for internal use to promote safety. 20:3 (March 1969).

————. Offutt AFB, NE: SAC in-house monthly pamphlet. 21:2 (February 1970).

Future Unlimited. Maxwell AFB, AL: AFROTC recruiting brochure—Training and Career Opportunities, 1961.

Gwynn-Jones, Terry. "Harold Gatty: Aerial Aviation Expert." *Aviation History* (September 2001).

Howland, John. *Through the Cloud Bombing.* Private brochure prepared by John W. Howland, Hondo Nav Class 43-11 and World War II pathfinder navigator, 1st Combat Wing, Eighth Air Force.

The Navigator magazine (Mather AFB, CA: USAF Air Training Command) 14:4 (Summer 1967).

————. 15:3 (Spring 1968).

Pilots and Navigators Stand Tall. Maxwell AFB, AL: AFROTC brochure outlining flight training syllabuses, 1966.

Professional Opportunities in the USAF. Maxwell AFB, AL: Air University, AFROTC, facts and figures for new officers, 1961.

UNT Class 67-20 Graduation Program. Mather AFB: Air Training Command, 1967.

306th Bomb Wing: Arc Light-1968-69. McCoy AFB, FL: Wing photo album of officers & enlisted men deployed in SEA, prepared mostly for private enjoyment/morale of Stateside dependents, 1969.

SELF-PUBLISHED WORKS BY B-52 COMBAT CREWMEN

Clonts, Jim. *When Penguins Flew and Water Burned,* 2006, ISBN: 978-1-4116-7465-3, Paperback. Clonts served as a BUFF navigator well after Vietnam, his book offering "a firsthand account of life during the last days of SAC and the paradigm switch from nuclear deterrence to conventional combat." Provides an extensive narrative about the lives of B-52 crewmen during the Desert Storm era. Interesting perspectives on the later modified Gs and Hs. To order, visit the author at: <www.jimclonts.com> or <www.lulu.com>.

Hooppaw, James. *Tall Tail Tales,* 2005, ISBN: 0-9722384-1-7, Paperback. "Buf Fellows" (see below) was so well received that Jim put together another book with more B-52 and Combat Crew stories.

————. *Where the Buf Fellows Roamed,* 1999, ISBN: 1-880222-33-7, Paperback. "Snake Crew" aircraft commander and retired USAF colonel Hooppaw flew B-47s and B-52 C, D, E, F, G, and H models, racking up some heavy-duty bomber flying experiences he shares in this book. Great Arc Light memories; lots of little stuff that sometimes tells tons about the big things. E-mail Jim at: <jwhoop@mindspring.com> or write: AV8R, 13518 Meadowview Lane, Nine Mile Falls, WA 99026.

Strickland, Wilton. *In the BUFF,* 2003, ISBN: 0-9747035-0-8, Hardcover. Retired lieutenant colonel and former B-52 radar navigator Strickland has put together a compact book of Black Hole remembrances from Stateside Alert, Arc Light, and Linebacker Two. Of particular interest are two rare ONC charts Wilton used during Linebacker, showing Vietnam GPI radar fixing points and the IP to target routes he flew against Hanoi and Haiphong. For ordering info write: Wilton Strickland, 618 Park Ave., Goldsboro, NC 27530.

Towery, Tommy, ed. *We Were Crewdogs,* 2006, ISBN: 1-59872-294-8, Paperback. A cooperative nonprofit effort put together by former B-52 combat crewman, including several individuals mentioned elsewhere in these pages. Mostly Vietnam War–era stories, with some Stateside SAC Alert stuff. "Their stories told in their own words and styles." Contact: <www.wewerecrewdogs.com> or write: Tommy Towery, 5709 Pecan Trace, Memphis, TN 38135.

——, **ed.** *We Were Crewdogs II*, 2006, ISBN: 1-59872-656-0, Paperback. The first "Crewdogs" was a big hit, so on its heels came number II. There are now also available numbers III and IV. All "bomber puke" lies of course, but good fun. Contact Tommy (a former B-52 EWO) as above.

WEB SITES

Air Force Association <www.afa.org>

Air Force Historical Studies Office <www.airforcehistory.hq.af.mil>

Air Force Navigators Observers Assn <www.afnoa.org>

AN/ASQ Equipment Listing <www.designation-systems.net/usmilav/jetds/an-asq>

B-52 Stratofortress Association <www.stratofortress.org>

Department of the Air Force <www.af.mil>

Global Security <www.globalsecurity.org>

Linebacker II 1972 Christmas Bombings <www.geocities.com/seavet72/LB2>

Military news <www.military.com>

Norden bombsight <www.twinbeech.com/images/bombsight>

Randolph AFB, TX <www.randolph.af.mil>

Strategic Air Command <www.strategic-air-command.com>

Strategic Air & Space Museum <www.sasmuseum.com/>

Teleproduction Group <www.teleproductiongroup.com/12_72-day-by-day.html>

National Museum of the USAF <www.nationalmuseum.af.mil/>

USAF OCS Class 60-C-David Zook <www.ocs60c.com/>

Vietnam War Resource Guide <http://www.amervets.com/warlib6/warlib6v.htm>

306th Bomb Wing Alumni Assn <www.306thbw.org>

INDEX

ABOUT THE AUTHOR

Robert O. Harder was an Air Force ROTC Distinguished Military Graduate at the University of Minnesota, Duluth. He served in the Strategic Air Command and flew 145 combat missions during the Vietnam War as a B-52D navigator-bombardier. He later became a commercial pilot and certificated flight instructor. A retired chain retail executive, he is pursuing a writing career. He and his wife, Dee Dee, live in Chicago and at their summer cabin on Big Sandy Lake, Minnesota.